All About Entertaining

✻ ✻ ✻ ✻   ✻ ✻ ✻ ✻ ✻   ✻ ✻ ✻ ✻

All About Entertaining

Everything You Need to Know
to Have
A Fabulous Social Life

BY

Kay Corinth and Mary Sargent

Including More Than 200 Original Party Ideas and Plans

DAVID McKAY COMPANY, INC. · *New York*

❀ ALL ABOUT ENTERTAINING ❀

❊ *To Mother, Dave, and Tom* ❊

 Contents

 Part One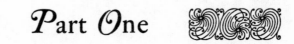

Finding Your Hostess Personality

Come in the evening, come in the morning,
Come when expected, come without warning;
Thousands of welcomes you'll find here before you,
And the oftener you come, the more we'll adore you.
(Irish Rhyme)

CHAPTER

1

Parties and people, places and play. That's the social whirl set off by prosperity and leisure time in America today. There are no barriers that prevent anyone from enjoying the fun. The Colonel's Lady and Mrs. O'Grady are on the merry-go-round together, each accepted and sought for what she can contribute to the enjoyment of others and to the occasion. The company *you* keep and the social life *you* enjoy can be as wide and as wonderful as you choose to make it.

Entertaining is every woman's privilege—and responsibility, too, if she and her family are to lead the good life. Whether you are single or married, young or mature, financially modest or well fixed—there's a place and a way for you in the social structure of the community. Your way may vary from another's, because every family unit varies, but the common denominator

3

for social success is the same—the ability to entertain with variety, gaiety, and charm.

The opportunities are great, but so are the challenges. The same prosperity that enables a wealth of entertaining has brought on a servantless period that has removed traditional help of almost every kind. And because of the abundance of entertaining, giving a party that's fresh and different challenges a hostess's ability and ingenuity as never before. To paraphrase the old nursery rhyme, it's Jan be nimble, Jan be quick, Jan jump from cook in the kitchen to party girl in the parlor in one quick trick. It's up to Jan to be able to cope with modern hostessing.

There's really no such phenomenon as a "born hostess"—or a born anything else, except a baby! Hostessing must be learned as a part of the great body of knowledge we must all acquire for living. The great pity is that most girls and women don't have access to organized training for the job of hostess, which really begins with the first childhood party. If there's a gracious social heritage in the family, it may be absorbed by osmosis and observation. If not, it may seem a terrifying task to the woman who must acquire the graces on her own. Strangely, it's a subject on which most women don't want to ask questions for fear of revealing their lack of knowledge.

The truth is that the art of being a gracious hostess is something anyone can learn, even though a good hostess must be schooled and skilled in writing (invitations and correspondence), designing (themes, decorations, tables), food (cooking and planning menus), serving (meals and refreshments), current events and the arts (conversation), interior design (her home and its appointments), and fashion (her clothes), among other things!

This book is written as an aid to all hostesses: for the young and inexperienced, as a complete guidebook; for the bride, as a key to establishing her social life as a young matron; for the experienced hostess, as a reference book of modern social life; and for all hostesses, as a stimulus to making each entertaining occasion a very special event.

The Social Give and Take

The element that makes society, in the larger sense of the word, is the social give and take among people. When you invite a group of guests to a party, it's like a pebble being pitched into the ocean. A chain of waves is set off that gets bigger and bigger and broader and broader from that time on. Your guests will include you in their next parties, where you become a part of a new chain reaction. You respond to certain individuals you meet, and new friends are made. Out of it all comes a social pattern that's distinctively your own and your family's. Your good relationship with others—both family and friends—is the precious kernel of life.

Fortunately, when entertaining, you can repay one kind of invitation with another. If you simply can't cook, you can repay a dinner invitation with a cookout—your husband at the helm. If you are invited to a ball in the house at the top of the hill, reciprocate with a cozy fireside supper in your house at the foot of the hill. It isn't *how much,* but *how* that counts.

Your entertaining has more charm and appeal if it is *appropriate* (a word we will harp on in this book) to your life. That's all anyone really expects of you. On the other hand, there's no reason for hiding behind excuses when you aren't fulfilling your part. Today there are more facilities available for entertaining than ever before—from undreamed-of appliances, to prepared foods, to myriad outside services. So whatever your situation, there's a way to offer hospitality with flair.

If you are a young business girl living alone or with other girls, you can learn little touches that give elegance to your necessarily smaller ways of entertaining. The menu of a dinner for two to four couples can be short but special. You can acquire a collection of beautiful tableware that will give a spaghetti dinner an air. Instead of a cocktail party with a staggering liquor bill, you can serve one kind of less expensive beverage, such as a tasty punch.

    If you are a bride, you will luckily be showered with all the equipment to set a pretty table, but you may not yet be skilled in managing all the details of a full-fledged party or of cooking a several-course dinner. You want to entertain with your new husband, and your friends are eager to be invited by you. You can start gradually with after-dinner groups of friends who come to see your new abode. What you serve can be the minimum of very good drinks and possibly only very good sandwiches, pastries from the bakery, and hot coffee (the first thing to learn to make well!). Your husband surely will be proud to assist. From there on you can take it in steps, learning to handle buffet suppers, luncheons, and, finally, a proper dinner.

    If you have reached the young matron status with several small children to care for, this doesn't entitle you to a social sabbatical. There's a way for you too. This is the time to call on outside services and help. Some mothers of young children can always find a baby-sitter when they want to go out, but when it comes to doing their share of entertaining, their excuse is that it's impossible with children underfoot. We say why not a baby-sitter when you stay at home, to enable you to give a party?

    If you have achieved the position of the mature matron whose children are at college or are married, you are in the vulnerable position of having the most expected of you socially. You are the ideal committee chairman, backbone of the charity ball, originator of great parties. In another day you would probably have come by at least one servant, but today chances are that you must discharge your larger social obligations without help, or with only part-time help. At this point in your social career you have undoubtedly acquired the know-how of doing many things yourself with uncommon skill, but you are the prime hostess for whom outside entertaining and outside services have been created.

ぺぴ The hostess of advanced years—the septuagenarian or octo-genarian—can enchant her guests with the simplest fare. Her responsibility is to be the ultimate in charm, understanding, and wisdom. A cup of tea proffered with rich conversation can be an exciting experience for guests. Our own octogenarian mother-in-law completely mesmerizes her guests of all ages, mostly half her age, by her ability to converse with spirit on any subject of interest to the guest. Accompaniment may be only a glass of the finest champagne or a cup of special tea with little biscuits ordered from the baker. Marie-Louise Bousquet, Paris editor of *Harper's Bazaar* for many years, is famous for her Thursday afternoons, when she is at home to friends. Only simple refreshment is served, but Madame Bousquet's guests are special and spark a feast of conversation.

Yes, you may say, I fit into one of those pigeonholes, but my situation is different. My house is so small, or my husband hasn't quite arrived, or he is just establishing a professional practice—and I can't keep up with my friends. No, you aren't that different. For you, too, there is a way to score as a hostess. In fact, it's extremely important that you contribute to your husband's development by providing an appropriate social background for his budding career.

Entertaining isn't limited to the financially fortunate or the socially select. Many deny themselves the pleasure of offering hospitality because of lack of self-confidence in planning and managing a party, shyness with other people, insecurity over culinary ability, small living quarters, or slim wallet. All but the last can be overcome with knowledge and practice. The last doesn't really matter. Elsa Maxwell, who called herself "World Party-Giver No. 1," was proud that she began to build her international reputation for parties when she was at her poorest and lived in only two rooms.

How to be the very "most" as a hostess is set out for all of you in this book. We have covered everything you need to know about giving a party from the first gleam in your eye until the door closes on the last departing guest.

A Way of Life

Though entertaining is first and foremost fun, it is and has been many other things to many people. Some have used parties to achieve status, as Mrs. Vanderbilt did almost a century ago when she gave a fancy-dress ball to the tune of a quarter of a million dollars just to impress her then social superior, Mrs. Astor. Perle Mesta, the "hostess with the mostes'" of party-giving fame, has used the medium frequently to bring important government officials together to settle differences in a social atmosphere.

Today, entertaining may mean more to you and your family than just having an enjoyable social life. It might quite likely influence your family livelihood, as well, for parties and entertaining are recognized as a part of business and professional life today. In this era of big business, they can be a powerful tool. The executive or professional man must be able to entertain right and well, which frequently involves his wife as a partner in the public-relations aspect of his position. We have a great deal to say about this later (Chapter 10).

Entertaining has strong new political overtones too, so that the word "party" has a double meaning. It refers not only to the political philosophy of the candidate, but also to the social side of the candidate's campaign. He must appear at numerous social functions planned specifically to expose him to the greatest number of prospective voters under the most pleasant circumstances. In many cases his votes are in direct proportion to his social activities. Here again, his wife plays an essential role as a companion to her husband and as a hostess herself. One candidate's wife described her husband's campaign as a "nonstop open house" with coffee perking day and night.

Both business and politics keep Americans mobile today, shifting from city to city, and even to foreign countries. Thus entertaining takes on still a different dimension as a means to building a social life and set of friends for a family in a new community. A bride can expect to move an average of six times during the balance of her lifetime, we are told. So the wife must be able to move as smoothly into a new social pattern as into a new house. Because her family's well-being and happiness depend on it, she must know the ways and means (see Chapter 11).

From the Heart

Whatever her way of entertaining, *sincerity* is the mark of the successful hostess. She offers hospitality from the heart with a sincere desire to do something generous, kind, and thoughtful for her guests. She proffers the comforts of her home and sets out her best in food and drink, whether modest and meager, or lavish and luxurious.

The French have a beautiful word for what counts most in entertaining successfully—*ambiance*. Though it doesn't translate literally into English, it connotes a sympathetic and pleasant surrounding atmosphere that doesn't cost money, and actually can't be bought with money. It's the gracious and graceful offering of heart and hearth to the guest in your home. It's sincerity.

$\mathcal{H}$ow to $\mathcal{O}$rganize
Υour $\mathcal{P}$arties $\mathcal{P}$ainlessly

In all things, success depends upon previous
preparation, and without such preparation there is
sure to be failure. —Confucius

2

"Getting there is half the fun," advertised a steamship line of
its crossings to Europe, thereby emphasizing that the time spent
on the way to the grand tour was fun, too. We can't think of a
more apt phrase to describe the preparation for a party. It's half
the fun! And like the ship's course, a party must be charted in
advance, with a leg of the course completed on schedule each
day.

We're always ones to recommend constructive mental atti-
tudes as the bridge to happiness and success. Your mental attitude toward entertaining should eliminate the negative, work-
drudgery angle and accentuate the positive, fun-creativity angle.
Entertaining is a creative pursuit, and it's the planning and
preparation that are the most creative part. Every aspect of a
party should be viewed as the creation of a pleasing picture—
home, flowers, decorations, food, even guests. Such an attitude
will reward you with a great feeling of accomplishment. Your

guests will appreciate the fact that you have given every possible thought and effort to their pleasure.

Aside from the aesthetic joys with which well-laid plans will reward you, the practical side is the payoff in mental and physical tranquillity for you when party time comes.

❋ You can schedule a few things to do each day beforehand. In this way every detail can be handled with more efficiency and thoughtfulness. The results will be infinitely better. At the end of this chapter you will find a "Party Progress Calendar" to help you schedule. Copy it and tack it in your kitchen or near your desk, next party you have. See what a help it can be.

❋ You will save money by planning ahead. When you can buy staples in a leisurely way, you can shop where the best buys are, instead of having to rush into the 24-hour delicatessen and pay a premium because the little man stays up all night. With time, you can make invitations, place cards, and decorations. You can pick flowers from your own garden—or beg from a friend—and arrange them yourself. Lacking a garden, you can buy flowers in bulk at a market, nursery, or florist and make the arrangements yourself the day before.

❋ You can avoid last-minute oversights or crises that are sometimes irreparable and can ruin a party.

❋ You will conserve your strength by spreading the preparations over a period of time. When party day arrives, you can be relaxed and fresh and able to have fun at your own party.

❋ Your guests will feel the organized and relaxed atmosphere that will prevail. They will feel that their presence in your home is a pleasure to you and not a hardship—comforting to any guest.

For the Record

Records are with us all of our lives, from the moment we're weighed in at birth. Without them we just couldn't be. And it's our considered opinion that without party records, a successful hostess just can't be.

The Party Log. One of the most fun as well as functional books in your bookcase or library can be a "Party Log." In this will be recorded a word picture of each party you give—kind of party, guest list, flowers and decorations, menu, and postmortem notes about anything that went wrong or should be improved next time. If you're an amateur (or even a pro) photographer and like to take pictures at parties, include these, too. Every time you plan a new party, this becomes the jumping-off point. For the new party you will want a different idea, a different guest mix, a different menu. The Party Log helps you plot it. The Log also becomes a happy—or sometimes comic—remembrance of sociable occasions with your friends.

Buy a loose-leaf notebook of convenient size. We suggest the 9-by-12-inch size that will hold an 8½-by-11-inch sheet of paper. The book itself can be a simple student's type that you can cover with pretty paper—perhaps wallpaper to match your dining room or kitchen, or it can be a handsome leather job. Begin the book with a copy of the Party Progress Calendar (copied from this chapter) as a permanent reference. A plan for the record sheets is given at the end of this chapter. Charm your husband into having it mimeographed for you at his office, or talk the mimeograph operator in your own office into doing it for you on her own time, for which you'll pay. Failing this, it's well worth the few dollars it would cost to have a local letter shop run off a supply for your book. You can even make the pages yourself, with a bit of time and patience!

Fill the Log, as you party, with all the pertinent bits and pieces, as well as the specifics, that made the day:

❊   *Vital Statistics:*   The date, place, kind of party, time, reason, and guest of honor, if any, are basic data to include to identify the party.

❊   *Guests:*   Nothing is duller than the same group of people always partying together, always conversing on the same subjects. This record will help you vary the group each time you entertain.

❊   *Menu:*   Ditto above. Who would want to eat the same menu at every party? Not even you, yourself! You may have a main-dish specialty or may specialize in a particular kind of cookery, but this record of the menu will help you at least vary the surrounding dishes. The same dish can be exciting served over and over again if everything else is different.

❊   *Decorations and Service:*   Record here any flowers or other decorations in the house, the table centerpiece, linens, dishes, and other tableware. Next time plan it differently, to add the essential surprise element.

❊   *Special Notes:*   This section can be a lifesaver when planning future parties. "Celeste fainted dead away at the sight of the snails, my pièce de résistance—next time try fruit first." "Peter is left-handed and kept locking elbows with sedate Mrs. Kitterage—should invite him only to buffets, or seat him where his southpaw can have full play." "Sandra is mad for my chocolate soufflé—repeat next time."

The Address File.   The greatest aid in your whole social life is a complete and always accurate record of the names, addresses, and telephone numbers of all of your friends and acquaintances. It's amazing how many of our own friends don't have this information handy. When it comes to writing or telephoning, they have to ferret through drawers for snips of paper and old envelopes, or resort to the telephone book—either way, a waste of time and a big irritant.

Personally we have kept our own list on 3-by-5-inch file cards in a little metal box purchased for the purpose. This has also served as a record of Christmas cards sent and received, and of birthdays of close friends and family. Recently our mother treated us to a beautiful big beige leather address book with monogram stamped in gold, from New York's most elegant purveyor of leather goods. It just makes us feel pampered every time we use it. We recommend such a luxury to you. Of course, we still keep our Christmas and birthday list on cards.

These are just two suggestions. You might prefer to make a book to match your Party Log. But compile this important list right now—some way.

Cookbooks. Don't scrimp on providing yourself with a shelf of several good cookbooks to your liking. First, and most essential, is a basic book that includes all pertinent information about cooking all classifications of food, measurements, can sizes, oven temperatures, meat and poultry cooking schedule, and so on. There are several famous ones, and each hostess has a favorite that she swears by. Go to a big bookstore and spend some time browsing through the possibilities before you decide on yours. These big basic books are a little more expensive than some of the more specialized ones, but having one is a must.

From here on, you can branch out in any direction that takes your fancy. If you are a busy business person, you may want to concentrate on casserole and quick cookery books. If you are a gourmet with time on your hands, you may want to collect magnificent French books. If your ancestry traces fairly directly to a foreign country, you may want to specialize in cookbooks with that accent, even in that language.

The Recipe File. This is the collection of recipes you have clipped from magazines and newspapers, or have wheedled out of your friends. New food ideas should constantly flow in, and unsuccessful ones should be deleted and thrown away. Here again, too many otherwise organized hostesses are in complete confusion. If *you* are guilty, organize now, because this can be one of your most important tools in becoming a successful hostess.

In the first place, clean out your drawers, cabinets, and desk, and gather all those loose recipes together. Read them over again and discard those you are no longer interested in trying. Then sort them into classifications, such as soups, hors d'oeuvres, entrees, breads, and so on, for filing.

Now put them in some permanent, organized, and usable form. It's easy to buy the accordion folders that are sold for this purpose, but for our money these become uncontrollable in no time at all. A loose-leaf book—to match your Party Log—can be easily indexed and is always workable with the recipes typed or pasted in. Pages can be removed and thrown away when a recipe is no longer desired, new recipes can easily be added, and recipes may be removed temporarily when you are using them. Then there is the card file, which has the same flexibility as the notebook. However, most of those made specifically for this purpose are too small. You can purchase larger sizes in an office supply store. The colors are usually as exciting as battleship gray or institutional tan, but with a small spray can of paint you can quickly transform this to an attractive color. Wooden file boxes are also available in these stores, and they can be covered with pretty papers (which won't adhere to the metal boxes).

David, Mary's husband, has made magnificent big boxes for both of us in his basement woodworking shop. Early American pine pieces are his hobby, so we have burnished pine boxes constructed to accommodate two parallel rows of 3-by-5-inch file cards. Guide cards separate the classifications. The insides of the boxes are prettily painted to match our kitchens—rosy brick for Mary and lemon yellow for Kay. The little brass latches are in keeping with the Early American design of the boxes. We hope you have as handy a husband or beau!

The Social Calendar. Now, don't rebel! Everyone needs a calendar on which to keep appointments. It will help you keep all

engagements straight and accurate, so that you'll turn up everywhere on the right day and at the right time. An amusing program of the "Candid Camera" television show rigged a situation
in which invited guests for a dinner party were greeted by a host
who pretended they had arrived on the wrong night. While
viewers of the show roared at the uncomfortable guests, the
guests themselves were mightily embarrassed. It could happen
to you—and not on TV!

The social calendar helps you pace your parties. If you see
there are many outside activities involving you and your friends
during a particular week or weekend, postpone your own entertaining to another time—for your comfort and that of your
guests too.

There are many pretty calendars available at the beginning of
every year. If you're a cat fancier, or a Paris buff, or an art lover,
or whatever, choose an inexpensive calendar showing your favorite subject, to give you pleasure the whole year through. Most
satisfactory from the standpoint of use is one in which each week
is on a separate sheet, with the days squared off with space for
notes. This is a good place to note birthdays you want to remember with a card or a party. Go through your address file and note
them on your new calendar at the beginning of each year.

The Guest Book.   This is a book about which we have mixed
feelings. Frankly we can't see much point to such a book unless
your social life is filled with many and varied people. If your
circle doesn't change much from party to party, it's a little pre-
tentious to ask guests to "sign in, please" every time they come
to your house.

There are some occasions when we believe a guest book is not
only delightful, but almost called for. Such an occasion is a very
special one when the book will be kept by the guest of honor
as a cherished souvenir of the event. It could be a christening
party with the book kept for baby to read years later. It could
be an important wedding anniversary such as the Silver or
Golden—or that of a sentimental couple who celebrate each year

and might want to keep a guest book with yearly signatures to watch their circle of friends expand and vary. A bridal shower is another occasion for a guest book. Or a party for friends who are moving to another city, state, or country so that they have a remembrance of the circle left behind. A guest book is essential for a business party where a record of those attending is necessary.

A couple who are friends of ours have a lovely idea for such a book. The husband's hobby is photography, so guests at their parties are snapped for a photographic guest book. Needless to say, this is a popular book frequently circulated at their parties —for who doesn't like to see how he looks in pictures!

Guest books come in all varieties, from simple stationery-store versions to handsome leather volumes. You may have an appropriate inscription for the occasion, or the name of the guest of honor stamped on it in gold by your stationer. Or make a guest book simply by covering a purchased notebook with pretty paper or fabric.

Write the Script

As we shall keep on reminding you, good parties don't just happen. They are carefully plotted, maybe even in several acts.

Good Timing. It's wonderful to be so flexible that you can suddenly decide to assemble a few friends for an impromptu party or dinner, but for a real party of any consequence the decision should be made *at least* two to four weeks in advance— even months ahead for a big affair. And this is, of course, the first step. There may be a reason for scheduling a party at a certain time—or you might just want to have a party and manufacture a reason! At this point, be sure to plan an appropriate (there's that word again) party for the occasion and for the guest of honor, if there is one, or for all guests. We mean, don't give a bridge party for someone who doesn't play bridge, or a cocktail party for someone who abominates drinking. This may sound farfetched, but it has happened.

In deciding on the kind of party you will have, make it appropriate for the time of year—or for fun or a gag, a party that is the complete antithesis of the time of year. For example, a group of teen-agers in winter-cold Denver decided to have a summer cruise party. Guests were asked to wear summer sports clothes appropriate for a cruise, and décor and food carried out the shipboard cruise idea. Personally, we think this is great fun for teen-agers, but not for adults unless carried out with sophistication. However, the great party-giver Elsa Maxwell thrived on ideas of this sort. So it's all in the way you do it.

An appropriate day of the week should be chosen for the party. Except for the very special occasions, a late-late party doesn't digest well in the middle of the week. It's better scheduled for a Friday or Saturday night when all the guests can dance the night away with a clear conscience. A tea or early cocktail buffet is perfect for midweek. Daytime parties for feminine guests are better during the week. On Saturdays and Sundays, most married women prefer their social engagements to be coeducational.

The Cast.   Selection of your guests follows right upon the decision to have a party, for they *are* the party. We have some pretty specific thinking on this subject that we're saving as the last section of this chapter. Here, we just want to say that the guest list is the first thing to prepare and that your invitations should be issued to them in plenty of time to assure their attendance. Of course, if there is a guest of honor, he or she will be checked first to be sure the date and time are agreeable. Chapter 3 gives complete information about all of the various kinds of invitations you may use, and how they should be answered.

The Props.   Plan on paper, as we have already plotted for you, your menu and all the equipment you will need to prepare and serve it. Use our Party Worksheet, as illustrated at the end of the chapter, for listing absolutely everything you will need. Work from this in assembling it all from your linen closet, cabinets, pantry, or wherever else you may keep your equipment. Be sure everything is shining bright and that linens are crisp and clean. Design your centerpiece and other decorations, such as greens and candles, and be sure you have on hand all equipment necessary.

The Sparkling Mix

You may be the greatest mixer of tasty recipes, or the most skillful mixer of frosty beverages, but unless you are knowledgeable about mixing the most important ingredient of a party—guests—you will never make it as a hostess.

First and foremost, when business entertaining is not involved, invite only people you really want to entertain as guests in your home. Don't be tempted to have someone who doesn't fit in, and whom you really don't want, just because it might be a coup to include her. It might make nice society column reading, but with all due respect to the newspaper, the refuse will just be wrapped in it next day! You don't need it.

Invite only people you know will be harmonious at a party. For example, during an election period, don't invite people who are too opinionated in one way or the other and would tend to become argumentative. If having an election-results party, be sure the guests are all on the same team, or that they are awfully good sports.

Generally, age must be considered in planning a guest list. As a rule, it is best to keep the group to a 10-year range. But as rules are made to be broken, you will certainly have ageless friends who are so interesting that they will fit into any group. To generalize again, usually the widest age range would be for a family party attended by everyone from Cousin Connie's new baby to Great-Aunt Gertrude. Exceptions again are mother-daughter, father-son (or vice versa) parties. These can be most enjoyable occasions.

A preponderance of females at a mixed party is to be avoided like the proverbial plague. Females that we are, we must admit that the most desirable guest mixture for a mixed party is one with a good dousing of attractive extra men!

The talented guest is one to be cherished, but not exploited. Frequently the talented guest volunteers to entertain, but never invite a talent with this ulterior motive. At a recent dinner party we attended, one of the guests spied a home organ and couldn't resist trying it out. A pleasant evening resulted for everyone. Be sure the guest volunteers, though, and that you don't so much as hint. The story is told of a hostess who invited a famous musician to a party and asked him to bring his violin. His answer was that in that event there would be a fee. The hostess quickly cautioned that in that case he was not to converse with any of the party. The artist's pointed retort was that in that case the fee would be considerably less!

In planning your mix of sparkling guests, these are the possible combinations:

a. You may mix people who don't know each other, but who you believe will enjoy one another and make a pleasant party.
b. You may always mix people who know each other well, or family, but there is danger here that your guest lists will become ingrown, with no surprises.
c. You may develop a combination of old friends, who know you and each other well, with a group of new friends. This has the best potentiality for a really lively and interesting party.

Within this framework, guests may be played against each other in many different ways to come up with the ideal sparkling mix. Be a bit daring about your "guest scheme," playing unusual or exciting or even quiet types against different personalities to come up with a colorful "people effect"—just as you might play orange against red in a color scheme for excitement and drama. To trigger your imagination:

❊ If you are single, try inviting only single men and women to a party, reserving your married friends for another time. An attractive magazine editor we know did this for a holiday cocktail party and found that the results were not only sparkling, but full of spark! All of the guests were able to make some new single acquaintances during the occasion, with possibilities of new friendshpis, or maybe more.

❊ A friend of ours gave an all-girl party for her husband on his milestone fortieth birthday, and he adored it. So did the girls adore pampering him. She invited all of the attractive women she knew her husband admired, counting on safety in numbers, we suppose!

❊ Parties for guests who are all interested in the same sport or hobby can be lively occasions. Get together groups that care about boating, or rug hooking, or surfing, or whatever interest a group might have.

❊ An international party can be fascinating if you have a circle of friends from far-flung places. Any peaceful and pleasant mixing of nationalities today can do a bit to help world friendships. Do what the Waldorf-Astoria Hotel does when expecting a distinguished foreign guest—in your decorations fly the flags of the countries of your guests. This can even be fun if you have foreign guests from only one country. Flags may be purchased or ordered from the Souvenir Shop at the United Nations in New York.

❊ The most glamorous mixture of guests we know of attends the semiannual party given by model agents Eileen Ford and Dorian Leigh in Paris during the couture openings. Highlighting the guest list are the world's most beautiful models. Beautiful girls or women can always glamorize a party, especially for the men present! As one great hostess said, they are cheaper than flowers!

❊ One of the most original guest mixtures was dreamed up by a couple we know. To widen their circle of friends and get out of a "same people" rut, they planned a party and asked each guest to bring someone he or she believed the hosts would like to meet. An ingenious idea because all of us love to bring good friends together.

❄ Guests may be mixed cagily with a specific purpose in mind. One of our female friends when single banded together with five other single girls to give a series of parties with the intent and purpose of meeting new eligible young men. Every two weeks for ten weeks, one of the girls hosted a party in her apartment for the other five. To it she was responsible for inviting eight young men in whom she herself was not romantically interested. Motto of the group was, "One girl's poison is another girl's man." The hostess forewarned each young man that she wanted him to meet some attractive girls, which was bait enough to insure the attendance of any red-blooded young male. The parties were simple after-dinner get-togethers of music and conversation. During the six parties each single girl met forty new single men. Result was that our friend married a man whom she invited to her own party, but who had not previously seriously interested her. A second realized after looking over the fabulous forty that she really loved the one she had been going with all along. And a third was enabled by this whirl to come out of a shell and be more of an extrovert, and soon she married a man she met on a plane!

To sum up, you can be sure of a pleasant, successful party if you invite pleasant, thoughtful, considerate, outgoing—and of course interesting—people. Don't worry if some are quiet, as every group needs listeners. Just beware of stony silence. Go light on people who tend to usurp the conversation and the whole party. The perfect party is an even give-and-take among the guests.

So give your imagination a whirl and see what interesting combinations of guests you can design. Anything can happen!

~~~ *Party Log* ~~~

Table arrangements or
seating plan (sketch
your own table shape)

Date:

Place:

Kind of Party:

Time:

Reason:

John

Guest of Honor:

Guests:

Anne   Susan

Menu:

Bill   George

Helen

Decorations and Service:

Special Notes:

23

(For easy reference, make a copy and keep it in your Party Log)

2–4 WEEKS OR MORE BEFORE:

Decide on kind of party.
Compile guest list.
Engage extra help, if needed.

2 WEEKS BEFORE:

Issue invitations.
Plan menu on Party Worksheet.
Plan flowers and décor on Party Worksheet.
Check clean linen supply in order to have time for any necessary laundering.
Order rental of extra chairs, tables, or other equipment.

1 WEEK BEFORE:

Make list of groceries.
Shop for staple groceries.
Check liquor supply and soft drinks, and order fill-ins.
List on Party Worksheet the tableware, service pieces, and other equipment to be used.
Wash dishes and glassware that haven't been used for some time.

4 DAYS BEFORE:

Polish silver and brass.
Order extra ice.
Check any invited guests not yet heard from.
Arrange seating and write place cards, if any.

(At this point, have everything done that does not absolutely have to be done the last three days.)

3 DAYS BEFORE:

Clean your house or apartment.

~~~ *Party Progress Calendar* ~~~

2 DAYS BEFORE:

Save this day for all the things you didn't finish yesterday and to get a jump ahead on tomorrow's schedule—also purchase fresh foods.

1 DAY BEFORE:

Check your dress and be sure it is pressed—and how about your husband's suit, too?

Have hair done and nails manicured, or do yourself.

Get out and assemble where needed all equipment to be used.

If using garden flowers, arrange (if you use leaves or other greens, can arrange any time during previous week—get out of way as early as possible).

Do quickie dusting and vacuuming (you have already cleaned thoroughly).

Press linens.

Set table or tables.

Prepare any food that can be done day before, such as washing greens, celery, making dessert—you can even measure all ingredients for hot breads and then quickly combine them on day of party for fresh baking.

DAY OF PARTY:

Prepare food as early in day as possible.

Set up bar, if any.

Ice is delivered.

Flowers delivered (if ordered from florist) and placed.

Freshen bathroom and mirror.

Put out clean towels.

Put out clean ashtrays.

Be sure coatroom and bathroom for women guests are properly equipped.

∾∾ *Party Worksheet* ∾∾

(Make one for each party)

MENU   SERVICE NEEDED

Cocktails/Hors d'Oeuvres

Appetizer

Soup

Entree

Vegetables

Salad

Bread/Butter

Dessert

Beverages

Liqueurs

EQUIPMENT AND SERVICE

Linens

Centerpiece/Décor

Candles

Tableware/Silver

Serving Pieces

The Complete Etiquette of Invitations, Acceptances, and Regrets

> Handsome is that handsome does.
> —Goldsmith, *The Vicar of Wakefield*

CHAPTER

3

First impressions are the most lasting, someone once philosophized. We'd like to paraphrase that truism to "First impressions of a party are made with the invitations, and can add a lasting memory."

The casual life led by most of us today has resulted in too casual an attitude about some of the traditional social amenities. Party invitations have gone this casual way, until a telephone call is too often the easy route taken. Granted there are times and occasions when a phone call is most expedient and appropriate, but there are more occasions when a little more effort and thoughtfulness will give luster to the invitation and to the party itself.

The very first impression and impact of your party are carried by the invitation. It can add immediate importance to the occasion, generate excitement and anticipation among your invited guests. There is a new trend developing toward more elegance and form (but not necessarily formality) in living and entertaining. This should be reflected in the way you extend invitations, as it may be in the decoration of your home, the way you dress, and the way you entertain.

The Pleasure of Your Company

Reason for Being.   An invitation has a twofold purpose, and both of these obligations must be observed by the hostess. Naturally, it is first of all *to invite as warmly and graciously as possible.* This is expressed in the type of invitation selected, in the quality of the paper used, in the typeface of the printing or engraving chosen, and in the wording. We have been invited to drop-in parties such as receptions or teas where the hostess has attempted to assure herself of an even flow of guests by inviting them in groups at different hours. For example, half of the invitations might give the time as 4 to 6 and half 5 to 7. This is dangerous and inhospitable. Some guests are likely to feel that their invitations are for the "wrong time." Or guests may want to come together who are invited for different times. Better to cut the guest list down if you can't handle peak periods when "everybody" is there.

The second function of an invitation is *to give information as completely as possible.* Your guests will want to know: day and date, time, place, kind of party. If special apparel is to be worn, this should be made clear. Nothing makes a guest more uncomfortable than to turn up in an outfit appropriate for another place and another time—but not that one! You can count on regular guests to know the kind of apparel usually worn for a specific occasion—but they can't guess the unusual.

If there is to be special entertainment that the guests should know about beforehand, say so. If you have a pool, swimming might be part of the occasion, so say "Be sure to bring your suit for a swim." A cookout might be a "pants party," with the girls asked to wear their casual pants, as well as the men. Naturally, a formal invitation bears the information "Black tie" or "White tie." This indicates the kind of dresses to be worn as well as the men's attire (see page 384).

Who Sends.   For almost every kind of party, the wife issues (and accepts) invitations for herself and her husband. She is the mistress of the household and director of the social life. Exceptions to this rule, when invitations are issued from "Mr. and Mrs.," are formal dinners, formal dances, weddings, debuts when both parents are hosts, and official functions when the husband and wife are co-hosts. One further exception to this rule is when an "informal" is used for an invitation (see page 42). Here it may be engraved or printed "Mr. and Mrs.," or the wife's informal may be used with her name alone.

The wife issues invitations with her full title: Mrs. David Allen Smith or Mrs. David Smith—never Mrs. David A. Smith, and never-never Mrs. Mary Smith. Each given name should be written out in full. Initials should not be used unless the name is just too long for normal use. Even so, it's better to drop out one or two of the given names. For example, Mrs. Archibald John Edward Gibson, Jr., could be shortened to whichever given name her husband is known by and the family name, as Mrs. John Gibson, Jr. (or junior).

Even if the invitation stems from business associations, the wife extends the invitation, although she may not personally know all the people invited. She would telephone or write the invitation to the other wife (or use whatever form of invitation is proper for the occasion). If by chance the husband should receive an invitation for his wife and himself transmitted by a business acquaintance on behalf of his wife and himself, the recipient should answer that he would like to check with his wife before giving an answer.

A single girl or woman issues invitations with the title *Miss*, as, Miss Deborah Blanchard.

A widow issues invitations exactly as a married woman would, using her married title, which is always her correct social name, such as Mrs. John Paul Johnston—never Mrs. Pamela Johnston.

A divorcee's correct social name is her family maiden name and the name of her former husband. If she was born Miss Deborah Blanchard and became Mrs. Thomas Fenton d'Arcy, her name as a divorcee becomes Mrs. Blanchard d'Arcy and her invitations should be issued that way.

Who Receives. Though invitations are usually extended by the female of the household, they are addressed to the persons you want to invite. This is so there will be no confusion in the minds of the guests as to just who is included. Thus Mrs. David Allen Smith addresses her invitation to dinner on behalf of her husband and herself to Mr. and Mrs. John Henry Hill. Invitations to single girls or women, widows, and divorcees are addressed as indicated in the section above. An invitation to a bachelor or widower should have the title Mr., as, Mr. Bruce Edward Jones.

When to Send. Invitations should be sent early enough in advance of the party to assure attendance by most of those invited. For most occasions, two weeks is correct and gives ample time for guests to "calendar" the party and respond. Invitations to a debut or formal wedding may be sent earlier, especially if a number of guests are expected to come from out of town. Also, if you live in a suburban area where weekends are heavy social periods, you may have to send your invitations as long as three to four weeks ahead.

R.s.v.p. If you expect your invited guests to answer your invitations, add at the lower left the letters "R.s.v.p.," which stand for the French phrase "Répondez s'il vous plaît" (Please answer). This may be written as shown or all in capital letters, "R.S.V.P." We prefer the capital "R" and the lower case "s.v.p.," although it is used both ways in this country. In England and France, it is always written in upper-case letters—"R.S.V.P." So you may take your choice. In some parts of our country the words "Please reply" are used instead, but this seems abrupt and not as smooth as "R.s.v.p."

If you are giving a tea or cocktail party and do not expect invitees to answer, just omit any reference to responding to the invitation. If you want answers only from those who cannot come, add the phrase "Regrets only" under the "R.s.v.p.":

R.s.v.p.
Regrets only

If your party is being held outside the home in a club, hotel, or the like, and answers are to be sent to your home, add your home address under the "R.s.v.p." Or if the invitation is from a club or organization, or from more than one host, add the name and address of the person who is receiving the answers under the "R.s.v.p.":

R.s.v.p.
Mrs. David Allen Smith
14 Shadow Lane

It seems elementary to say that all invitations received *must* be answered—either yes or no—if an answer is requested. We frequently hear of cases where no response at all is forthcoming from some of the invited guests. This can only be attributed to ignorance. Even if no answer is requested, it is thoughtful if you telephone or drop a note to your hostess and say you are looking forward to the occasion—or that you are disappointed that you cannot come. Furthermore, invitations should be answered *promptly,* within one or two days if possible, and in the same way in which they are extended. A formal third-person invitation requires a formal third-person answer, a telegraphed invitation demands an answer by telegram, and so on. If you cannot give a prompt answer because of some contingency, tell your hostess when you will be able to let her know and ask whether that is ample time for her. Never, never stall in giving an answer with the hope that something more exciting will turn up. And once you have accepted an invitation, never renege because something more enticing does arise. If you must legitimately regret an invitation after you have accepted, do so at once and give the reason. If you regret by telephone, don't leave the message with Junior or anyone else who might not relay it. *Be sure* it reaches the hostess.

Abbreviations. Socially, abbreviations are usually taboo if there is room to write out the word:

❊ In names, you may write out junior, third, fourth, as Mrs. David Allen Smith, third. However, if you prefer, or if the name is too long, abbreviations are acceptable: Jr., II, III, etc. A comma is placed before Jr., but not before the Roman numerals: Mrs. David Allen Smith, Jr.—but Mrs. David Allen Smith III. (Never use Senior after a name under any circumstances!)

❊ In street addresses, the number may be written out if it is twenty or under; for easy legibility to aid the post office, numerals may always be used:

> Fourteen Shadow Lane *or* 14 Shadow Lane
> 225 Shadow Lane (a number this large is never written out)

❊ Names of cities and states should always be written out without any abbreviations.

Handwritten vs. Typewritten.   In tune with modern living, the typewritten letter or note appears in many places where it formerly would never have dared. Even so, an invitation and acceptance or regret are still nicer and prettier if written. The typewriter should certainly never be used for a formal or semiformal invitation. Also, it should never be used for a fill-in on a printed or engraved invitation.

The Ink Color.   Dark-blue or black ink is standard for writing invitations and should always be used for formal invitations and acceptances. However, there are many colors today that are acceptable in writing papers, and so it follows that ink colors may broaden to coordinate with the paper colors when used for informal invitations. For example, on white notepaper with a turquoise monogram, turquoise ink may be used.

Addressing the Envelope. Ink used on the envelope should match that used on the invitation. The title (Miss, Mrs., Mr., Mr. and Mrs.) should always be used before the name unless it is a girl or boy under thirteen. The name goes on the first line, street address on the second, city on the third, state and zip code on the fourth. No punctuation is used at the ends of the lines. Each line may be slightly indented, or the lines may be written block fashion with the left side even:

Mr. and Mrs. John Phelps
123 East Drive
New York
New York, 10021

or:

Mr. and Mrs. John Phelps
123 East Drive
New York
New York, 10021

The sender's address may be printed or engraved on the back flaps of the envelopes that go with informal notepaper, but is not shown on the envelopes that go with visiting cards, informals, fill-in, and other formal invitations. In these latter cases, it may be written in the same ink on the back flap or in the upper left corner of the face of the envelope.

Stamp of Approval. We may seem to be batting at gnats to talk of the kinds of postage stamps to place on envelopes containing invitations. But the post office surprises us today with a multitude of stamp designs. We'll never forget our embarrassment one time when a commercial letter shop mailed invitations for us and used a memorial stamp to some dead hero all done up in black crepe. Hardly a happy note on which to introduce a party. So go to the post office and look at the stamps available. Usually, the best rule is: The simpler, the better.

Never put invitation envelopes through a postage meter, even if they are mailed as business invitations. There are some things that just never can be accepted socially, and this is one of them. We are still shocked over the young girl we heard about who, short on budget, took her wedding invitations to the office and sneaked them through the postage meter.

At a stamp auction in London a charming story of an imaginative hostess came to light when a 116-year-old envelope with stamps was sold for a record $78,400. The hostess was Lady Gomm, wife of the governor of the island Mauritius, and the party was a fancy-dress ball she and her Lord were hosting in 1857. Lady Gomm had heard of the new custom of paying postage by placing stamps on the upper right corner of the envelope. To give special flair to the invitations to her ball, she commissioned a local watchmaker to engrave a set of stamps for her. The watchmaker, not as au courant as Lady Gomm, made an error by engraving "Post Office" instead of "Post Paid," as it should have been. Lady Gomm proudly applied the stamps to her invitations—and a philatelic treasure was born!

Zip Codes.   Our only counsel here is, please! Be sure to obtain those of your friends, keep a record of them in your address file, and speed the mail by using them.

A Friend in Need.   It can throw off a hostess completely, and even spoil her party, when a guest asks to bring someone who is visiting him or her (an extra him is usually more welcome than an extra her!). It is better not to ask. Instead, say that you would love to come to the party, but that you can't because your old college roommate will be visiting you at that time. This gives the hostess leeway to invite the roommate, too, or to say she is sorry and hopes that next time you can come. Remember Shakespeare's comment that "unbidden guests are often welcomest when they are gone."

This is a good place to discuss compiling a guest list for a hostess who is giving a party in your honor. A guest of honor is usually asked whether there is anyone he or she would like to have invited. *Always* feel out the hostess as to how far she expects you to go in this case.

One of our friends planned a small, quiet post-wedding Sunday night supper party for the two sets of parents the day after a wedding and was completely set back when the bride's mother answered, "How nice, I'll send over my guest list"—and did, to the tune of 28 names. This is more than any hostess should be expected to do unless she has indicated that she wants to give a big party for you and that you are free to suggest as many names as you would like. If you are the hostess, don't pussyfoot around, but let the guest of honor know exactly how far you can go on the guest list.

To Postpone or Cancel.   There comes a time when because of some unexpected emergency or mishap, a party must be postponed or canceled and the invitation changed or withdrawn. It goes without saying that guests must be notified immediately. It is best to follow the form of the original invitation, if there is time. If not, telephone calls may be made, or telegrams may be sent. Forms for postponing or canceling are given later in this chapter.

If a party has to be postponed, you must re-invite *all* of the guests originally invited. You can't change your mind and leave out someone. Of course, you may add guests.

A reason must be given if you cancel a party. If you postpone it, you may or may not give a reason.

Children's Invitations.   Children love to receive mail, so to a child, an invitation to a party is just about as exciting as the party itself. There are many charming invitations available in card and stationery stores. Always send them for young people's parties.

Teen-age Invitations.   Teen-agers like to give different and unusual parties, and they like to send and receive invitations with a difference. So if you are giving a party for a teen-age group or helping your own teen-ager plan a party, do give special attention to the invitation. Many attractive fill-in invitations can be purchased. Or with a little ingenuity and time, attention-getting invitations may be made at home.

Business Invitations. A business invitation should follow the general ground rules for social invitations. However, some adjustments may be necessary to meet business requirements:

❧ The invitation may come from the company itself, or from one of its representatives.

❧ In a formal invitation it may be necessary to give a title and company name after the host's name so that it is clear to invitees (who may not know) exactly who the host is. For example:

Mr. Taylor Randolph
President of the Acme Corporation
requests the pleasure of your company
[etc.]

❧ Invitations are addressed to the guests as they are known professionally. Many married women in business, for example, use a given name with the title Mrs. and their husband's family name. Thus a business invitation would be addressed to: Mrs. Eleanor Jefferson Thompson, rather than to her married title, Mrs. John Robert Thompson, which the inviting company probably doesn't know, anyway. This is, of course, the complete opposite of correct social usage. If a married woman uses her maiden name in business, then an invitation is sent that way—to Miss Eleanor Jefferson, rather than to Mrs. Eleanor Jefferson Thompson.

❧ To encourage a prompt answer (which is sometimes not forthcoming in business because of tentative appointments or just plain neglect), a response card is usually enclosed with a hand-stamped self-addressed envelope. This is generally not done with social invitations. This card might be worded simply:

M (for guest to fill in own name)

accepts   regrets
(guest crosses out word that does not apply)

for Monday, October tenth

Or a name of a secretary and a telephone number may be given under the R.s.v.p. line:

R.s.v.p.
Miss Sara Whitney
321-2345

Correctly the R.s.v.p. should be followed by the address to which an acceptance or regret should be sent, but this confuses many persons in business who do not know how to write a reply. To answer this kind of R.s.v.p., use the best business paper available and write or type:

Miss Eleanor Jefferson

accepts with pleasure

Mr. Taylor Randolph's

kind invitation

for Friday, October tenth

❧ Invitations to a business party are frequently specially designed to tie in with a theme and are often quite elaborate. This is perfectly proper and adds zest to the party.

The Hostess's Paper Wardrobe

It is well worth the money and effort for any young hostess to provide herself with a wardrobe of all the writing papers and cards she may need for any occasion, and to reorder these as she uses them up. It may seem like an extravagant expense at the outset, but it costs no more in the end to have the right paper provisions always on hand. We nominate for an ideal wardrobe:

Personal Writing Paper. This is the most basic necessity for writing informal invitations, acceptances or regrets, and "bread-and-butter" letters (see Chapter 13). Tradition has always strictly prescribed folded notepaper for women, about 5 by 7 inches folded, in white, cream, blue, or gray. Newer colors are now acceptable if pale and not garish, such as pale pink, pale mauve, pale green, pale yellow. A monochromatic or contrasting border is the usual accent. These papers may be printed or engraved in a harmonizing color to match the border. Engraved paper is the finest and most expensive. In engraving, an individual metal plate must be made on which the name and/or address or monogram is etched or incised. This gives a raised effect to the letters. You must pay extra for the plate, but it becomes your property to use each time you order new paper. A similar effect is achieved in a less expensive way by using thermographic printing. Or just plain printing is perfectly acceptable on personal writing paper. The paper may be engraved or printed in *any one* of these ways:

❧ Three-letter monograms in upper left-hand corner or upper center. Choose a size that is compatible with the size of the paper, and choose a typeface that is simple—no fancy flourishes, please.

❧   Name centered at the top in a discreet typeface and harmonizing color. Your correct social title should be used (as
outlined in the section "Who Sends" on page 29). The only
exception is that a single girl may omit the title *Miss* if she
chooses. The address may be printed or engraved under the
name if desired. Or name and address may appear on one line.

❧   Address only, centered at the top in an attractive typeface
and harmonizing color.

Matching envelopes of the size to fit the note when folded
once may be lined or unlined. But do be sure that an unlined
envelope doesn't tell tales and reveal the message inside. The
back flap of the envelope should be printed or engraved with
the address of the sender. In order to save an additional engraved plate, it is also acceptable for the flap to carry the name
as well as the address. If the address is an apartment, so that a
street address is not sufficient, the name may be used also, or the
apartment number may be added after the address, as: 925 Park
Street, 18-H, or 925 Park Street, Apartment 18-H.

Another caution about abbreviations: never use them in the
markings on your personal writing paper or on the envelopes.

In using personal writing paper, the pages may be used and
numbered in any way that suits your whim: 1-2-3-4, or 1-3-2-4,
or 1-4-2-3. If you write in the 1-4-2-3 order, you may turn the
paper sideways and use the center pages as one large page.

In folding and inserting folded notepaper, fold the bottom
up to the top and insert in the envelope with the fold down.

Although Aunt Millicent may be a stickler for form and insist on folded notepaper, changing mores in our casual world
today have given the nod to other papers that are also socially
acceptable. You may choose single sheets from about 5 by 7
inches to a maximum size of 6 by 8 inches, frequently bordered.
These sheets and their matching envelopes are marked exactly
as are the folded ones described above. However, you would use

a plain sheet without any marking for the second sheet of a letter. You may write on the backs of the sheets, numbering them in order.

A handy and acceptable notepaper to use is the "semi-note" size. This is about half the size of a folded sheet, about 5 by 3½ inches, doubled with the fold at the top. It slips into its envelope without any further folding. It looks prettiest with a border and matching monogram in the center of the front side. The inside and back are used for the message. Or if you prefer, the semi-note may have your monogram at the left, with address at the right. Or it may have an address only at the top, in which event you would start the message on the front.

Tiffany, recognized arbiter of social papers and invitations, prefers a folded sheet or a semi-note for an invitation, rather than a single sheet. They feel that it looks "more gracious and generous."

Visiting Cards.   Next to notepaper, the most useful and versatile social paper is the visiting or calling card. Granted, the formal call with a clutch of cards left on the butler's silver salver is pretty much a thing of another day. However, the visiting card has assumed an important role as a medium for invitations and acceptances or regrets. It has other uses too, such as an enclosure with gifts or flowers.

There is no one set size that a visiting card must be. Actually, there are two types in two different sizes:

1. The regular visiting card for an adult woman, which may be around 2 by 3 inches. Tiffany's most popular size for women is 2¼ by 3¼. (For no apparent reason, a man's card is longer and narrower than a woman's. Standard is around 1½ by 3 inches.)
2. The other size is for a young girl who is not yet in her teens. Her card should be about 2 by 2¾ inches, or even smaller. (A boy's card is slightly smaller.)

The visiting card *must* be on kid-finish or parchment paper in white or off-white. Popular today is creamy parchment color. Engraving (never printing) *must* be in black. Panels or plate marks are not used on visiting cards.

A woman's name is engraved exactly as her name is used socially.

Girl under 13	Phyllis Potter
Girl over 13	Miss Phyllis Potter
Married woman	Mrs. Arthur Charles Garnett
Husband and wife	Mr. and Mrs. Arthur Charles Garnett
Widow	Mrs. Arthur Charles Garnett
Divorcee	Mrs. Potter Garnett

A caution once more that a woman's own given names are never used except when she is single (or on a business card, but that should never be used socially). A man may or may not use the title *Mr.* before his name. An unmarried woman always uses the title Miss on her cards.

If you are permanently settled at one address, it is handy to have your street address also engraved on the card in smaller letters at the lower right corner. Or you can go Continental and have the address placed at the upper right corner. If you move around and don't want the expense of a new plate for each move, leave off the address.

When you purchase visiting cards, be sure to order matching envelopes if you are going to use them for invitations. The minimum size that the post office will accept today is 3 by $4\frac{1}{4}$ inches, so your envelope will be larger than your card. You can, of course, order larger cards to fit this size envelope. These look quite chic when used for invitations. Tiffany and Cartier show cards up to about $3\frac{1}{2}$ by $4\frac{3}{4}$ inches in size. Of course, you would never leave a card this size when calling on someone!

There are several typefaces that are correct for use on visiting cards, but only two that are widely used. These are "Script," which has a distinguished traditional look, and "Antique Roman," which is a handsome shaded type.

Informals. The informal is similar to a visiting card except that it is double, with the fold at the top, and is usually a larger size. Today the most accepted size is the 3-by-4-inch, which is mailed in an envelope that meets the postal minimum-size specifications.

The paper is kid-finish or parchment, usually of lighter weight than that for visiting cards. Colors are white or off-white with black engraving, the name (and address if used) exactly as on a visiting card, in the same kind of type. A panel border may be used, but it isn't recommended because it makes writing more difficult. Matching envelopes are always delivered with informals.

When using an informal, the invitation may be written on the outside or inside. Either is correct. If used for a note, the message goes on the inside and may continue onto the back if needed.

Note Card. This is exactly like an informal except that it is a single card on card stock. In other words, it's a large visiting card with an envelope. It may be used for a note or an invitation. The name may be centered as on a visiting card, or it may be engraved a little above center.

Fill-In Invitation Cards. A serious hostess who entertains with any degree of formality will find it worthwhile to have a fill-in invitation card engraved, which can always be used (as long as she keeps the same name!). If she is married, these should carry the couple's name, as: Mr. and Mrs. John Allen Jackson. Matching envelopes with no return address always come with these. The card should be of white (most popular) or off-white kid-finish paper, about $4\frac{1}{4}$ by $5\frac{1}{2}$ inches. Use Script or Antique Roman in black ink for the lettering. The husband's coat of arms or crest may be embossed without color at the top center of the card, but no other marking is correct. An invitation in the name of a woman alone never carries a coat of arms, which is a masculine family insignia. A widow may use a lozenge (a diamond-shaped outline containing the heraldic insignia from her husband's shield), but a divorcee would not. A single woman may use a lozenge of her father's arms. Actually, any woman may use a lozenge from her father's coat of arms if she wishes, although it may not be technically correct in every instance.

See page 66 for the correct wording of the fill-in invitation. On each occasion for which you use this form, fill in the invited guests' names and the pertinent information in black ink in the spaces provided.

Some chic hostesses are now also using a fill-in invitation card for informal parties. Though the wording is the same as on a formal card, color gives a casual look. The message may be printed in a gay tone, such as turquoise, on a white card. There may even be a matching colored border on the card and the envelope flap. The very nature of this card indicates that the party is informal.

Formal Writing Paper. Everyone needs a box of notepaper for answering semi-formal and formal invitations. This should be good-quality perfectly plain double sheets or semi-notes in white or off-white kid-finish paper with matching envelopes (no return address). It is perfectly correct and usual for the paper and envelope to have no marking at all. However, if you prefer your papers personalized, the paper may have a monogram or lozenge (if entitled to use one) at the top center or top left. No borders of any kind should be used on this paper.

Minimum Paper Wardrobe. If your social life does not demand that you keep a supply of all of the papers described in the ideal wardrobe, you can manage nicely with only three: personal paper, visiting cards, and formal writing paper.

Casual Invitations

A new kind of invitation has come into being as a new kind of casual entertaining has taken over a large part of our social lives. The occasion has a casual, almost spur-of-the-moment feeling, such as . . .

"drop in for a cup of coffee"
"come over for lunch"
"let's go to the movies together"
"come for dinner"
"come for potluck supper"
"drop in for tea"
"stop by for a drink"

The invitation follows suit and is equally casual. It is extended only a few days before the occasion, or even as late as the same day. It would be ostentatious to employ any other form than a telephone call or a direct personal word. Naturally, if the person you invite lives in a suburb or the country or a nearby town, and you prefer to send a note, that is certainly correct. But remember that the note must be sent in time for an answer to be transmitted.

When telephoning an invitation, be short, sweet, and to the point. There is no need to enter into a prolonged conversation unless you are calling one of your intimates and just want to chat.

Telephoned Casual Invitation.

1. *Invitation:* Hello, Jane. This is Constance. George's sister and her husband surprised us with an overnight visit, and we'd love to have you and Bob come by for a cocktail and buffet tonight. About seven o'clock would be fine.

2. *Acceptance:* We'd love to. We're so fond of George's sister and brother-in-law. It'll be great to see them. Thanks for ask-.ing us . . . we'll see you at seven.

3. *Regret:* Oh, Jane, we just can't make it, because Bob has a business meeting this evening. Do give them our very best . . . and tell them we hope for better luck next time.

4. *Cancellation:* Hello, Jane. This is Constance. I'm calling regretfully to say that we're going to have to cancel our plans for this evening. Suzy was sent home from school with a fever and sore throat. The next time George and Helen are here, we'll try again.

Casual Invitation by Personal Note.

5. *Invitation:*

Dear Meg:
  Dick's boss gave him
four tickets to Cinerama
for this Saturday night
at nine. We're hoping
you and Phil can go
with us - the reviews
say it's great. Come
at seven for dinner
beforehand.
  Let us know - and
do come.

              Affectionately,
                  Sally
July First

6. *Acceptance:*

> Dear Sally:
> How did you know
> we've been dying to
> see Cinerama! We
> wouldn't miss going
> with you and Dick ...
> and will arrive at
> your house around
> seven. Thanks - thanks!
>
>   Affectionately,
>   Meg
>
> July second

7. *Regret:*

Dear Sally:
  I could weep! We've
been dying to see
Cinerama -and most
of all to see you. But
Saturday is Jan's
birthday, so our house
will be bursting with
teen-agers. Phil and
I have to be around
to keep the roof on.
  Thanks for the
generous invitation.
Again - we're sorry.

                 Affectionately,
                     meg
July second

8. Cancellation:

Dear Meg:
   A quick note to let you
know that the plans for
Cinerama and dinner
Saturday night have
had to be canceled.
Dick has to make an
urgent business trip to
Chicago and will be
away over the weekend.
We're going to try to
exchange the tickets
for a later date — and
will let you know.
   We're so disappointed,
but hope we can all
have an evening
together soon.
                    Affectionately,
                      Sally

July third

Informal Invitations

Any party that involves more than six persons, except strictly formal occasions, calls for informal invitations. Some of these occasions are:

> breakfast
> coffee
> brunch
> lunch
> dessert
> shower
> tea or cocktails
> open house
> dinner
> supper
> card party
> picnic or cookout
> informal dance

Invitations to these and many other similar affairs may be given in a number of ways. As we have urged you before, we urge you again to give extra flair and excitement to your parties by varying the types of invitations. Each time choose a different form from the many possibilities:

> personal invitation
> telephone call
> personal note
> visiting card
> informal card
> informal fill-in card
> printed purchased invitation
> hand-made special invitation
> telegram

Many attractive printed invitations may be purchased for informal parties. There is a particular abundance of printed cocktail invitations that are in very good taste. All that is necessary is to fill in the party information and mail. It's quick and easy, and does give variety to your party bids.

If the party has a specific theme or purpose—and if you're the do-it-yourself type—you can carry out the idea by making invitations that tie in. For a tot's party, a felt cutout of a teddy bear or other animal can be pasted on a card with the written invitation. For a barbecue, it might be a leather cutout in the shape of an animal hide that adorns a rough-textured invitation paper. Or for a hootenanny and bagged supper, write the invitation on a brown grocery bag, fold it, and close with a colored seal. Let your imagination soar, and come up with your own original ideas.

Informal invitations should be extended or sent two weeks before the party. If given personally or by telephone, it's a good idea to send a written reminder that can take the form of a written note, a visiting card, an informal card, or almost any written form. Just add the words, "A reminder," or "To remind you." The value of the follow-up reminder is to give the guest all of the information about the party in writing so that hostess and guests will all be synchronized as to day and time.

Informal Telephoned Invitation.

9. *Invitation:*   Hello, Mrs. Johnston? [Or Sarah, if an intimate friend.] This is Mary Sheridan. We would like so much to have you and your husband come for dinner on Thursday evening, July tenth, at eight o'clock. We're having a small group of friends, and it will be informal.

10. *Acceptance:*   We'd love to come! I'll put it on my calendar right away—for Thursday, July tenth, at eight. Many, many thanks . . . it will be so good to see you.

11. *Regret:* You're darling to include us ... but we're going to be at the shore the whole month of July. We'll certainly miss being there, but look forward to seeing you when we get back.

12. *Follow-up Reminder:* *

Dear Mrs. Johnston:

We're delighted that you and your husband can come for dinner on Thursday evening, July tenth, at eight o'clock. It will be so good to see you both.

Sincerely,
Mary Sheridan

July first

* Note should use informal first-name address if person is well known.

(On visiting card or informal)

a reminder

Dinner, Wed., July 10, at 8

MRS. JAMES SHERIDAN

10 Waverly Street

(Note: If card or informal is small, this is the one time when abbreviations are acceptable.)

13. *Cancellation:*   Hello, Mrs. Johnston? This is Mary Sheridan again. I'm so sorry to have to call and tell you that we have had to cancel our dinner on Thursday, the tenth. My mother is ill, and I'm flying to Boston tonight. We hope to be able to plan another party as soon as Mother is better.

14. *Postponement:*   Hello, Mrs. Johnston? This is Mary Sheridan again. I'm so sorry to have to call and tell you that we have had to postpone our dinner scheduled for Thursday, the tenth, until Thursday, the seventeenth. My husband has to be away on urgent business the tenth. We do hope you will be able to come on the seventeenth at the same time— eight o'clock.

Informal Invitation by Personal Note.

15. *Invitation:* *

Dear Mrs. Jamison:
My husband and I
would love to have
you and Mr. Jamison
come to a small
buffet supper on
Sunday evening,
March tenth, at
nine o'clock. After
supper we have a
marvelous old Valentino
movie to show.
Do let us know that
you will be able
to come.
Sincerely,
Janis Fielding

February twenty-fourth

* Note should use informal first-name address if person is well known.

16. *Acceptance:* *

> Dear Mrs. Fielding:
>
> We are delighted to accept your kind invitation for supper and a Valentino movie on Sunday evening, March Tenth, at nine.
>
> Sincerely,
> Phyllis Jamison
>
> February Twenty-sixth

* Note should use informal first-name address if person is well known.

17. *Regret:* *

Dear Mrs. Fielding:

We are so sorry that we will not be able to be with you on Sunday evening, March tenth. My sister and her husband will be visiting us from Chicago at that time. Our sincere appreciation for the kind invitation.

Sincerely,
Phyllis Jamison

February twenty-sixth

(Note: The hostess may at this point telephone Mrs. Jamison and say that she would like very much to have the Jamisons come and bring Mrs. Jamison's sister and her husband. Or she may simply accept the regret, if she does not want to include additional guests.)

18. *Cancellation:* *

Dear Mrs. Jamison:

My husband and I regret that we must cancel our buffet supper for Sunday evening, March tenth, because of emergency surgery which our son Tommy has had to undergo.

As soon as Tommy is well again, we hope to see you.

Sincerely,
Janis Fielding

March first

* Note should use informal first-name address if person is well known.

19. Postponement: *

Dear Mrs. Jamison:

We have had to postpone our buffet supper and film from Sunday, March tenth, to Sunday evening, March seventeenth, at the same time — nine o'clock. The change in date is necessary because of illness in our family.

We are sorry about the tenth, but hope you will be able to come on the seventeenth. Please let me know whether you can.

Sincerely,

Janis Fielding

March third

Informal Invitation on Visiting Card, Informal, or Note Card.

20. *Invitation:*

> To meet Mr. and Mrs. John Downing
> Cocktails, Tues., June 5, 5 to 7
>
> *Mrs. David George Dailey*
>
>   *17 East Drive*
>
> R. s. v. p.

(Vary wording to suit event—at home, to honour, etc.)

21. *Acceptance:*

> Accepts with pleasure
> for Tues., June 5, 5 to 7
>
> *Mrs. Robert Chancelor*

22. *Regret:*

> Sorry, unable to come
> Tues., June 5
>
> *Mrs. Robert Chancelor*
>
> will be away

23. *Cancellation:*

Sorry, must cancel
for Tues., June 5th

Mrs. David George Dailey

because of my
husband's illness

17 East Drive

24. *Postponement:*

Party to meet
Mr. and Mrs. John Downing
postponed from June 5
to Fri., June 8, 5 to 7

Mrs. David George Dailey

R. s. v. p.   *17 East Drive*

(Note: As mentioned before, abbreviations are acceptable
on visiting cards, informals, or note cards if there is not
room to write out all the information.)

Informal Invitation on Fill-In Card.

Wording is the same as for formal fill-in cards. The difference is that here informal paper stock, colors, and typeface may be used. For forms see: Invitation 30, Acceptance 31, Regret 32, Cancellation 33, Postponement 34.

Informal Invitation by Telegram.

25. *Invitation:*

MAY 18

MR. AND MRS. JOHN HENRY HESTER
500 PARK LANE
NEW YORK CITY

HOPE YOU CAN JOIN US FOR LUNCH ON SUNDAY, JUNE FIRST, AT ONE O'CLOCK TO MEET MR. AND MRS. GEORGE JENKINS OF BEVERLY HILLS. R.S.V.P.

KAY KEITH

26. *Acceptance:*

MAY 19

MRS. WILLIAM KEITH
123 EAST PLACE
NEW YORK CITY

WE WOULD LOVE TO COME SUNDAY, JUNE FIRST, AT ONE TO MEET THE JENKINS.

MILDRED HESTER

27. *Regret:*

MAY 19

MRS. WILLIAM KEITH

123 EAST PLACE

NEW YORK CITY

THANK YOU FOR INVITATION FOR SUNDAY, JUNE FIRST. REGRET WE ARE UNABLE TO COME AS WE WILL BE OUT OF TOWN.

MILDRED HESTER

28. *Cancellation:*

MAY 25

MR. AND MRS. JOHN HENRY HESTER

500 PARK LANE

NEW YORK CITY

REGRET WE MUST CANCEL THE LUNCH ON SUNDAY, JUNE FIRST, BECAUSE OF ILLNESS IN THE FAMILY.

KAY KEITH

29. *Postponement:*

MAY 25

MR. AND MRS. JOHN HENRY HESTER

500 PARK LANE

NEW YORK CITY

LUNCH ON SUNDAY, JUNE FIRST, HAS BEEN POSTPONED TO

SUNDAY, JUNE EIGHTH, AT ONE BECAUSE THE JENKINS'S TRIP

WAS DELAYED. DO LET US KNOW THAT YOU CAN COME ON

THE NEW DATE.

KAY KEITH

Formal Invitations

For most of us today the formal invitation is a rarity, either to send or to receive. The reason is again our wonderfully down-to-earth life, which takes most things in casual stride. On the other hand, there's hardly anyone who doesn't at some time or other have to extend, accept, or regret a formal invitation. If this kind of party isn't the usual thing in our personal lives, we do encounter it in connection with clubs and organizations to which we belong.

But let's just say an encouraging word in favor of going all out once in a while and "going formal." Spring is a propitious time for a formal dinner and dance, or a dance followed by supper. The debut party for young women is another occasion that is growing all across the country, and should be encouraged. Holiday time between Thanksgiving and New Year's just cries for dress-up parties. So corral your friends, lasso your men, and see what a great time you will have.

The usual occasions that demand formal invitations are:

> formal dinner or banquet
> formal dance or ball
> debut party
> official functions
> sorority and fraternity dinners and dances
> junior and senior proms
> formal parties of clubs and organizations
> weddings and receptions

Formal invitations *must* be sent two weeks in advance of the party date. If a number of invited guests are expected to come from out of town, as for a debut or wedding, the invitations can go three to four weeks ahead. Better too early than too late. The means of issuing a formal invitation are limited to these, *all written in the third person:*

> telegram
> engraved invitation
> engraved fill-in invitation
> formal handwritten invitation

"Black tie" may or may not be noted in the lower right corner. The very form and appearance of a formal invitation imply "Black tie"—but we are for being specific if there is a chance of any doubt. If "White tie" is expected, this must be noted in the lower right corner. (See page 384 for type of dress required.)

Formal Fill-In Invitation.   This handy social tool must be engraved or thermographically printed on white or cream card stock with kid finish. Most popular size is about 4¼ by 5½ inches. The basic form is shown on the card, with the specific information for each party written in by hand with black ink. In the forms below, note how the date and time are written, how the lines are spaced, and that lower-case letters are used at the beginning of each line (information to be filled in is in parentheses). (When these forms are used for informal invitations, the paper, colors, and typeface are informal.)

30. *Invitation:* *

> Mr. and Mrs. John Thomas Love
> request the pleasure of
> (Miss Smith's)
> company at   (dinner)
> on (Thursday, the fifth of June)
> at   (eight o'clock)
> 10 Broad Avenue
>
> R.s.v.p.

or:

> Mr. and Mrs. John Thomas Love
> request the pleasure of the company of
> (Miss Smith)
> at   (dinner)
> on (Thursday, the fifth of June)
> at   (eight o'clock)
> 10 Broad Avenue
>
> R.s.v.p.

---

* When these forms are used for informal invitations, the paper, color, and typeface are informal.

31. *Acceptance:* Handwritten on formal note or semi-note paper.

Miss Helen Smith

accepts with pleasure

Mr. and Mrs. Love's

kind invitation for

Thursday, the fifth of June

at eight o'clock

32. Regret: *

Miss Helen Smith

regrets

she cannot accept

Mr. and Mrs. Love's

Kind invitation for

Thursday, the fifth of June

---

* When these forms are used for informal invitations, the paper, color, and typeface are informal.

33. *Cancellation:* Engraved, thermographed, or written by hand on formal note or semi-note paper.

Mr. and Mrs. John Thomas Love
regret that it is necessary to
recall their invitation for dinner
on Thursday, the fifth of June
because of the illness of Mr. Love

34. *Postponement:* *   Handled in the same way as a cancellation.

Mr. and Mrs. John Thomas Love

regret that it is necessary to

postpone their invitation to dinner

from Thursday, the fifth of June

to Thursday, the twelfth of June

at eight o'clock

10 Broad Avenue

R.s.v.p.

---

* When these forms are used for informal invitations, the paper, color, and typeface are informal.

Formal Invitation by Telegram.

35. Invitation:

JUNE 10

MR. AND MRS. JOHN HENRY HESTER
500 EAST AVENUE
NEW YORK CITY

MR. AND MRS. WILLIAM KEITH REQUEST THE PLEASURE OF
YOUR COMPANY AT A SMALL DANCE ON SATURDAY, THE
TWENTY-FIFTH OF JUNE, AT HALF AFTER TEN O'CLOCK.
BLACK TIE. R.S.V.P.

(No signature)

36. Acceptance:

JUNE 11

MR. AND MRS. WILLIAM KEITH
123 PARK PLACE
NEW YORK CITY

MR. AND MRS. JOHN HENRY HESTER ACCEPT WITH PLEASURE
MR. AND MRS. KEITH'S KIND INVITATION FOR SATURDAY, THE
TWENTY-FIFTH OF JUNE, AT HALF AFTER TEN O'CLOCK.

(No signature)

37. *Regret:*

JUNE 11

MR. AND MRS. WILLIAM KEITH

123 PARK PLACE

NEW YORK CITY

MR. AND MRS. JOHN HENRY HESTER REGRET THAT THEY ARE
UNABLE TO ACCEPT MR. AND MRS. KEITH'S KIND INVITATION
FOR SATURDAY, THE TWENTY-FIFTH OF JUNE, BECAUSE OF
A PREVIOUS ENGAGEMENT.

(No signature)

38. *Cancellation:*

JUNE 20

MR. AND MRS. JOHN HENRY HESTER

500 EAST AVENUE

NEW YORK, NEW YORK

MR. AND MRS. WILLIAM KEITH REGRET THAT BECAUSE OF
THE SUDDEN ILLNESS OF MR. KEITH THEIR INVITATION FOR
SATURDAY, THE TWENTY-FIFTH OF JUNE, IS RECALLED.

(No signature)

39. *Postponement:*

JUNE 20

MR. AND MRS. JOHN HENRY HESTER

500 EAST AVENUE

NEW YORK, NEW YORK

MR. AND MRS. WILLIAM KEITH REGRET THAT IT IS NECES-
SARY TO POSTPONE THEIR INVITATION TO A SMALL DANCE
FROM SATURDAY, THE TWENTY-FIFTH OF JUNE, TO SATUR-
DAY, THE SECOND OF JULY, AT HALF AFTER TEN O'CLOCK.
R.S.V.P.

(No signature)

(Note: In issuing any kind of invitation by telegram, the
guest list, together with the invitation message, is simply
given to the telegraph company. This may be handled
over the telephone, but it is much safer and more likely
to be transmitted correctly if you write it out and deliver
it to the telegraph office.)

Formal Engraved or Handwritten Invitation.

40. *Dinner Invitation:*

Mr. and Mrs. Charles Reese duBois

request the pleasure of your company

at dinner

on Thursday, the first of October

at eight o'clock

500 Sutton Avenue

R.s.v.p.   **Black tie**

41. *Acceptance:*

Mr. and Mrs. Alexander McKnight

accept with pleasure

the kind invitation of

Mr. and Mrs. du Bois

for dinner

on Thursday, the first of October

at eight o'clock.

42. *Regret:*

Mr. and Mrs. Alexander McKnight

regret

that because of a previous engagement

they will be unable to accept

Mr. and Mrs. du Bois's

kind invitation

for the first of October

43. *Formal Dance:*

Mr. and Mrs. Jamison Guest

request the pleasure of your company

at a small dance

on Saturday, the third of December

at half after ten o'clock

The Empire Room

Waldorf-Astoria

R.s.v.p.

123 North Street

44. Acceptance:

Mr. and Mrs. Albert Downing

accept with pleasure

the kind invitation of

Mr. and Mrs. Quest

for Saturday, the third of December

at half after ten o'clock

45. *Regret:*

Mr. and Mrs. Albert Downing

regret

that because of a previous engagement

they will be unable to accept

Mr. and Mrs. Guest's

kind invitation

for the third of December

46. *Debut—Afternoon Tea:*

Mrs. John Howard Payne

Miss Susan Payne

will be at home

Thursday, the tenth of December

from five until seven o'clock

100 North River Drive

(Note: No response required because no R.s.v.p.)

47. *Debut—Ball or Dance:*

Mr. and Mrs. John Howard Payne
Miss Susan Payne
request the pleasure of your company
on Saturday, the tenth of December
at ten o'clock
One Lake Drive
R.s.v.p.   Dancing

or:

Mr. and Mrs. John Howard Payne
request the pleasure of your company
at a dance
in honour of their daughter
Miss Susan Payne
on Monday, the tenth of January
at ten o'clock
One Lake Drive
R.s.v.p.

or:

Mr. and Mrs. John Howard Payne
request the pleasure of the company of
(Mr. Bartlett)
at a dance
in honour of their daughter
Miss Susan Payne
on Monday, the tenth of January
at ten o'clock
One Lake Drive
R.s.v.p.

48. *Acceptance:*

Mr. Charles Edward Bartlett

accepts with pleasure

Mr. and Mrs. Payne's

kind invitation

for Monday, the tenth of January

at ten o'clock

49. *Regret:*

Mr. Charles Edward Bartlett

regrets

that because of a previous engagement

he will be unable to accept

Mr. and Mrs. Payne's

kind invitation

for Monday, the tenth of January

50. *Wedding Anniversary:*

1931   1966

Mr. and Mrs. Robert Waters
at home
Thursday, the first of June
from five until seven o'clock
21 Turtle Creek
R.s.v.p.
Regrets only

or:

Mr. and Mrs. Robert Waters
request the pleasure of your company
at a dinner celebrating
the fiftieth anniversary of their marriage
on Tuesday, the first of June
at eight o'clock
21 Turtle Creek

R.s.v.p.

51. *Regret:* (For either invitation)

Mr. and Mrs. John McHugh

regret that they are unable to accept

Mr. and Mrs. Water's

Kind invitation

for the first of June

52. *Acceptance:*

Mr. and Mrs. John McHugh

accept with pleasure

Mr. and Mrs. Water's

Kind invitation for dinner

on Monday, the first of June

at eight o'clock

53. *Invitation from School:*

The President and Trustees of Smith University

request the pleasure of your company

at a dinner in honour of

Doctor Charles Raney, Dean of the School of Medicine

on Friday, the fifth of October

at eight o'clock

The Faculty Club

R.s.v.p.   Black tie

Miss Sarah Johnson

100 Quadrangle

54. *Acceptance:*

Professor and Mrs. John Scott

accept with pleasure

the kind invitation of

the President and Trustees of Smith University

for dinner

on Friday, the fifth of October

at eight o'clock

55. *Regret:*

Professor and Mrs. John Scott

regret that they are unable to accept

the kind invitation of

the President and Trustees of Smith University

for Friday, the fifth of October

56. *Invitation from Club or Organization:*

Alpha Beta Gamma

requests the pleasure of your company

on Saturday, the first of March

at ten o'clock

State Room

Student Union Building

R.s.v.p.   Dancing

Miss Mary Samuels

Alpha Beta Gamma House

57. *Acceptance:*

Miss Pamela Powers

accepts with pleasure

the kind invitation of

Alpha Beta Gamma

for Saturday, the first of March

at ten o'clock

58. *Regret:*

Miss Pamela Powers

regrets

that she is unable to accept

the kind invitation of

Alpha Beta Gamma

for Saturday, the first of March

59. *School Prom:*

The Senior Class

of Central High School

requests the pleasure of your company

at the Senior Spring Prom

on Friday, the tenth of May

at nine o'clock

The Starlight Roof

Waldorf-Astoria

R.s.v.p.   Black tie

60. *Acceptance Card:* (Enclosed with invitation)

M   (name to be filled in)
will attend
the Senior Spring Prom
on Friday, the tenth of May
and will have as guest
M   (name to be filled in)

Subscription: $5.00 a couple

(Note: Where there is a subscription for a party, as for a
school prom or a charity ball, it is better to use an acceptance card that shows the amount, rather than note this on
the formal invitation. If the recipient of the invitation
does not wish to attend, no regret is necessary.)

Cancellations or postponements of the formal invitations from
No. 40 through No. 56 would follow forms 33 and 34, respectively.

❧❧ *Quick Key to Party Invitations* ❧❧

Here is a fast guide to any and all problems concerning the giving and answering of invitations. The numbers refer to the preceding examples on pages 44 to 91. If the reference is made to several types, such as informal and formal, choose the one that suits the degree of formality of your party. Change the wording to fit your occasion. Numbers in parentheses refer to notes appearing on page 95.

❊ CASUAL ❊

	Invitation	Acceptance	Regret	Cancellation	Postponement
Barbecue	1, 5	2, 6	3, 7	4, 8	—(1)
Breakfast	1, 5	2, 6	3, 7	4, 8	—
Brunch	1, 5	2, 6	3, 7	4, 8	—
Buffet	1, 5	2, 6	3, 7	4, 8	—
Cocktails	1, 5	2, 6	3, 7	4, 8	—
Coffee	1, 5	2, 6	3, 7	4, 8	—
Cookout	1, 5	2, 6	3, 7	4, 8	—(1)
Dessert	1, 5	2, 6	3, 7	4, 8	—
Dinner	1, 5	2, 6	3, 7	4, 8	—
Luncheon	1, 5	2, 6	3, 7	4, 8	—
Picnic	1, 5	2, 6	3, 7	4, 8	—
Soup	1, 5	2, 6	3, 7	4, 8	—
TV Party	1, 5	2, 6	3, 7	4, 8	—

❀ INFORMAL ❀

	Invitation	Acceptance	Regret	Cancellation	Postponement
Anniversary	20[2], 30	21, 31	22, 32	23, 33	—[3]
At Home	20[4]	—[4]	22	23	24
Barbecue	9 & 12, 15, 25	10, 16, 26	11, 17, 27	13, 18, 28	14, 19, 29
Birthday	9 & 12, 15, 20, 25, 30	10, 16, 21, 26, 31	11, 17, 22, 27, 32	13, 18, 23, 28, 33	—[3]
Breakfast	9 & 12, 15	10, 16	11, 17	13, 18	14, 19
Brunch	9 & 12, 15, 20, 25	10, 16, 21, 26	11, 17, 22, 27	13, 18, 23, 28	14, 19, 24, 29
Buffet	9 & 12, 15, 20, 25, 30	10, 16, 21, 26, 31	11, 17, 22, 27, 32	13, 18, 23, 28, 33	14, 19, 24, 29, 34
Card Party	9 & 12, 15, 20	10, 16, 21	11, 17, 22	13, 18, 23	14, 19, 24
Christening	9 & 12, 15, 20[7], 25	10, 16, 21, 26	11, 17, 22, 27	—[6]	14, 19, 24, 29
Cocktails	9 & 12, 20[4]	10	11, 22	13, 23	14, 24
Coffee	9 & 12, 15, 20[4]	10, 16	11, 17, 22	13, 18, 23	14, 19, 24
Cookout	9 & 12, 15, 25	10, 16, 26	11, 17, 27	13, 18, 28	14, 19, 29
Dance	20, 30	21, 31	22, 32	23, 33	24, 34
Dessert	9 & 12, 15, 20	10, 16, 21	11, 17, 22	13, 18, 23	14, 19, 24
Dinner	9 & 12, 15, 20, 25, 30	10, 16, 21, 26, 31	11, 17, 22, 27, 32	13, 18, 23, 28, 33	14, 19, 24, 29, 34
Engagement	20	21	22	23	24
Luncheon	9 & 12, 15, 20, 25	10, 16, 21, 26	11, 17, 22, 27	13, 18, 23, 28	14, 19, 23, 24, 29
Open House	20	21	22	23	24

Chart continues on following page

❧ I N F O R M A L (*continued*) ❧

	Invitation	Acceptance	Regret	Cancellation	Postponement
Picnic	9 & 12, 15, 25	10, 16, 26	11, 17, 27	13, 18, 23	14, 19, 29
Reception	20	21	22	23	24
Shower	9 & 12, 15, 20	10, 16, 21	11, 17, 22	13, 18, 23	14, 19, 24
Soup	9 & 12, 15	10, 16	11, 17	13, 18	14, 19
Supper	9 & 12, 15, 20, 25, 30	10, 16, 21, 26, 31	11, 17, 22, 27, 32	13, 18, 23, 28, 33	14, 19, 24, 29, 34
Tea	20	21	22	23	24
TV Party	9 & 12, 15	10, 16	11, 17	13, 18	14, 19

❧ F O R M A L ❧

	Invitation	Acceptance	Regret	Cancellation	Postponement
Anniversary	50	52	51	33	—(3)
At Home	46	—(4)	49	33	34
Ball	43, 47, 56, 59	44, 48, 57, 60	45, 49, 58	33	34
Birthday	30(5), 35, 40, 43	31, 36, 41, 44	32, 37, 42, 45	33, 38	—(3)
Dance	30, 35, 43, 47, 56, 59	31, 36, 44, 48, 57, 60	32, 37, 45, 49, 58	33, 38	34, 39
Debut	46, 47	48	49	33(8)	34
Dinner	30, 35, 40, 50, 53	31, 36, 41, 52, 54	32, 37, 42, 51, 55	33, 38	34, 39
Engagement	30, 40	31, 41	32, 42	33	34

Chart continues on following page

❧ FORMAL (*continued*) ❧

	Invitation	Acceptance	Regret	Cancellation	Postponement
Open House	46	—	—	33	34
Prom	59	60	—	33	34
Reception	46, 50	52	51	33	34
Supper	30, 35	31, 36	32, 37	33, 38	34, 39
Tea	46	—	—	33	34

1. A casual invitation is so spur-of-the-moment that the event would ordinarily not be postponed.
2. The visiting card or informal used should be in both names— Mr. and Mrs. If given in honor of a couple, wording would be "To honour" (this spelling always used in invitations). If given by the couple themselves, the wording would be "25th Wedding Anniversary."
3. It is unlikely that a birthday or wedding anniversary celebration would be postponed to another date, although it might be canceled because of an emergency.
4. An invitation to a cocktail, tea, or other "drop in" party usually does not call for an R.s.v.p. unless for "Regrets only," which is noted right under the R.s.v.p.
5. A birthday party may take the form of any formal party— dinner, dance, etc., so formal invitations 30, 35, 40, 43 would apply. The words "To celebrate the birthday of Mrs. (or Mr.) Smith" may be included if desired.
6. It is unlikely that a christening would be canceled, although it might be postponed because of a family emergency.
7. An invitation to a christening sent on a visiting card should be on the "Mr. and Mrs." card.
8. It is unlikely that a debut would be completely canceled except for a family death or serious illness. In this case it might be canceled completely at the time and re-scheduled at some later time.

A Treasury of *T*able *S*ettings and *K*itchen *E*quipment Guide

After all, you can't expect men not to judge by
appearances. —Ellen Glasgow.

4

Attractive surroundings bring out the best in people. We asked the parents of two teen-agers how they manage to have such successful parties for the high school crowd and yet avoid the rowdiness and crashing that we frequently read about. Their advice was to put the emphasis on the setting itself. Although they have an attractive recreation room, they make it a practice to use their living room, dining room, and best china and silver when their children entertain, disregarding the rumpus room entirely (even the name suggests havoc). The young guests come dressed in their best clothes and always respond to the beautiful setting with beautiful behavior. Decorations and entertainment are carefully planned so that all will have a good time. Summer parties are held in the yard, but dress consists of simple sports clothes with never a hint of the beatnik—except for the possible exception of a costume party.

We experienced a similar reaction to setting when we once invited to lunch the housekeeper of an apartment hotel where we were living. Because of her many favors to us, this was our way of reciprocating. She was as rough and ready as they come when bossing her staff in the building, but when she sat down at the table, spread with our best china and silver, she underwent a personality metamorphosis and became a dignified, soft-spoken lady with perfect manners. We do believe in using our best whenever we have guests, whether there are two or twenty. It's not a matter of trying to impress someone, but rather a desire to make the occasion a very special one. Almost everything on your table will outlive you, including the table itself, so enjoy what you have. A friend often remarks when getting out her best for family use, "After all, who is better than we are!" We once knew a gracious lady who was dining-room hostess in a New York girls' club. She always enjoyed making things pretty for the girls and planning little treats. While her husband was alive, she told us, dinner was planned each evening as though it were a party, using seasonal and holiday decorations whenever possible so that each meal was a delightful experience. When she became a widow, she transferred these attentions to the girls in the club, and they loved her for it. With just a little extra thought and effort you can make any meal a very special event for whoever shares your board, and that last full measure of devotion that you put into the occasion will long be remembered by the guest.

Here once again that word "appropriateness" rears its head. Your way of entertaining should be not only appropriate to your style of living, but also appropriate to the theme within your home. Fashion authorities have been hammering away at us for years about being understated rather than overstated in our dress, and the same rule applies to the home. Vermeil befits the elegance and formality of the manor house on the hill staffed with servants, but it is ostentatious in the do-it-yourself abode where the husband on the way up is straining to pay the mortgage.

With shops crammed to capacity with tempting treasures to accent hospitality, it's a real struggle to resist them. We have a friend whose most consuming vice is collecting innumerable sets of unusual dishes to set off her parties. Where she stores them is still a mystery to us, but her table is always a delightful surprise, and we anticipate each meal there, wondering what will it be this time—chile con carne in a Mexican clay tureen, or bird's-nest soup in Chinese rice bowls. The fact that she is also a superior cook, the kind who can whip out a Baked Alaska to dazzle her guests, becomes almost incidental.

It would be a luxury for any hostess to have a choice of dishes for each party, but most of us have to make do with only a few variations. It takes years for a young wife to accumulate an adequate hospitality wardrobe, but you can manage quite nicely with the minimum in equipment if sufficient thought goes into every purchase. Thank goodness, the days of everything matching are gone—forever, we hope! How dull it is to use the same pattern in dishes throughout every single course of every single meal. It makes for much more interesting parties, as well as more interesting shopping, to poke around in unusual boutiques and antiques shops for dessert plates that are the real you. Far more fun than telephoning for six desserts to match the dinner plates. One of our most exciting finds happened unexpectedly when we had no thought of purchasing more dishes. We stumbled upon a set of very early French Quimper plates, each one handmade and charmingly individual. They are conversation pieces whenever used.

Smallest details can make a difference in the party beautiful, for they add up to a pleasing total. The tray on which you serve the sherry seems inconsequential, but the tray can set off the glasses just as the mounting sets off a fine diamond. And if small details make such a difference, how much more important are the large considerations, such as dishes, silver, and linens. It is important that individual selections for your table contribute to an altogether look. Each thing is an integral part of the whole and not to be chosen indifferently or carelessly. Do linens, china, silver, and glassware complement each other? Do they fit into the overall decorating and color scheme of the dining room? Is there a good balance between pattern on the table and pattern on the walls or at the windows? Do linens clash with carpeting, or make pleasing eye travel from one to the other? Try to carry the same general feeling throughout, either formal or casual. This doesn't mean that you can't have fine china and crystal in a room of simple pine furniture and braided rugs. But do choose patterns suitable to the surroundings.

If you feel unsure of your own taste, you can acquire a sound education in what goes with what by spending no money, but time. And the more time you spend, the more knowledge you will acquire. Shop, shop, shop the good stores where they sell high-quality merchandise. You can study the handsome displays in stores throughout the year of table and room settings, fabric and color combinations. It's well worth every minute you spend looking and taking notes before buying a major item. Constant study of home magazines and books by decorators can be of great help, too. When you feel that you have thoroughly covered the field, spend time thinking. Sort things out in your mind; consider the type of entertaining you wish to do, your home, and the amount of money budgeted for this purpose. Then make your decision. As brides we did this, and we are as happy now with our selections as we were then. Many additions have been made through the years, but all for the purpose of expanding, not replacing, our original choices. Once you've made all the big decisions, it's clear sailing ahead, and you're on your way to becoming the gracious hostess your husband will be proud of.

A Word About Borrowing

The gracious lender is a friend indeed, but too much borrowing puts a strain on the most solid relationship—especially if damage occurs to the borrowed item. This subject always brings to mind a neighbor of our youth. Every time she gave a party, she called upon our mother to supply card tables, dishes, Mah-Jongg sets, and even leveled our garden periodically for her supply of flowers. Mother never seemed to mind until the day when she in turn asked to borrow a silver tray. Mrs. "X" declined with a limp excuse, and after that we were less than enthusiastic when the neighbor gave a party.

It's helpful and inoffensive to borrow a rarely used item from kissing cousins or close friends, but we don't advocate borrowing with any degree of regularity. It's habit-forming and should be avoided whenever possible. We never acquired this habit and even as youngsters seldom borrowed each other's clothes. Hence our system of building a party around what we already possess comes naturally. We do have the same silver and crystal patterns, so we can exchange occasionally for large parties. These things are replaceable in case of accident, but we'd never want the responsibility of borrowing anything irreplaceable, such as an heirloom punch bowl. In this age of easy party rentals, there is actually no need to make a habit of borrowing (see Chapter 7).

Color Scheming

When you enter a home, the color scheme is probably the first thing that strikes you. It makes either beautiful music or crashing discords, or like a lost chord it registers nothing. When you select your hospitality wardrobe of dishes and linens, remember that color coordination is just as important here as it is in wallpaper, paint, draperies, upholstery—or your clothes. Fortunately, today you have greater freedom in combining colors than ever before. A few years ago, who would have dared combine blue and green, or orange and pink (established twosomes now)? The secret, of course, is in coupling the right value and intensity of the various colors.

Most of us expect to use the same dishes throughout our married lives, because they represent a substantial financial investment, yet no one expects to have the same paint on the living-room walls or the same paper in the dining room twenty years hence. If you are worried about future decorating bouts and a possible change in color scheme, be reassured by the fact that whether you realize it or not, you will always lean toward a particular color. Everyone is a color—one of us is yellow, the other is blue; one friend is green, and another gold. Your color will run throughout your life in many different ways, but ten to one it will always be present.

If you are among the fainthearted who won't take chances, choose basic white, which is always correct. Shops offer an impressive variety of white dinnerware that you can vary with other textures in white. The early white ironstone is being copied today using authentic lines of antique pieces. Many collectors complete old sets by filling in with new, and only an expert can tell the difference. Milk glass makes an interesting contrast with other whites. There are beautiful earthenware patterns, produced by the best manufacturers, all white with embossed designs, gadroon borders, and graceful shapes. If yours is a strictly modern taste, there is pure-white china with clean-cut lines. A white setting shows off handsomely on colored linens. And if you want to highlight your 18th-century table, place stark-white dishes and silverware directly on the wood. Use napkins in a color, and emphasize this same color in candles or centerpiece. Achieve a dramatic effect by combining black and white in a contemporary home. With so many possibilities, there is a color scheme for everyone. So don your beret and give the palette a whirl.

Turning the Tables

A dinner can be a feast in more ways than one, because a beautifully set table is a feast for the eyes. If you "design" your entire meal, the food is sure to taste better than it really is. This is a legitimate form of brainwashing guests that every hostess is entitled to do. The beginner cook can cover up the sins of commission in the kitchen by camouflaging the dinner in a lovely-to-look-at environment. One hostess has carried this so far that her reputation as a cook has reached the point of becoming a strain to live up to, even though she secretly insists that she is not a great cook.

Every home, including the smallest apartment, should have some sort of table for dining. No one wants to spend a lifetime balancing meals on his lap. And the table can become the center of many of the happiest occasions in your life. There are miraculous expanding and collapsible creations for small places. One table can grow from breakfast to banquet length; another elevates from cocktail to dining height. If you are selecting a table for the first time, do try to find one that provides comfortable seating arrangements. No one enjoys straddling table legs, but where it's unavoidable, see that the men are the straddlers instead of the women—unless you're giving a pajama party!

Many antique tables present seating problems. A few cases of outright discomfort are justified if the table itself is sufficiently rare. We are frequent dinner guests in a pre-Revolutionary home furnished with choice Americana. One of the prized possessions of the owners is a very early 18th-century tavern table, worthy of the most discriminating collector, which they use for dining. They take a good bit of ribbing about the way guests must sit sidesaddle because the supporting rail for the table top is too low for knees to go under. But it's worth the discomfort to be able to gaze upon the patina of the aged wood and the interesting distressed areas, probably brought about by much tankard tapping on the part of early-day settlers. In the glow of candlelight we retreat two centuries into the past when our forefathers were tall in the saddle but obviously short in the tavern.

A dining table should comfortably seat at least six persons and preferably eight, a cozy number around a table that makes for easy conversation and togetherness. Whatever your table, do keep greasy fingerprints and sticky spots cleaned off, or the effect will be spoiled, no matter how fine the table or the setting. (Furniture wax sprays are most effective.)

Each hostess must work out her own best way to serve a dinner. If buffet is your way, provide individual trays or snack tables. It's important that guests have a place to set their dishes, both while eating and after they finish. Men especially dislike balancing plates on their knees. When the little snack tables first came into use, many of them were unattractive, with their gaudy designs and cheap construction. Now that they have become standard equipment, they are made to fit into any surroundings, from the simplest to the most elegant. It is certainly money well spent to invest in them if you entertain often, for they have many uses.

You may prefer to have guests eat at card tables. They are now sturdily built and come in smart colors and a variety of styles. The new round ones are a welcome change from the old squares. If storage space is too limited to keep your own supply, it's easy to rent them—good-looking ones, too.

Be Seated. Adequate seating is important for any group beyond the teen-age set, which enjoys sitting cross-legged on the floor. For guests seated at a dining table, chairs shouldn't be so close that they touch. Have enough space to sit down gracefully without awkward maneuvering. Folding chairs are a help at large parties and, like card tables, they have come a long way from the old-fashioned functional but ugly ones. There are attractive styles in all colors, and pretty wicker ones that can double as porch chairs. Folding chairs can be rented, too. You no longer have to depend on the local undertaker—it always seemed so un-partylike to see his ad on the back! Small campstools are a practical solution to the seating problem, especially around card tables, and take up little storage space. They can be painted and covered in bright colors. But don't expect guests to sit on them an entire evening without backaches.

Choose China Carefully

Women are now blessed with a wealth of china patterns for their tables—something for everyone's taste. We have talked about color, but you must also consider scale and design when selecting china. Pale pastels and delicate flowers are at home in a setting of soft colors and with the delicate lines of Sheraton furniture. But this same china would be overpowered in a house featuring heavy wood paneling and primitive pine furniture, or in a contemporary setting where bold color, texture, and medium are emphasized. It is more important to consider design, color, and scale than period. All periods can combine in contemporary homes; the mixture depends on your personal taste. Think, too, about how a plate will look with food on it, in case you're like the person we know who has an aversion to seeing flowers underneath the roast beef and gravy. Her own china has only a border design. Whatever pattern you choose can bring about different effects by what you put with it. China takes on the character of the environment and will look different if you change the other appointments you use.

Mix and Match.   Patterns can be mixed and varied for different courses. Use perfectly plain dishes interspersed with patterned dishes. Or if your china is heavily decorated, tone down the busy look by combining it with glass salad or dessert plates. During the past few years the fad of collecting assorted teacups and demitasses has been a popular hobby, as was spoon collecting in our mothers' and grandmothers' days. Bread-and-butter plates can be different, too. We have found unusual ones in teak with matching spreaders, besides silver and pewter ones. Just be sure that your mixtures are simpatico, not hodgepodge. Colors must be compatible, and also designs.

Fine China vs. Earthenware.   Chinese export porcelain became widely used in America after the Revolution, when our country could trade directly with China, the source of all fine china up to that time. Then in 1794 Josiah Spode perfected a formula in England for bone china (it actually contains bones—ox bones, not human!), which has been imported by Americans ever since. Now there are other bone chinas available. Whether bone or not, all fine china is made of refined clays and stone and is fired at a high temperature for long periods. It is translucent, and its hard, non-porous quality makes it extremely durable. Cost of production is a great deal more than for earthenware, principally because of the skill required in making it.

China is considered the finest dinnerware, but in making your decision don't discount good earthenware. Either china or earthenware is appropriate for almost any occasion you would have, and many people actually prefer earthenware because of its more informal look. Money doesn't buy good taste, and it's choice of style and pattern that counts. A good quality of earthenware is a mixture of clays and ground stone, but it is fired at a lower temperature and for shorter periods than china. It is opaque, has a hard glaze, and is very durable, but less so than china, although it will last a lifetime with proper care.

What and Why. Time was when a person would buy a complete 92-piece set of matching dinnerware, but today most china is purchased in 5-piece place settings: a 10-inch dinner plate, a teacup and saucer (which can also be used for clear soup if you don't have soup cups), a bread-and-butter plate, and an 8-inch plate that can be used for dessert or salad. The other way to buy china, which we prefer, is from "open stock." This means that each piece is priced separately, so that you may buy exactly what you want or replace a broken piece. You can let your imagination take over and design your own place setting.

Some sweet young brides reach the altar with no more than a nodding acquaintance with the kitchen. Their cooking experience has been limited to Girl Scout camping trips, which hardly prepares them for the impressive array of dishes they receive as wedding gifts. Consequently they may store them in little-used cupboards, not knowing exactly what to do with them. Later, when they do more extensive entertaining, the dishes are retrieved from dark corners, but may still present a puzzlement. The following list tells what to do with the various dishes and will also serve as a guide for purchasing. On pages 116-120 of this chapter you will find sketches to guide you on how to place dishes properly when setting a table.

10-inch service plate—purely decorative and used only at formal dinners as a cover plate when guests sit down to tables; never used for serving food—is removed when the first course is served.

10- or 10½-inch dinner plate for main course.

8½-inch breakfast or luncheon plate—used for main course at breakfast or lunch.

7- to 8-inch plates—can be used for salad or dessert, or as tea plate. Crescent-shaped plates are also pretty for salad and occupy less space on crowded tables.

5- to 6-inch bread-and-butter plate—used at informal meals for bread and butter and now sometimes at formal meals.

7- or 8-inch rim soup bowls—can be used anytime, but no others are correct at formal dinners.

Cream soup and stand—low soup bowl with handle at each side and small plate similar to a saucer, used at lunch or informal dinners.

Bouillon cups and saucers—cup with two handles, used for clear soups at lunch or informal dinners.

6-inch cereal dish—always placed on a breakfast, tea, or dessert plate.

5-inch fruit dish—used for fruit and other desserts; always placed on a tea or dessert plate.

Oval or rectangular platters, 10 to 16 inches for meats.

Chop plate, 12 to 16 inches—round serving platter for meat, salads, cake, pastries, or whatever looks pretty on it.

Sauceboat, uncovered, for sauce or gravy—usually has attached stand and a lip for pouring.

Covered tureen, 9- or 11-inch, with platter underneath—for serving soups; useful at buffet suppers for anything in large quantity.

Sauce tureen with cover and stand—for any sauces or gravy.

Open oval dish, covered oval dish, and covered round casserole—all used for vegetables.

Square cake plate, 9 by 9 inches, for cake, bread, pastries, cookies.

Teacup and saucer—used by everyone for all hot drinks.

Coffee cup and saucer—larger than teacup; used for breakfast, but few people now bother with two sizes.

Demitasse—small cup and saucer used for serving black coffee after lunch or dinner.

Crystal Clear

It's always a surprise to learn that the things we take for granted in daily living were once either non-existent or rare luxuries. Most modern-day housewives have several sets of glasses, yet glasses did not come into common usage on the American table until early in the 19th century. Before that, glass was within the means of only the most affluent and was considered a status symbol of the day. Others had to make out with pottery mugs, pewter tankards, or wooden noggins. At that time there was no pressing need for anything else, since the favorite drink for both adults and children was cider at any time of day. And from what we hear of early-day cider, we wonder how they ever got on with their business of founding the country! Glassware owned by the wealthier pioneers came from England and Ireland, but after the war of 1812, when such imports were no longer available, American manufacturers forged ahead at full speed. From then on, as production increased, almost every housewife had glasses on her table.

We have advanced to the point of having so many styles and qualities in glassware that at present the trend is to start cutting down and to use one glass for several different purposes. We haven't yet come full circle and adopted a single glass or returned to the all-purpose mug, but people have rebelled against the ridiculous notion of having a different-shaped glass for every drink, when often there is almost no difference in capacity. The trend today is toward impressive large sizes—only partly filled, of course.

Glasses are the most space-consuming item that a housewife owns, because they are extremely fragile and can't be stacked. Therefore, if she has dozens of glasses that are brought out but infrequently, she must sacrifice valuable cupboard space. Since the lives of most of us are geared to informality, we have no desire to imitate the formal dinner where service often consists of four different glasses at each place—for water, sherry or white wine, red wine, and champagne. This alone would keep one servant busy. In the average home, picture the frustration, first of the hostess in providing that many glasses—48 at a dinner for 12—and then of the host when it's his problem to pour the right thing in the right glass at the right time. No wonder everybody is jumping at the chance to adopt the tulip glass! The number of glasses at one meal reached a new high when the Lucullus Circle, an exclusive group of 48 true gourmets, met for dinner awhile back. Ten large wine goblets were lined up at each place —480 glasses in all!

The tulip glass, which was originated by Lalique in France, can now be bought in many qualities and sizes at a wide range of prices. By its utter simplicity, it will serve almost any purpose. It is pretty to look at and will go with any other glassware you have. This shape, which comes in different heights, is fast becoming a standard requirement because of its versatility and is now being used as an all-purpose wine glass, as well as for water, too. However, if you are using it for wine, use another type of glass for the water for a more interesting effect.

Another all-purpose shape in wine glasses, used by many good French restaurants, is a bulb-shaped glass that may be found in different heights and sizes. The bowl of this glass is fuller and rounder than the tulip. It is equally versatile.

For years everyone considered the wide, shallow glass as the only proper one for champagne. Now we are told by one who would surely know that we must not make this mistake again. Vicomte Bernard de la Giraudière of the Champagne Producers Association of France rules that the *only* way to serve champagne is in a long-stemmed tulip glass. It is easy to hold and keeps the champagne cool, since the hand never has to touch the bowl of the glass. If you own the traditional type of champagne glass, it is of course perfectly proper to use it.

Designs In Glass. Our phrase "safety in simplicity" applies to glassware along with everything else—but this doesn't mean jelly glasses! We mean you don't have to have the tallest goblets to reach the highest rung on the social ladder. Again selection and pattern take precedence over price. There are lovely patterns with geometric designs, such as circles or diamonds, which make the perfect complement to almost any china. And perfectly plain glasses with graceful lines, or with a little decoration on the stem, will suit any table. Steer clear of would-be grandiose goblets etched with busy little flowers overall or edged with imitation gold. If you lean toward the more formal type of setting, go all the way and buy the very best crystal, with 14-karat gold or no gold at all! This brings up a question often asked by young wives. Should gold-rimmed glassware and china be used on the same table with sterling silver? Of course they should, but quality is of utmost importance with gold trim (and extra care must be taken in washing it).

When most young women first establish homes of their own, they have the idea that it is necessary to buy the most expensive glassware in order to set a beautiful table. It is true that eggshell-thin crystal can make a table come alive as it reflects light and color. But after a few years, many young hostesses become discouraged when they discover that in spite of careful handling, many of the glasses have tiny chips around the rim or the base. We've even heard stories about guests accidentally biting pieces out of very thin glasses. Then the disillusioned hostess begins to have second thoughts about how she has spent her money. Thin crystal is so delicate that rims of the glasses can't touch even when stored on a shelf, because the slightest jiggling can cause chipping. It goes without saying that an automatic dishwasher is out. Women usually end up buying other sets of heavier glasses for a lot less money so that they can relax and enjoy them.

One winter day we met a young friend whose budget was quite limited. She had been invited to a crystal shower for a bride and had just purchased her gift of *one* goblet to the tune of $12. At that point she was praying that if she slipped on the ice and broke the goblet she would also break her leg, giving her a plausible excuse to miss the shower and thus eliminate the necessity to purchase another goblet.

We're not for a minute implying that you shouldn't consider fine crystal, but it's wise to weigh both advantages and disadvantages. If you still prefer the best, it is advisable to have plenty of other glasses for more informal use. And if you decide to forego the luxury of the finest, do make up for it in table interest. Much of the early glassware found in antique shops is durable as well as beautiful. Of course, prices on antiques go ever upward, so they are not inexpensive, but some of the glass —either pressed or blown in a mold—is more durable than thin crystal. Make a collection of mixed patterns in similarly shaped clear goblets so that each person at the table has a different glass. If you do this be sure they are *all* different, or it will look as though you are using remnants of several broken sets! These can frequently be picked up very reasonably, as they are lone survivors of sets. Or make a hobby of collecting one pattern. This is a challenge, and it sometimes takes years to complete a set, but if you're a collector at heart, you'll relish the hunt. If you're not game for the chase, you can buy reproductions of these old patterns that are modestly priced. Colored glassware is pretty on a table, but should be used sparingly. It can be mixed with clear glass—a colored water goblet and a clear wine glass, with either clear or colored salad plate. Wine should never be put in colored glasses, for the wine itself provides the color.

A Good Beginning.

It's not wishful thinking to suggest starting out as a young hostess with but four different types of glasses. It *can* be done, and without apologies.

❋ A short, chubby stemmed glass, used for juice and also sherry.

❋ A tulip-shaped stemmed glass—used for water or wine, including champagne.

❋ A standard footed cocktail glass for manhattans, martinis, and other cocktails not served "on the rocks."

❋ A large chunky glass, popularly known as a "double-old-fashioned," used for all other drinks—highballs, on-the-rocks, carbonated, and non-alcoholic.

It's desirable to expand the glassware department of your home with the addition of footed sherbets or low glass fruit and dessert dishes, and possibly glass salad plates, either round, square, or crescent-shaped. Also cordial or liqueur glasses, if you serve after-dinner liqueurs. Strictly optional are pieces such as a salad bowl, cake plate, punch bowl, large berry or fruit bowl, and relish dish. There are so many more interesting substitutes

for these that we certainly wouldn't suggest having everything
match. We do find that a footed glass cake plate deserves every
bit of space it takes in the cupboard, because it is not only attractive for cake but also pretty for molded salad or mousse.
Crystal individual salt dishes are lovely and coming back into
use.

There is a revived interest in pretty glass finger bowls. Don't
think that you have to have servants to indulge in this nicety.
Simply place the finger bowl with a little doily on the dessert
plate and let each guest lift it off with the doily before the dessert service. The dessert fork and spoon may also be placed on
this plate, to the left and right respectively. Finger bowls are
useful for many other purposes, too—small flower arrangements,
nuts, mints, cold soup, fruit, and berries.

The Language of Glass.   Don't be confused or frightened by
words you may hear to describe different kinds of glassware.
There are only a few terms you need to know and understand:

❧   *Handblown crystal*—This means that the article is actually
   blown by the glassmaker and shaped entirely by hand. This
   makes it easy to see why this type is most expensive.

❧   *Hand-molded crystal*—This means that the glassmaker
   blows the molten glass into a mold which makes it easier and
   quicker to fashion the article. Today molded glass can be
   made entirely by machine, which makes it less expensive. It
   is thicker than handblown crystal and not so fragile.

❧   *Pressed glass*—This is a method of actually pressing the
   glass into a mold, invented in this country at the beginning
   of the 19th century. The glass has a duller look, and patterns
   pressed in have dull edges.

❧   *Lead glass*—Lead oxide is added to the basic glass formula
   to make a finer product. It gives a heavier feel, a more brilliant look, and a clearer ring.

Sterling Qualities

If the ghost of an 18th-century New England housewife were to crash a 20th-century dinner party, she would be bewildered at the miscellaneous assortment of silverware laid before her for the purpose of consuming one single meal. Etiquette books of her day could hardly help her, since they were concerned with such questions as how to eat with a *knife* properly. Anyone who has used only a knife, fork, and spoon would be overwhelmed when faced with so many as eight or nine pieces, not at all unusual today. That New England ghost would have to do the same as any other uncertain guest—follow the lead of her hostess.

The "dowry" of silver that most wives now bring to their mates is indeed lavish. And blessed with such a number of things, they certainly should be as happy as kings. The purchase of sterling is not really extravagant. Most couples buy it sooner or later, so it's economical to start early in acquiring what you need and plan to use it every day. With care there's little that will damage it short of holocaust. Outside of kitchen equipment, there's no need to have any other flatware unless you especially want it. In fact, silver becomes more beautiful with constant use, and by alternating pieces daily, only an occasional cleaning with silver polish is necessary.

Weight, pattern, scale, and whether or not it is "open stock" are the only important considerations in selecting sterling flatware. If your china is extremely plain or all white, we suggest that you'd be happier with design on your silver, simply to break the monotony and to bring pattern into the overall scheme. And by the same token, if everything else is ornate, a plain or simple design in silver would be better. There is an idea afoot that ornate silver is hard to clean, but there again it's prettier when use and aging develop enough darkening around the design to serve as a foil. It isn't necessary to clean out every little crevice. Neither do we go along with the theory that plain flatware should be avoided because it shows scratches.

The first few scratches hurt, we grant you, but after that they all blend together into a soft mellow patina.

Silver may be purchased either in 6-piece place settings or from open stock. A place setting consists of knife, fork, salad fork, teaspoon, individual butter knife, and dessert spoon, which is also used for soup and cereal. Knives and forks come in dinner size and slightly smaller luncheon size. We recommend the dinner size for general use, unless you plan to have both. After acquiring these basics, add the following whenever possible: several serving forks and spoons, round-bowled soup spoons, demitasse spoons, dessert forks, beverage spoons (if you like iced tea or coffee), a butter knife, sugar tongs or shell, a ladle, salt spoons (if you use individual salt dishes), oyster forks that can be used for shrimp cocktail also, a cake and pie server. For variety, select a different pattern for demitasse spoons and salt spoons, and also for some of the serving pieces. A double quantity of teaspoons and salad forks is almost necessary, because these are the pieces so often needed in quantity. The diagrams on pages 116-120 of this chapter show how silver is properly placed on the table.

If a couple simply cannot afford to start out with sterling flatware, there are attractive substitutes in stainless steel and silver plate. (A comparatively new process in silver-plating makes the plate last indefinitely.) Some of the stainless steel patterns have ebony, teak, walnut, or bamboo handles, which give added interest, and the finest among them can probably be considered among the heirlooms of tomorrow.

Silver Setting. One very important thing to remember when setting a table is to see that all pieces of flat silver are lined up straight as soldiers. And this goes for everything else in a place setting. The plate should be centered, and place mats should be equal distances apart. We are compulsive picture-straighteners, and it carries right over to the dining table. It's distasteful to see a sloppily set table with everything askew. Silver and place mats should be placed about an inch from the edge of the table.

Forks should be at the left of the plate, tines up, arranged according to courses; start from the outside and work toward the plate, except for the oyster fork, which is at the right of spoons. When forks first came into use in this country, tines were turned down, as a carry-over from Continental forks (and spoons, too). Some are still designed to turn down, with design on the back —but in America, it's tines up.

Knives are placed at the right of the plate with blade toward the plate. (And when using the knife, be sure to keep the blade turned in toward the center of the plate when you rest it for a moment, or when you finish.) Spoons are to the right of knives according to use, again using them from outside in. An individual butter knife is laid horizontally (this is the generally accepted way, although it may be arranged vertically) across the top of the bread-and-butter plate with handle to the right and blade turned toward center of plate. Dessert fork and spoon can be put on the dessert plate when it is served along with a finger bowl (fork to the left, spoon to the right), or arranged horizontally, spoon above the fork, in the center above the dinner plate. Spoon handle is on the right; fork handle is to the left. This is the Continental arrangement and is a convenience for the hostess if there is room on the table. Demitasse spoons are placed on the saucer when coffee is served.

Glasses go above the knives and spoons. If there is only a water glass, it goes directly above the knife. If one wine glass is added, it goes to the right of the water glass and a little toward the edge of the table. If four glasses are used at a really formal dinner, the water glass is above the knife closest to the plate; the white wine or sherry, red wine, and dessert or champagne glasses are staggered toward the edge of the table, starting a little above the water glass.

The bread-and-butter plate belongs above the forks on the left, while a salad served with the main course goes to the left of the forks. At breakfast, the coffee cup is placed to the right of the spoons. (See diagrams of place settings.)

1. *BREAKFAST*

The place is set with an 8½-inch breakfast plate under a cereal dish. Cereal spoon is placed to the right of the knife, while the fork goes to the left of the plate. The coffee spoon is on the saucer, but it is equally correct to place it on the right of the cereal spoon, as coffee is generally served at the beginning of breakfast (and throughout the meal). Bread-and-butter plate is above the fork, salt and pepper above the plate, and glass above the knife. Napkin corner is toward the diner, to make it easy to pick up and open halfway across the lap.

2. *LUNCH*

Plate is the 8½-inch size. Fork goes on the outside, and salad fork on the inside to the left of the plate. (If the salad is served as a first course, the forks would be reversed.) To the right of the plate, from the outside in, are a teaspoon for a fruit cocktail, a soup spoon, and the knife. The dessert spoon and fork are placed above the plate, but are equally correct placed on the dessert plate when it is brought in with the finger bowl, as shown on page 120. Water glass is above the knife, while bread-and-butter plate is above the forks. Spoon for coffee or demitasse would be placed on the saucer when served.

3. DINNER

A larger 10- or 10½-inch plate is used for dinner. Fork and salad fork are on the left; cocktail or oyster fork, soup spoon, and knife are on the right, from the outside in. Water glass and one wineglass to the right of it are shown above the knife. If a fish course is included, the fish fork is placed on the outside at the left, while the fish knife goes between the knife and soup spoon on the right.

4. FORMAL DINNER

Though a dinner with a setting this formal is rare, this is the correct order of placement. Service plate is the 10-inch size. Napkin is laid on the service plate. Oyster fork, tipped over the soup spoon, is used for the first course (this fork could also be laid straight, or placed at the far left on the left side of the plate). Soup spoon (for a rimmed soup plate) is used next. The three knives and forks, used from the outside in, are for fish, meat, and salad courses. Traditionally, the bread-and-butter plate is eliminated, but it may be used if preferred. The four glasses, left to right, are for water, white wine or sherry, red wine, and champagne. Since there is so much silver on the table, the dessert spoon and fork should be brought in on the dessert plate, as shown on page 120. Demitasse spoon is placed on the saucer when served.

5. *ALTERNATE DESSERT SERVICE*

If the dessert spoon and fork are not placed on the table at lunch or dinner when the table is set (as shown in diagram 2), they may be brought in on the dessert plate (7- or 8-inch size) with finger bowl and doily. Diner places the flatware on the table as shown and sets the doily and finger bowl on the table to the left.

Pretty and Practical. Silver hollow ware can be decorative in the corner cupboard as well as useful on the table, and silver always lends distinction to any home. No matter how rustic the setting, a few pieces of well-polished silver will make a home a castle— assuming it *is* well polished. If it isn't, hide it!

The accessory pieces not in daily use, such as platters, vegetable dishes, and gravy boats, can be Sheffield or regular silver plate if you can't afford sterling, or they can be of an entirely different content. Plated silver will last for years and can be replated when necessary. Pewter is becoming almost as popular as it was in the 18th century and requires little care. You can find both traditional and contemporary patterns that combine beautifully with silver. Bread-and-butter plates are pretty in either pewter or silver. When not used for bread, use them for cocktail snacks or under iced tea glasses as coasters and to rest the spoon. There are also handsome pewter "glasses" in different sizes for sherry, cocktails, and highballs, and tiny pewter mugs for liqueurs and cordials. Stainless steel used to be confined to the kitchen, but it is beginning to rival pewter in looks. Some of the salad bowls and platters are equal in beauty to those of silver.

Unexpected combinations are sometimes more dramatic than the obvious. A silver tea set doesn't have to be put on a silver tray. In Williamsburg, Virginia, we were attracted by a beautiful silver service on a mahogany Chippendale tray, and ever since, silver on wood has been our choice. A tole tray is also pretty under a tea service. A silver sugar bowl and creamer can be used with a china teapot, or china sugar bowl and creamer with a silver or pewter pot.

Linens to Live With

Once the big decisions are made on the more permanent items such as china and silver, selecting linens is sheer delight. It's like the icing on the cake. There are all sorts of beautiful combinations that accent both the table and the entire dining room. White is always correct, but color lifts the spirit as nothing else can. So have at least one color ensemble among your linens. Choose colors from walls, draperies, or china. Don't have too much pattern on pattern; let each set off the other.

Place mats have taken over where domestic help left off, and they have virtually become a way of life. As a result, time-consuming and difficult upkeep of huge tablecloths has been eliminated. Most of us find the enormous white damask banquet cloths, which were always brought out for company dinners by our mothers, are nothing more than white elephants taking up space. They have gone the way of the 92-piece set of matching dinnerware. If you're wondering what to do with the one you inherited, don't overlook the possibility of cutting it into huge squares to hem by hand for oversize dinner napkins. We have also cut ours into dish towels, which are the envy of some but appear unorthodox to others. A fine damask still makes a beautiful setting for a formal dinner, but taking the shortcut with place mats has emancipated womankind for the more interesting phases of entertaining. Place mats are now used at both formal and informal affairs. At formal parties, the mat is often round and barely larger than the plate itself.

In addition to several sets of place mats, every hostess should own at least one tablecloth, either white, off-white, or a solid color with matching napkins. We prefer the texture of linen for ours, but this is simply a personal choice. Prices range from a very moderate amount for a simple cloth to a very great amount for an exquisitely hand-embroidered one. In a setting of country furniture and homespuns, now found in both town and country houses, nothing lends more charm to a table than one of the old turkey-red tablecloths you can sometimes find in antiques shops, especially when set with blue-and-white dishes.

If you are looking for the easiest and most economical way of acquiring a tablecloth suitable for all occasions, purchase one of the unadorned Belgian linen cloths, which come in all sizes and colors, with matching napkins. Rip out the machine-stitched hem of the tablecloth and sew it by hand with tiny stitches. If the hem is too narrow, make it wider, about an inch and a half. This takes away from the commercial look, and it will provide a background that you need not be ashamed of for any table setting. If you crave a touch of elegance, sew a pretty lace or fringe around the edge. Better to put your money into sterling silver than into costly linens, if you are on a limited budget. Wait for your husband's next promotion to buy the one you dream of with lots of magnificent cutwork.

The size of a tablecloth should be sufficient for adequate overhang all the way around (10 to 12 inches) to prevent it from looking skimpy, unless it is one of the sheer organdy or handkerchief-linen cloths, pretty at teatime, which come just to the edge of the table on all sides. Using the table bare and having pretty napkins has become an optional choice for any time of day—assuming the surface of the table is in good condition.

Great-Aunt Effie may abhor the idea of a bare tea table, but it's now being done, with trays under coffee and tea services. To give softness and perhaps color, you can use a runner down the center of the table with a 6- to 8-inch overhang at each end. Always cover card table tops completely—no place mats here. They look pretty with two cloths, one in a color with a deep skirt on all sides, and over it a standard-size card table cloth in white or a harmonizing color. If it's a square table, place the top cloth catty-cornered so that the corners fall over the four sides of the table.

Because of America's preoccupation with laborsaving devices, the demand for plastic table mats and covers and paper napkins has soared. These are all right in the privacy of the family, but not for guests, except at a picnic, barbecue, or children's party. Even then it's more effective to use inexpensive casual fabrics such as burlap or denim with bandanna napkins. Occasionally paper napkins of high quality can be used to carry out a particular theme at an informal party, but not at lunch or dinner. Straw place mats, which come in luscious colors, are every bit as easy to take care of as plastic and more attractive.

Yards and Yards. If you sew a fine seam, the possibilities are endless for making one-of-a-kind ensembles for your table; they require very little work and the minimum expenditure. Use your imagination when wandering through the rows of drapery or dress fabrics. Selection is important, not price. Sometimes you can find a bargain at mill-end shops on remnants that are just enough for a set of place mats and napkins. Almost any fabric will do except rayon, which we consider taboo on the table. Choose from linen, polished cotton, lace, eyelet embroidery, theatrical gauze, homespun, pillow ticking, madras, felt, fishnet, organdy, your own drapery fabric if cotton or linen, crewel, flowered sheets, and even textured silks. Some of the early handloomed bedspreads or paisley throws make beautiful table covers, and for either a Victorian or contemporary interior make a table runner of velveteen lined with silk or edged with gold braid. For an informal tablecloth that is sure to amuse guests, there is patchwork madras by the yard. Use stripes, polka dots, geometrics, checks, florals, paisleys, or plaids. Tablecloths and place mats can be round, square, rectangular, or oval. Edges can be scalloped, pointed, or straight, with deep hems or narrow.

Few linens sold by the yard are wide enough for a dining table, but there is an easy solution for this. Measure the length of your table, allowing adequate overhang at each end. Buy two lengths of 36-inch-wide linen, or any other fabric you wish, and use one length for the center panel. Split the other length in half for the side panels. Attach the side pieces to the center panel by means of a lace or eyelet embroidery insertion. Hem by hand. You can make any size cloth you need. It is important to pre-shrink both fabric and trim before sewing them together because they shrink differently when washed. Cotton fringe shrinks badly, so we always dip it in hot water and dry it before using.

For those who enjoy handwork—and have twenty-twenty vision—there are linen tablecloths stamped for cross-stitching. These are especially beautiful when worked in one color only, or in white on white, and worthy of posterity. Keep more feminine table dressings for parties that are strictly feminine affairs. Men are not at home with lace and delicately sheer fabrics.

Trims and Whims. There are almost as many different ways to trim table linens as there are fabrics. We think of the Victorian era as promoting fringe, but present-day manufacturers have literally gone on a fringe binge. There is long fringe and short, tied and untied, silk and cotton, giant or midget cotton balls, and tiny velvet balls no bigger than a blueberry—all in a wide range of colors. There are also braids with flowers and hearts, bindings, lace, eyelet, and even gold rickrack. These trims can be used on full-size cloths, card table covers, or place mats. Again, be sure to pre-shrink anything you plan to wash. For special party themes, attach temporary felt appliqués by tacking them on with a few stitches. Line up felt Christmas trees around the sides of a tablecloth. Or scatter cutout Christmas trees, baubles, or bells of felt decorated with gold braid and sequins over the top of the table without tacking. Velvet bows on the skirt of the tablecloth are effective and look luxurious.

Napkins, Too. In the early days of our country, napkins weren't used, so the tablecloth had to suffice for wiping mouths. When the napkin finally became an essential part of a place setting, it certainly improved our culture, to say nothing of what it did for the tablecloth. Since then, the napkin not only has become important in a practical way, but also is important as an accessory to the general decorating theme. Napkins should be made of comparatively soft and absorbent fabric, as opposed to a hard cotton or glazed chintz, and may be unstarched or lightly starched. They can be white, colored, or printed and, like china, mixed or matched. You can improvise in any way that brings added interest.

There are many ways of folding napkins, and whatever strikes your fancy is all right as long as it looks pretty. Place the napkin at the left of the forks (but not under them), or in the center where the plate will be set, or on the plate itself if it is already on the table. Be sure the fold is neat, and if it is rectangular have the open edges of the napkin toward the plate so that it can be picked up easily and opened. Napkin rings used to be for family use only, but are new as decoration, too. There are up-to-the-minute styles in silver, brass, wood, and colored raffia. However, guests still expect clean napkins at each meal!

At a buffet party, arrange napkins on the table in any interesting way. They can be folded and placed in a neat row, each one slightly overlapping the next; or, when folded in squares, divided into three or four stacks, each stack turned diamond fashion overlapping the next. They can also be lined up in a row with knife and fork on top of each, ready for guests to pick up all three at once. For patio parties, roll the knife and fork inside the napkin and place them on a tray or pile them in an antique knife box. Always keep several pretty napkins for the bread tray or basket—a lacy one for dressier occasions, and colorful checks, stripes, and coarse homespuns for more informal use.

Come Clean.   No table covering can possibly look attractive, regardless of quality, unless it is absolutely spotless and pressed to perfection, with the only crease down the center and in a straight line. If you put away spotty and soiled linens after entertaining, a day of reckoning is inevitable. Make it a practice to launder them immediately after use to avoid last-minute crises. Then if you have unexpected company, or your husband telephones that he is bringing an important client to dinner, you will be ready. When linens look dowdy, so does the dinner.

We make quite a production of getting a tablecloth onto the table, which means that it must be done the day before a party. We always give it a fresh press, even if the cloth was ironed before being put away. The best place to do this is as close to the table as possible; then when it's finished, a quick flip in the right direction will cover the table without a wrinkle. Another way is to pull the cloth gently from ironing board to table as you iron, to prevent wrinkles. When finished, flip it open and straighten. It really takes two people, one at each end, to put a large cloth on a table without mussing it, and this is where our husbands come in. Lillian Rogers Parks let us in on a secret about crisp tablecloths in her book, *My Thirty Years Backstairs at the White House*. Whenever a state dinner was given, the tablecloth was ironed right on the table—but don't try this yourself without a heatproof table protector. And Henrietta Nesbitt revealed in her *White House Diary* that when there was a series of parties in one day, one tablecloth was put on top of another, with a layer of plastic in between. As each party ended, the used cloths and the plastic were whipped off, and the tables were all ready for the next party with fresh cloths. But entertaining in the average home is not likely to reach this fever pitch.

Table Silencers.　Very little needs to be said about table silencers and protectors. They are not as important as many think. Most dining tables now have a heat-resistant finish and, in addition, there are all types of interesting trivets available in stores. The added protection of the heavy, stiff cover is needed only where undisciplined little Indians hammer on the table. Felt silencers under a tablecloth do provide a more pleasing surface. These can either be purchased or be made by cutting felt to table size. Or simply fold a white sheet and fit it smoothly to the table before putting on the cloth. It is neither necessary nor desirable to put any type of protection under a place mat. Sheer cloths should be placed right over a bare table or over an opaque colored cloth. Lace cloths are put directly on the bare wood or over a colored liner.

In the Gloaming

Only a hundred years ago candles and open-flame lamps were utilitarian. No longer a necessity, they are a romantic route to soft light with sweet music. Any woman who has a desire for glamour—and who hasn't?—will use candlelight at the slightest excuse. Even if she has reached the bifocal stage and can no longer see well, she is willing to develop eyestrain rather than forego this romantic lighting. We know one lady who always dines by candlelight, even when she is alone. Men frequently protest, but they are merely putting on an act. They like it, too!

It's ironic to think that when people had to depend on candles, there was little or no variety, while in this age of electricity we have the most elaborate selection the world has ever known. Candles are tall, short, thin, and fat; round, square, and pointed; shaped like fruit, angels, and animals. And now we can buy vegetable-shaped candles the same way we buy our vegetables— in tin cans appropriately labeled. But the current generation has gone one step too far by producing the *gas* candle. This is one of those miserable, functional inventions destined to rob us of all romance, and we don't encourage it.

The general rule is not to light candles in the daytime, since their purpose is to give light, but they are pleasant and proper in late afternoon at tea or cocktail time. And if a dining room is unusually dark, there is really no reason not to light them when they are needed. Keep candles high and centerpiece low on the dining table at a seated dinner, but on a buffet, both centerpiece and candles can be high. If a candle doesn't fit the candlestick, heat the bottom end of the candle over a flame, or dip it in hot water for a few seconds, then quickly put it in the holder while the wax is hot. Or use a small daub of florist clay when the hole in the candlestick is too large.

Classic candlesticks of silver, crystal, or brass always contribute to the beauty of a party scene. But don't limit your thinking to the idea that all your candlesticks should match. Arrange a clutch of candles of different heights and shapes, or combine silver and brass, or silver and glass. The small colored hobnail glasses containing short candles (like altar candles) give a soft glow set at each place on a table. And the very long slender dripless tapers spreading out at an angle from a centerpiece add to line and pattern. One hostess we know owns an unusually beautiful five-way silver candelabrum that she places in the very center of her table. She confided that in spite of the cost, she considers it an excellent investment and has actually convinced her husband that it's money in the bank, since she no longer orders flowers for every party. Instead, she creates table interest by entwining ivy around the candelabrum, covering the base with greens, or filling a gigantic center bobêche with small flowers from her garden or bright red strawberries in season. At times she places a bowl of fruit at each side of the candelabrum. It's always different and always attractive.

Now that manufacturers have almost run the gamut in candles, a new interest has been stimulated in holders and containers to put them in. There are ceramic and stoneware lanterns in various shapes. We've found owl and pussycat lanterns, but so far haven't discovered their pea-green boat of nursery rhyme fame. There are solid cast-iron lanterns that don't tip over, perforated metal lamps, antique lanterns, clear and colored containers of crackled and uncrackled glass. And there are the charming hurricane lamps that protect the candle flame with a gleaming glass chimney. Then there are always the old wine bottles—standbys for extra candles in recreation room or outdoors. These can be grouped together on a picnic or barbecue table in different sizes and shapes. Egg cups make unusual holders for short, chunky candles. A variation to candles is the tiny wicks that float in salad oil and burn safely in a glass.

Since outside parties have reached epidemic proportions throughout the country, one of the greatest additions to the party scene has been the innovation of unusual outdoor lighting that has the desirable quality of candlelight and in many cases has an insect repellent built within to discourage the enemy without. Citronella candles that burn for 1,000 hours come in pretty bowls that can later be used for flowers. Garden torches that can be set in the ground and moved easily from place to place are among the most useful lights for large parties in the yard. A novel way to light a driveway or swimming pool is with candles set in about 3 inches of sand inside foil bags. These are called "luminaries" in Mexico and are used at festivals. They can be used outside the year round. We remember a Christmas party where they formed a veritable fairyland set on the snow along the drive to the house. On turning the corner, the guests at their first glimpse of this gay welcome were put in a party mood before they ever reached the door.

For a patio party, strings of Japanese lanterns (now weather-resistant and electrified) make the most festive lighting of all. Perhaps it's a throwback to childhood, but these lanterns fascinate everybody. When one new family moved into our neighborhood, the people surrounding thought that they were continual party-givers, because every weekend their yard was aglow with gay lanterns. After an entire summer of this illusion, the neighbors were amused to discover that the lanterns were merely for the enjoyment of the family. Little did they know how much the neighbors were enjoying them, too! There are also outdoor

gas lamps that can be hung from porch, patio wall, or tree, and
set on the table, too.

The lighting story wouldn't be complete without a mention
of plain ordinary electricity. Lamps should be spaced in a room
so that it is evenly lighted throughout. Be sure that your lamp-
shades and light bulbs give soft lighting. When candlelight is
used in the dining room, have enough candles so that guests
can see what they are eating, or supplement the candlelight
with one or two small lamps. Avoid a harsh glare from over-
head, the most unflattering light of all. There are handsome
reproductions of 19th-century chandeliers that are usually electrified, but they can be illuminated with tiny flame bulbs that
give a soft glow comparable to candlelight. You can also buy
dimmers that control the degree of light in any chandelier.

Front and Center

The centerpiece of any table is always the focal point. A table
would be incomplete without it, no matter how beautifully set.
And whether your table decoration is of permanent value or
whipped up for one occasion, it's not to be tossed off lightly as
an afterthought. Avoid itty-bitty things that make itty-bitty impressions. A large arrangement of nothing but greens is more
effective than a thimbleful of rare flowers on a dining table.
(Card tables are an exception and call for small arrangements.)
So here again, think of scale as well as color. Either symmetrical
or asymmetrical groupings make interesting centerpieces. If the
table is against the wall, decorations can be arranged on the
side near the wall. If you have only four to six guests at a long
table, group them at one end, with decorations at the other.
Or group them at the center, with floral arrangements at the
ends.

Flowers, Trees, Birds, and Bees. Almost anyone who has a
yard can look to nature and find something for decoration.
Postpone pruning evergreens until just before Christmas and

make use of the clippings. Each section of the country has its specialties, whether it's magnolia blossoms in the South, or driftwood and bayberry bushes on the East Coast. Even the desert has its cactus flower. So take advantage of what is available to you.

There's no prettier bouquet than a mixture right out of an old-fashioned garden. And with these a casual arrangement is much better than a stiff, formal one. Flowers still growing in pots are always good as decoration and can be planted later—a beautiful azalea, a pot of tulips, or a collection of African violets in different colors. Pots can be painted any color or set inside other containers so they won't show. Make a row of three potted geraniums down the center of the table, alternating with candles. If your linens are casual, let the pots show, but be sure to scrub them first and put them on a decorative saucer. We prefer seeing a nice red earthenware pot to all that fancy foil that usually surrounds them.

Even in winter months, when gardens are snow-covered, evergreens are available and can be used in many ways. Fill a basket with them, and for color perch little painted wooden birds on the branches. An individual touch such as one or two bees is amusing, but don't overdo it. Avoid the commonplace such as water lilies on a mirror base; such typecasting falls into the category of fish wallpaper in the bathroom. We'd rather follow the spirit of the girl in the song who tied roses on the lilac tree.

Try for the live instead of the artificial whenever possible. Of course, artificial flowers are not the monstrosities they once were. They are now so real-looking you sometimes have to sniff. Or they are crazily unreal and whimsical. But the effect of the artificial can be enhanced by the live. Combine artificial flowers with live green leaves, or use live flowers with artificial greens. Big bunches of rhododendron, laurel, or lemon leaves are inexpensive at the florist's and add much to a room without needing a single flower. They're wonderful for filling bare corners, and they last for weeks.

Mix flowers and berries, berries and leaves, or pussy willows with spring flowers. In the fall, big green leaves streaked with red and gold are pretty with fall flowers, and during the Christmas season, gilded leaves combined with green are pretty. Trailing ivy is always good to fill in a bouquet because of the graceful way it grows and gives width where needed. Tall, thin models do great things for clothes, but tall, thin vases filled with tall, thin flowers can't do anything for a dining table. Put high vases with long-stemmed flowers on a table or on the floor in an obscure corner. It's much easier to avoid awkwardness with short, full floral arrangements in a room, unless the room is exceptionally spacious with very high ceilings.

Dried flowers make charming decorations and last indefinitely. You can select them in bulk at shops or country stands in the fall and arrange them yourself at a fraction of the cost of expensively boxed ones. You can even learn to dry your own flowers at almost no expense. We have a friend who has mastered this art, and she makes magnificent bouquets to enjoy the year round. In fact, one of her most beautiful decorations cost but a trifle. She sprayed a pair of ordinary pound-size coffee tins with gold paint, then made a border of inch-wide mauve velvet ribbon around the top edge of each. Filled with identical arrangements of small dried flowers, and made with exquisite taste and skill, they measured up to the setting of fine paintings in this home when used to adorn the mantel.

This seems a fitting time to say that a wife can always help her husband to have a more gracious home than they might otherwise be able to afford if she will draw on her inner resources and talents, whether it's gardening, arranging flowers, making table linens, or refinishing furniture. During many hours of volunteer work in thrift shops, we have been astonished to learn how unwilling many people are to put forth a little effort. Dresses with the best labels, priced at a dollar or two, are sometimes turned down only because they need shortening, a job that would take less than an hour.

Art in Edibles. If you have any hesitancy in using vegetables or fruit as your centerpiece, look to the masters. The artistic value of these edibles is indicated by the number of still-life paintings exhibited in museums. And we have enough Scotch blood mixed in our veins to appreciate the economy of a centerpiece that can be consumed. It's not unusual to catch guests sneaking grapes to nibble on at the end of a meal. Almost any fruits make a pretty combination—as long as they are fresh! Lemons, apples, plums, pineapples, bananas, grapes, peaches, pears, avocados, oranges, and grapefruit—all are possibilities. Always wash the fruit and polish it with a dry dish towel. Nothing is easier to arrange or prettier to look at than polished red apples in a silver bowl. You can combine fresh fruit and artificial fruit with walnuts and pine cones. Autumn leaves or greens with pine cones can be arranged on the tablecloth around a bowl of fruit.

Select vegetables that are the prettiest in color and shape, and only odorless ones—eggplants, red and green tomatoes, artichokes, green peppers, cucumbers, and squash. Combine fruit and vegetables with ivy. (Cut the ivy as late as possible so it will keep fresh out of water, or let it stand in water for a few hours before using.) Of course, the centerpiece should be in keeping with the general table theme. Where it's fitting to the décor, nuts, fruits, and vegetables can be gilded, but *don't* plan to eat them afterwards; they may be poisonous when painted. Vegetables are especially appropriate and attractive when put in rustic containers such as baskets, little wooden tubs, small trunks, antique wooden cheeseboxes, and in old washbowls and tureens. They can also be arranged on a simple flat board and in the enameled colanders that you find at gift shops in such pretty colors. These informal centerpieces look their best with casual table linens such as textured homespuns and on gaily colored cloths. Pumpkins are always fun in autumn, and the little runt pumpkins can be combined with gourds and dried wheat in a basket. Jack-o'-lanterns are not new, but both adults and children always enjoy them. To be different, have boy and girl pumpkins. Don't make the same mistake we did one Halloween when we replaced the top of the pumpkin after lighting the candle inside. Halfway through dinner we noticed an odd odor and discovered that Mr. Pumpkin was sagging. Our Jack-o'-lantern was cooked!

A big cake for an occasion such as a birthday or anniversary can be used as the centerpiece and later be eaten, if it is decorated in a special way and put on a pretty tray or plate. The effect is more decorative if greens or flowers are arranged around it. A tiered epergne or compote filled with skillfully decorated petits fours makes a centerpiece for an informal tea, and guests can help themselves to the goodies.

Well Contained.   The container is every bit as important as what goes in it. Don't fall into the routine thinking that all flowers belong in vases and all fruit in bowls. A silver vegetable bowl isn't limited to serving vegetables. Put spring flowers in it, and see how pretty it looks. Even the ordinary brown earthenware casseroles and saucepans can be used for colorful mixed flowers on patio tables. Large Portuguese bowls made to look like real cabbage leaves are ideal for an arrangement of vegetables. There are lovely Italian ceramics, and with the current interest in Spanish clothes and furnishings, the stores are filled with unusual Spanish items. Brass and copperware of all shapes and sizes, old and new, make attractive containers—kettles, small buckets, and saucepans. A birdcage can be painted and filled with flowers and ivy; for a realistic touch, add an artificial bird. We crave baskets for holding anything and everything. Only one person surpasses us in this craze, and she has hung her kitchen ceiling with antique baskets for decoration, so she always has one of an appropriate size ready for use. Old molds, of copper, pottery, or ironstone, can be used for flowers, fruit, or vegetables. A bright-red geranium in a beach hat makes a centerpiece suitable for a beach party. And sometimes a pretty teacup is just the right size and color for flowers on a small table.

There is a surprisingly large assortment of tiered epergnes

and compotes in shops. They are a delight to work with and come in silver, brass, porcelain, ceramic, crystal, and wicker. These are practical, though sometimes expensive, because they can be used in so many different ways. We have seen them filled with fruit, berries, flowers, nosegays, Easter eggs, vegetables, and greens.

Reserve one shelf in a cupboard for any basic equipment you will need in making arrangements. Have on hand at least a half-dozen good frogs for flowers, either the pottery and glass ones with holes, or spiked metal ones, and florist's clay for anchoring them. Always have extra containers on hand, in case you are confronted by large bouquets from late guests! Styrofoam is easy to use and can be purchased in quantity and cut to any shape. It can be used to build up arrangements of flowers, either real or artificial, and keeps them in place. Always camouflage it with greens so that it won't show. When used in water, it has to be anchored with wire or florist's clay. Of course, it's much cheaper to buy flowers and greens in bulk and arrange them yourself, instead of paying the florist to do it for you. Always submerge cut flowers in deep water for several hours or overnight before arranging, to keep them at their best.

Inanimate Objects. Not long ago, rules of etiquette specified to the letter exactly how one must decorate the center of a table with flowers and candles. Even the spacing of the candles was spelled out. We won't go so far as to say anything goes, but certainly originality and individuality are now encouraged, with the happy result that tables are more interesting. It's no longer necessary to limit the decoration to flowers or fruit. Inanimate objects can be equally attractive as a focal point.

Start by thinking of your own interests and hobbies. If you are a "collector," consider a grouping from your collection, if the individual pieces are important enough. It could be several beautiful porcelain cats or birds, a cluster of antique decanters or apothecary jars in different sizes and shapes, or some of the sizable Royal Doulton figurines. Group several odd pieces from a pewter, copper, or toleware collection. A great conversation centerpiece could be composed of all your small objets d'art simply cluttering the whole center of the table. Arrange as prettily as possible such items as tiny easeled pictures, china eggs, small figurines, tiny floral pieces, little boxes. For those with a nautical bent, a ship model would be appropriate on an informal table. Victorian washbowls make attractive centerpieces, with or without anything in them. There are charming tureens topped with lovebirds, bunnies, cows, chickens, or even in the shape of a big cauliflower or other vegetable.

Since the special holidays come but once a year, we're all for going along with traditional decorations, but try to give them a new twist. At Easter, colored eggs look pretty in a footed milk-glass compote or in a silver bowl. At Christmas set a beautiful antique pitcher beside a matching bowl of greens, or fill apothecary jars with bright Christmas balls. The unique flat Mexican tin Christmas trees make ideal decorations for a buffet table set against the wall.

Large, fat candles of varied shapes and heights always make a pretty grouping, and since they come in every color imaginable, they are not limited to Christmas, as some seem to think. They can be used in autumn colors with autumn leaves around the base, or in pastels for spring. Put them in the center of a glass flower ring of pansies, ivy, or any small flowers. Of course, colors must harmonize with other colors on the table. Place one large candle inside a glass chimney and surround the base with flowers.

Shops are overflowing with magnificent ceramics. We tend to think of ceramics in modern terms only, but they have an extraordinary quality of being adaptable to any setting. The Italian pieces are somewhat bolder in design than the French, which are done with a lighter touch. But all have flair. Some are strictly decorative pieces and made for table ornaments, such as various fruits and whimsical birds, while others are containers only. There are also bowls of ceramic fruit and vegetables, molded all in one piece, which make attractive centerpieces.

These may appear expensive, but they have the advantage of always being ready. Therefore, it's practical to buy a really good one that will be an asset to your table, since it can be used forever, if you're lucky enough not to break it. Put it away for part of the year and bring it out after the flower season has passed. Besides the ceramics, decorative fruits are also made in glass—either colored, clear, or gold-dusted Venetian.

A simple but novel decoration for an outdoor table is a fruit basket, such as apples come in, lined with loosely crushed tissue paper in several different colors. Put three attractive bottles of wine in the basket with colored tissue crushed gently between them. And there are pretty wine baskets with handles, which hold six bottles. Why not have three bottles of wine alternating with flowers in the other sections?

The invention of the spray paint can is a boon to party people who enjoy playing around with decorations. You can quickly paint practically anything these days, and it's easy to change color. If you prefer colored baskets to match décor, you can do it in a jiffy with spray paints. Cucumbers or pineapples can be changed to glamorous gold in a centerpiece. For those who are not imaginative by nature, there are stores that specialize in party ideas to help you. Some of the paper party items for very specialized themes are clever, such as paper palm trees for a luau.

Outside, Too

When decorating your home, don't forget the outside. A touch of something seasonal on the front door makes a guest feel welcome the moment he arrives, and it's fun for neighbors, too. Don't wait for the Christmas wreath. Whimsical touches are amusing the year round. There are a few houses in our neighborhood that never fail to have holiday touches, always in good taste, and we'd be disappointed if they didn't appear—a chubby cupid on St. Valentine's Day, a big bunny at Easter, a basket of flowers on May Day, and of course the American flag on national holidays. Personal flags are quite the vogue, so design one to fly whenever you give a party. Use an arrangement of motifs that appeal to you or that express some part of your life. Or use your family coat of arms. Appliqué the design in bright colors of felt on a flag of felt. Edge with fringe, if you like. Fly from a regular flagpole on your lawn, or suspend on a stanchion by the door.

Dress up porch and patio, too, with flowers, greens, and hanging baskets. It's a lot easier than inside, because nature is the limit on color schemes and you can have the fun of a complete change from winter. If you're not the gardener you'd like to be, cheat a little with pots of artificial flowers. If you use only the very realistic ones, you're likely to catch a guest with a watering can doing what Hogan did in Lawrence Roman's play "Under the Yum-Yum Tree." As he carefully tended plants, his companion cautioned, "Look, I hate to tell you this but those plants aren't real." "Doesn't matter," Hogan answered, "the can was empty."

When entertaining outside, be sure that such eyesores as garbage cans are out of sight. You can hide all "skeletons" in the garage temporarily and park the car in the street, if necessary. And any time you plan an out-of-doors party, do set an alternate date in case it rains, or else be ready for an instantaneous shift indoors, since the weatherman often puts the whammy on picnics. Cold, wet guests are miserable guests. We remember a steak party in a downpour when everyone was shivering and husbands with big black umbrellas were sloshing around in soggy grass to tend grills. They were so eager to get back to shelter that we had to eat our steaks not rare but almost raw!

Place Cards

Place cards are optional, but are appropriate any time you choose to use them. At a formal dinner the card should be plain white Bristol board written with title and surname (Mr. Brown), unless it is an intimate group. If there are two guests with the same surname, the given name is also used (Mr. Thomas Brown). At informal parties, write in the name as you are accustomed to using it. For holidays such as Christmas or Easter, decorated place cards look festive; frilly valentines are especially pretty to mark places on St. Valentine's Day. But it's wise to keep on hand plain white cards that can be used anytime. If you are entertaining in a club or hotel, place cards may be a part of their service, but be sure they are of good quality.

There are different ways to arrange place cards. Without holders, they can be laid flat just above the plate or on the folded napkin. A folded place card or one in a card holder stands above the plate in the center. If you wish to use holders, there are sterling ones in the shape of shells, roses, and leaves. Or you can find holders made of Dresden china flowers, or tiny gold pineapples (the symbol of hospitality). If you can't afford really good ones, use the place card alone. Better than resorting to plastic holders!

Music, Maestro, Please

Most party-givers are equipped with some sort of record player. Unless you are more interested in the science of sound than in the music itself, a medium-priced machine will serve you just as well for party purposes as one with the kind of paraphernalia that requires an engineer. It is of more importance to have well-cared-for records and high-quality needles.

Background music helps to get a party started and is pleasant during dinner. But regulate the sound so that it is background, not foreground! And don't have music continuously. When conversation is going strong, turn it off. Unless yours is a really swinging party, music without a heavy beat and with the least brass is better music to chat by. Of course, if guests are invited for dancing, lay in a good supply of records for all types of dances. Even the golden-age set may want to learn the latest steps.

At large parties, indoors or out, occasionally treat the guests to "live music." One instrument will do, if sufficiently musical —no drums! A guitarist or an accordionist wandering among guests will make an ordinary party become a festival. And wherever there is a good pianist, there is usually a lively party. Banjos and ukuleles have made a comeback, and zithers have for some time been appearing on the scene.

Extra! Extra!

Even with a good supply of everything for the individual place setting, it takes a heap of extras to entertain well. There are so many things in shops to be bought for party-giving that discrimination must be used to keep from ending up with a lot of things you don't like and needing a lot that you don't have. The many electrical appliances are a great aid to a hostess, but don't go overboard. We lean toward the things that make for more attractive serving, instead of being purely functional, but this too can be overdone. A happy medium is always best.

Now we are blessed with battery-operated appliances that eliminate the ugly, treacherous cord and the necessity of an outlet within reach. One of their greatest blessings is out-of-doors use. There are cordless electric carving knives, ice crushers, and portable mixers available, with more to come in the future.

Encourage your family to make your birthday and Christmas gifts some of the luxury items for entertaining. By doing this you can build up a very impressive party wardrobe within a few years. Some of the extras that can add to your convenience and the guests' pleasure are listed below.

Plainly Practical.

❋ A tarnishproof silver chest saves you hours of cleaning time and keeps flatware ready for use.

❋ Electric coffeemakers come in many sizes for home use, from 12 to 35 cups. They are being designed with more eye appeal than the old purely functional ones, but serving is still more attractive from a silver, pewter, or china pot at the table. However, there are electric percolators (12 and 15 cups) in silver plate on copper that look as though they belong to your silver service.

❊ Electric trays for keeping things warm come in different sizes. These are especially useful outdoors, if you have an electrical outlet within reach.

❊ Blenders are helpful only if you use enough blender recipes to make one worth while.

❊ Small electric rotisseries can be used right at the table for cooking steaks, chickens, roasts, and shish kebab—no spatter, no spill, no smoke. Be like the French restaurateurs, who are famous for cooking in the open, before the eyes of the guests. It always impresses onlookers. "Dress rehearsals" are very important, however, or your serving table may look like the kitchen. Perfect for apartments as a substitute for suburban outdoor cooking.

❊ Nonsticking cookware is available in casseroles, Dutch ovens, skillets, muffin pans, loaf pans, cookie sheets and saucepans. Saves a lot of scrubbing time, but it's very important to follow directions carefully.

Plainly Pretty.

❊ Matching ashtrays for the dining table and containers for cigarettes. Don't gather together an odd assortment and think they will do.

❊ Individual salt dishes are nice—and pepper dishes, too, if you use coarse pepper (so guests won't sneeze). There are also tiny pepper mills in sterling silver. These individual conveniences should be put at each place, or between every two guests.

❊ Giant pepper mills—but not too giant—if you don't use individual ones.

❊ Muffineers, antiques or reproductions, make pretty accessories for nutmeg, powdered sugar, or cinnamon and sugar combined.

❊ Decorative trays, and plenty of them. Half a dozen are none too many.

❊ Pretty coasters that don't stick to the glass. There *are* such things.

❊ Numerous trivets that are both attractive and safe for hot dishes. There are brass, iron, and silver ones, and colorful tiles set in wooden frames.

❊ Wooden boxes with hot tiles or little slates in the bottom to keep rolls warm. And baskets are indispensable in all sizes and shapes for rolls and snacks.

❊ Pretty wooden boards in various shapes and sizes for serving. These are handy for cheese, coffee cake, and special breads such as nut bread at casual parties.

❊ Large, unusual serving plates, round or square, for cakes, tortes, or desserts made in a mold. Our favorite is a 12-inch-square marble slab on little brass feet. Footed cake plates in ceramic and glass are also pretty.

❊ Individual casseroles in the shape of chickens are an amusing way to serve a baked chicken dish, chicken salad, or chicken soup.

❊ Glass mugs for Irish coffee can double for "nosewarmers" (cups of hot madrilene or bouillon). There are also pottery mugs in bright colors and stripes that sit right on a luncheon or dessert plate for morning coffee or Sunday night supper.

❊ Individual wine carafes not only are good conversation pieces, but also free the host from pouring. Naturally, the wine must be one that can be decanted.

❋ Don't stint on salad bowls. You need a good number in different sizes and shapes, and it's fun to have changes. Wooden ones, old or new, are favorites; there are stunning gigantic teak bowls an inch thick. Victorian washbowls or a glass punch bowl are the answer to serving large quantities of salad. There are exquisite black wooden hand-rubbed bowls with matching trays for contemporary homes, clear crystal ones for elegance, and colored enamelware for casual use. The individual enamelware bowls make a cheery table when different colors are combined. They can also be used for cereal or soup. And individual wooden bowls are always popular for salad. We saw a life-size watermelon bowl in authentic colors that would be a dazzling party dish filled with fruit salad.

❋ Salad servers can be wooden, silver-plated, sterling, stainless steel—whatever is in keeping with your bowl. A convenience at a buffet supper is the wooden scissors type of server, for it can be used with one hand.

❋ Platters of different sizes are needed and can contrast with other dishes. Use china, sterling, silver plate, ironstone, pewter, stainless steel. For sizzling steaks and chops there are heavy cast aluminum ones to put right under the broiler and then to fit into a wooden tray for serving, meanwhile keeping the meat hot.

❋ Oven-to-table cookware is a big thing now. Just about everything you can think of to cook in is made in porcelainized cast iron or other ovenware. Colors are bright, and styles are varied, but all are practical as well as pretty. They keep the heat in, can be brought right to the table, look attractive, and are easy to clean. What more could you ask for? There are handsome Dutch ovens, casseroles, and skillets in various sizes. There is also good-looking pure-white ovenware.

❋ A collection of egg cups. Especially if you have frequent breakfast guests. They can be matched or varied.

❋ Ice buckets are no longer the fairly unattractive containers they once were. They too are now a part of the general decorating scheme, and some are so beautiful they can be brought right into the living room to be admired.

❋ Chafing dish and fondue chafer—make for attractive serving and keep food hot.

❋ Serving stands with warming candle or Sterno come in silver, brass, enamelware, and various ovenwares for one, two, or three casseroles.

❋ Punch bowl. Not used often, but nice to have. Any large bowl can be used, such as a tureen or an old washbowl. If you buy one for once-a-year occasions, an inexpensive bowl will do. Plain glass in the low price range looks much better than fancy designs. If you can't give it houseroom, rent one with cups when needed.

❋ Serving carts today are pretty racy, compared with grandmother's tea wagon of long ago, but they still have the same objective. They save steps and make serving attractive. Especially convenient for kitchen-to-terrace use. Cozy in winter by the fireside, too. There is a wide price range and a variety of styles.

Tools of the Trade

If you have a husband who is gadget-minded—and most are—you will probably end up with a cupboard full of eye-catching items, some of them utterly useless but the rest indispensable. You may find the same old standbys coming out to help every time, whether for parties or for everyday routine. Undoubtedly you have your own special loves, but here are some of the things we think should be found behind the scenes in any well-run kitchen, besides the usual supply of pots and pans and skillets.

Three Dozen K.P. Keepies:

1. Pressure cooker—a must in our kitchen, and a great time-saver.
2. Earthenware pie plates—the only way to bake a pie.
3. Wooden mixing spoons—never bend, and are great for stirring sauces and gravy.
4. Carrot scraper—speeds up that tedious job.
5. A good bottle opener and corkscrew.
6. A really workable jar opener.
7. Several tubular molds—can be used interchangeably for salads or cakes.
8. Efficient food shredder, grater, and chopper.
9. Large tongs for hot food such as potatoes and corn on the cob.
10. Pepper mill—freshly ground pepper is always best.
11. Extra ice-cube trays.
12. Ice crusher; a good hand-operated one works fine, and, for more money, an electric one works better.
13. Garlic press.
14. Onion chopper—saves tears.
15. Corn scraper—if you have elderly guests.
16. Large board for chopping or rolling pastry.
17. Hand pastry blender with metal blades, for cutting shortening into flour.
18. Juicer, hand or electric, depending on how much squeezing you do.
19. Electric mixer, portable or stationary—we find portable more versatile.
20. Baster—the kind that looks like a giant medicine dropper, for basting anything that needs it.
21. Meat thermometer—does away with guessing.
22. Adjustable metal rack for roasting pan—keeps meat from sticking to the bottom of pan.
23. Good, big vegetable brush with strong bristles—so much better than little flimsy ones.

24. Several wire cake racks—the only proper way to cool cakes, cookies, and bread.
25. Several paring knives and meat knives—nothing fancy, just plain, sharp knives.
26. Springform cake pan.
27. Release-type tubular cake pan—bottom and sides of pan separate so that cake doesn't.
28. At least two loaf pans, standard size.
29. Small lemon strainer that fits over cup.
30. Small Mouli hand grater for nuts, hard-boiled eggs, small amounts of cheese, etc.
31. An oversized cake cover to keep cake fresh after baking. Large enough to keep from touching cake on top or sides. There are lovely clear glass ones, a big improvement over the old commercial-looking metal ones.
32. Large flat-sided spoon for stirring—gets down to the bottom of things.
33. Large spoon for stirring that can be hooked on side of pan —keeps from dribbling on the stove and from getting lost.
34. Automatic timer, either attached to stove or separate—absolutely essential, unless you have an elephant's memory.
35. Teakettle—don't deny yourself; you'll use it much more than you'd ever imagine.
36. Good spot remover—to take care of the spills on clothes and carpets that are sure to happen occasionally.

Always keep a good supply of aluminum foil on hand, and plastic or glass containers for leftovers. Remember to reserve space in the refrigerator so that you can whisk away the perishables quickly (after the guests have left the table, of course) and get on with the party. In your haste, don't do what the mother of a friend did years ago. In her concern over getting the remains of the Thanksgiving turkey put away, she didn't notice that Smokey, the cat, had jumped into the icebox, hot on the trail of the turkey. The family went off to bed, unaware of what had happened until the following morning, when the icebox was opened for breakfast. Out leaped the cat, very cold, but obviously stuffed with turkey. Lucky it was the day of the old-fashioned icebox, instead of modern electric refrigeration, or old Smokey never would have survived.

Be sure your kitchen aids are of adequate size. It's so inefficient if they are not. We had one last-minute crisis as a result of owning only a small colander. When pouring a big quantity of noodles into a small-capacity colander, we ended up with oodles of noodles all over the sink. Since the rest of the dinner was already on the table and hungry guests were waiting, there was nothing to do but scoop them up and carry on. But the following day we rushed to the nearest premium store and exchanged our trading stamps for the biggest colander they had.

Know Your Own. We heartily recommend a good solid relationship with your kitchen; be sure you are on speaking terms with all equipment in it before trying it out on guests. We also urge you to read directions for all electric appliances, so that you know their limitations and won't expect the impossible. We were proud recipients of a beautiful combination bean pot with electric plate beneath. In our eagerness to use it, we immediately invited friends in for a baked bean supper. We put the beans in the pot a good three hours before the guests' arrival, turned on the electric switch, and went about other preparations. Two hours later, we decided to check on the beans and were stricken to find that they weren't even hot. On reading the directions, we found that the electric plate was not for baking at all, but merely to keep the beans warm *after* they were cooked. So our baked bean party turned out to be a midnight supper!

It seems unnecessary to mention that the oven and range are the most important equipment in any kitchen. Great strides are being made in cooking equipment, and we are promised a microwave oven any day now. This miracle worker cooks at an incredible speed of four to six times faster than the pokey ones we have presently. A 14-pound turkey will cook in 30 minutes, an egg in 20 seconds. We can't help thinking that there is going to be a lot of burned food on the table, but for any wife who has dragged herself out of bed wearily at 5:30 A.M. on Christmas morning to put the turkey in the oven, things are looking up.

When entertaining outdoors, check furnace or grill several days ahead, to be sure that everything is clean and in good working order. A neighbor sent her husband out to start the fire in the open-air furnace an hour before a large party. When he didn't reappear, she went out to investigate and found him still in work clothes, busily repairing and even cementing the furnace—and guests fifteen minutes away! As for his unconcern, this is typical husband timing, which all wives learn to live with.

Twenty Tempting Tables

We hope that the tables described here will not only tempt you to give a party, but will also tease your imagination and ingenuity. Of course, you won't have on hand all of the objects described, but similar objects can be substituted. Almost all of the linens can be made, if you can sew a straight seam; they require very little special skill. Even if you can't sew, you can fringe edges by raveling. Although party colors do follow nature and the calendar, they can be altered to harmonize with your own color scheme.

1. Madras County. Cover the table with a patchwork madras cloth (fabric can be bought by the yard). Instead of one important center arrangement, load the table with wooden objects, spacing them at random, such as coffee grinder, 12- or 16-inch pepper mill, wooden candlesticks, small wooden board with bottle of wine and cheese, antique wooden tea box, and a cheesebox. Use stark-white ironstone dishes. Make napkins of the different colors included in the patchwork. Give a country or informal party—luncheon or supper, buffet or sit-down.

2. Ship Ahoy! Use any blue cotton or linen cloth and cover it with white fishnet (can be bought by the yard). Ship model for centerpiece, and ship lanterns to light the table. Solid-color cotton or linen napkins alternating in red, white, and blue. Again, white ironstone dishes.

3. Yippee! Blue denim tablecloth with bandanna napkins, for a children's Western party. Use square cake for centerpiece enclosed in tiny square fence. Letter cake "Bar 6 Ranch" (use birthday year for number). Fly small flag on top that says "Don't fence me in." Toy horses surround cake. Tie box lunches with small rope and enclose favor in each. Use enamelware mugs, cowboy style, for milk.

4. Paisley Pretty. Use old paisley shawl for table cover. (Can substitute cotton or linen paisley in autumn colors; purchase by yard and edge with fringe.) Pick up one color in the paisley for napkins. Brass three-tiered compote for center of table with tiny runt pumpkin on top tier. Fill middle tier with fruit-shaped marzipan candy and lower tier with gilded walnuts on bed of green leaves. Brass candlesticks with gold-colored candles. Use good china and amber glassware. For autumn or Thanksgiving entertaining—buffet or seated supper, open house, or cocktail party.

5. Merry Christmas! White felt cloth edged with white cotton ball fringe. Victorian washbowl filled with evergreens in center. Decorate greens with many small bright-colored birds (either wooden, feathered, or the old-fashioned glass ones made for Christmas trees) and small tree baubles (about an inch in diameter) in red, green, silver, and gold. Tuck a little bird's nest among the greens, complete with bird and tiny baubles in place of eggs. If you can't find an abandoned nest, buy an artificial one—don't rob the birds. Alternate solid-color napkins in red and green. Silver candelabrum on each side of bowl, with red or green candles. Christmas dishes. Give a holiday sherry party, tea, open house, or buffet—or use for your family Christmas dinner.

6. Ring in the New.   Cover New Year's table with two layers of pastel theatrical gauze—green over blue, or mauve over pink. Select one of the colors for napkins. Sprinkle table with silver glitter. Large silver Revere bowl in center filled with toy tin horns and big silver and pastel baubles. Silver candlesticks with pastel candles. Best china.

7. Olé!   Mexican sarape tablecloth or runner for a Mexican- or Spanish-themed party. Alternate solid-color napkins in red,. yellow, and orange. Piñata animal for centerpiece. Very tall wrought-iron candlesticks with red candles. Informal dishes, such as brown pottery, clay, or Mexican tin plates. Perfect for informal patio party or on terrace.

8. Happy Landing!   Fill a small leather or wooden antique trunk about 12 inches long (doll's trunk will do) to overflowing with laurel or pachysandra leaves. Conceal Styrofoam in container in bottom of trunk to secure arrangement. Stick miniature flags in the Styrofoam among the leaves representing countries to be visited. (These can be purchased from United Nations Souvenir shop in New York, as we have mentioned.) Use place mats and napkins of natural linen or homespun in a color to blend with your dining room. Give a luncheon for a traveling friend.

9. Here Comes the Bride.   Make it really pretty for the bride-to-be with a white organdy appliquéd tablecloth. Fill a crystal or cut-glass bowl with pink carnations or roses (whichever are in season) combined with white babies'-breath. Among the flowers arrange an opened white fan. Crystal candlesticks with white candles. On each white napkin, place a pink rose or carnation tied with moss-green velvet ribbon. Best china and crystal.

10. Midnight Magic. Deep-blue linen tablecloth with large silver paper stars scattered over it. Matching blue napkins in silver napkin rings. Large five-armed silver candelabrum in center of table with metallic silver candles. Blue-and-white dishes. Silver goblets and silver bread-and-butter plates. Give a late supper party after theater, concert, or ball.

11. Quilted Splendor. Select a quilted floral pattern in rich, subtle colors from drapery fabrics for a table runner and cut to 20- to 24-inch width. Line with lightweight fabric to make neat edges. In center, place round silver tray that is filled with a mound of fruit, a clear glass decanter of red wine, and a footed silver compote full of green grapes that trail over the side. Silver candlesticks. Choose one of the colors in the fabric for candles and napkins, or make napkins of unquilted matching fabric, if it is of suitable weight. Seated dinner, buffet, open house, or cocktail party.

12. Easter Sunday. Any pastel tablecloth would be pretty— soft gold, aqua, pink, or yellow. As a centerpiece, use a handsome double scale, antique or reproduction, and fill each suspended section with colored, decorated Easter eggs on a nest of greens. Place a decorated egg in an egg cup at each individual place. Invite friends or family for Easter dinner.

13. Black and White. Make round black linen place mats edged with pure-white cotton fringe (either ball fringe or knotted). Plain white linen napkins. Spray birdcage, either metal or wicker, with white paint and entwine a few sprays of artificial ivy among the bars; place inside it a sassy black stuffed toy cat with bright-red ribbon around his neck. Perch an all-black bird (you can spray him black) outside on top of the cage, looking in at the cat. White milk-glass candlesticks with white candles. White dishes and milk-glass goblets. A whimsical table for an informal supper party.

14. Very Victorian. Make a rich red velveteen table runner, 20 to 24 inches wide (depending on width of your table), edged with gold braid or fringe. Fill a giant hurricane glass chimney about 18 inches high with an arrangement of fruit. On each side use brass candlesticks with clear glass hurricane chimneys. Red candles. Shape red linen or damask napkins into a roll and tie with gold cord and tassel. Gold-rimmed china or glassware.

15. Sweet Sixteen. Give an "in-the-pink" luncheon or supper for a girl's sixteenth birthday. Make two pale-pink 11-inch-wide runners to stretch the length of table down each side to take the place of individual mats. Any cotton or linen will do; polished cotton would be pretty, or a pink-and-white checked gingham. One table length plus 12 inches to take care of overhang at each end will make both runners, with enough left along the side for napkins. Use bare center of table for three stages of birthday girl's life: childhood, school days, and a grown-up sixteen wearing flowers to the prom. Arrange pink carnations for all the guests in a mound on a footed cake stand or compote of white ceramic or china in the center of table. Tie flowers with pink ribbons that lead to individual places, so that each girl takes home a flower. Dress birthday girl's favorite childhood doll in spanking new pink dress and lean it against centerpiece. On other side of centerpiece, place several schoolbooks wrapped in pink-flowered gift-paper jackets. Pink and white dishes.

16. Americana. Cover table with old turkey-red cloth. Matching napkins or white. Group 19th-century blue-and-white Staffordshire tea set in center. Fill creamer, sugar bowl, and teapot with small dried flowers. Why not tuck a tiny flower in the spout? Invite friends to lunch and use blue-and-white dishes, pewter bread-and-butter plates, and any pewter serving pieces you might have.

17. Luscious Luau.   Green burlap tablecloth. Cover all of table center with large, shiny green leaves; then fill table with coconuts, pineapples, bananas, melons, and any other fruit available, for a lavish look. Place pineapple-shaped candles among the fruit. Make inexpensive cotton napkins in different pastel colors. Informal dishes. Great party for summer evening outdoors.

18. Denim and Daisies.   Welcome spring with yellow-and-white-striped denim table cover with matching or plain yellow napkins. Set a large basket of daisies in center of table and smaller baskets of lemons at each end. Tuck a few daisies among the lemons. Cheerful for morning coffee on the terrace. Yellow-and-white coffee mugs.

19. Cabbages and Queens.   Bare table centered with green ceramic cabbage-shaped bowl filled with several pieces of white ceramic fruit. Polished-cotton napkins in blue-and-green floral print. Serve a salad lunch in matching individual cabbage-leaf bowls set on white plates. Cobalt-blue goblets Luncheon or Sunday night supper.

20. Purely Patriotic.   Cut a circle 18 inches in diameter from bright-blue felt with pinking shears. Glue—or tack with blind stitch—white felt stars about an inch in diameter all around the edge. Place this in center of table, and over it place a circle of red felt, 14 inches in diameter, so that a blue border of white stars shows from beneath. Center with toy drum from which one side has been removed. Line with glass dish and fill with white flowers. Group three toy soldiers in Revolutionary uniforms, 8 or 10 inches tall, with the drum. Let one hold a small American flag. Red-white-and-blue-striped napkins. Table suitable for Independence Day, Flag Day, Memorial Day, Washington's or Lincoln's Birthday. Use red or blue glass goblets.

Planning for Faultless Food and Drink

Feast, and your halls are crowded;
Fast, and the world goes by.
                    Ella Wheeler Wilcox, *Solitude*

"Sit down and feed and welcome to our table."
                    Shakespeare

CHAPTER

5

The breaking of bread with others has long symbolized the establishment of a bond of friendship. It is only through sharing someone's board that you actually get to know the real John Buck or the real Jane Doe. The French have a unique way of expressing this thought when they say, "Never judge anyone before eating a pillow of salt with him."

Right here at the beginning of this chapter, without so much as an apology, we're going to say that it's not our intention to make this a cookbook. There is already an abundance of cookbooks available on how and what to cook, whether you are planning an Eskimo wedding celebration at the North Pole or a lion-hunt breakfast in an African jungle, so our true aim is to stress the importance of balance, interest, and variety in menu, of food and color combinations, and of ease of preparation. We'll leave it up to you to compile your own recipe file.

Planning the Menu

Once you have decided on the date of your party and your guest list, start immediately to plan your menu. It's a good idea to glance over your menu file and favorite cookbooks to refresh your memory on certain dishes that have been especially successful and have made a hit previously with guests. Don't, however, use your guests as a test panel. If you have that adventurous spirit, so necessary in becoming a gourmet cook, use the family for your trial run. They'll complain, of course, but don't be intimidated by heckling. Have the courage of your convictions, if you think a recipe worth trying. With experience you'll soon learn to change a recipe here and there to make the sauce a little thicker, or the cookies a little crisper. So don't fail to have rehearsals before opening night.

Know Your Capacity. Undertake only what you can handle. Don't *overestimate* your ability, but neither should you *underestimate* it. The day of the poor helpless female who just "can't boil water" has long since passed. Friends are more likely to admire your culinary ability than your coy affectation. With enough determination you are bound to succeed, but plan your menu within reason. Some people have a compulsion to do everything single-handedly and to show off all their accomplishments at one time. Such a hostess takes too much on herself— and consequently out of herself—so that she can't do justice to any one thing.

"Case" Your Kitchen. Thoughtful planning of the menu in relation to service is as necessary as any other preparation for a party. Consider all your equipment, from size of utensils to the appliances that actually do the cooking. You may make the highest soufflé in town and the puffiest popovers, but if you try to serve both at the same meal, you will be in trouble—unless you have two ovens. The soufflé must bake undisturbed for a longer time and at a lower temperature than the popovers, so don't get yourself in a bind by failing to realize this in time.

Personally we do not believe that a double oven is at all essential. Life can be beautiful without it, although most of our friends disagree. In fact, the subject has become quite controversial in our circle. We still maintain that we are not inhibited when entertaining or cooking because of this void in our lives, but if you feel a desperate need for two ovens and have charmed your husband into buying them for you, make the most of it; get in there and cook up a storm. If you need additional oven space but rarely, the answer to your problem is one of the small electric oven appliances that fit neatly on the counter. This will take care of warming rolls, toasting bread, and baking a few potatoes, and leaves the main oven free for large casseroles or roasting pans. Many people enjoy the present-day craze for outdoor cooking because of the variety of foods you can cook at one time on a large grill, from steaks to fresh corn on the cob. An added benefit is keeping the cooking heat and steam out in the wide open spaces on a hot night.

It's amazing what a hostess can do with the minimum in equipment and the maximum in thought. A memorable dinner was one served by a glowing bride with only an electric hot plate and a tiny refrigerator in a pullman kitchen. The climax of the dinner was a magnificent pie made with graham cracker crust, refrigerated filling, and a whipped cream topping, all done without benefit of oven. You can always get around any inconvenience with the proper ingenuity.

Precision Timing. Thoughtful planning must also go into serving. Perfect timing is probably the most difficult thing for the ambitious cook to conquer. You can excel in creating three or four different dishes, but unless you can manage to complete all of them at the same time and serve them gracefully, victory will not be yours. The hot dishes must be kept hot and the cold dishes cold. It's much better to plan a menu that doesn't require such careful synchronism. Casseroles are a boon to the uncertain hostess because of the flexibility in cooking time. They can always be started a little early or held a little late in the oven. With the "Cook and Keep" feature of modern ranges, such dishes can be held indefinitely without spoiling and drying out.

One way to keep your timing on schedule is to note in your recipe file the increased amount of time that it takes for preparation when you double or triple a recipe. You may be surprised how much longer it takes, and if you are prepared for this additional time, your dinner will be better coordinated. Don't leave it to guesswork. For instance if you double a soufflé recipe for four, it will take an hour and a half to bake, instead of an hour. This could throw off your entire schedule.

Ingredients for a green salad can be prepared a few hours ahead—washed and even cut or broken (whichever school you follow). But please, please, don't wilt their crispness, the secret of a good tossed salad, by mixing too early with the dressing. Time your work so that you can do this at the very last minute while rolls are warming and coffee is perking. Any molded salad, such as an aspic or mousse, should be turned out on a serving plate early in the day, then returned to the refrigerator. This not only will save those last precious minutes, but also will reset any softening that has occurred during the unmolding process. Then voilà—it's ready to set on the table after everything else has been done, without so much as a jangled nerve. We'll let you in on another secret of successful molds that never look limp and sagging on the plate. If you use a flavored gelatin, reduce every two cups of liquid to one and three-fourths; and if you use the unflavored type, which is usually dissolved in a little cold water, add an extra half envelope of gelatin for every one that is called for. We guarantee that your fish molds will stand up sturdy and strong on the plate and look the guests proudly in the eye. No more of those embarrassing apologies.

Among our greatest delights from the dessert section of our recipe file are the steamed puddings—chocolate, almond, date, and our holiday plum pudding. What a joy to be able to set a steamed dessert on a burner—you don't even have to use oven space—two hours before the party and forget about it until dessert time. Or make it the day before, and reheat it in a double boiler while the entrée is being served. Besides being easy to make, it is always a conversation piece among guests and causes no end of comment. Even if you're only a so-so cook, this is the way to con your friends into crowning you "Queen of Cuisine." For some unexplained reason, most people think it's extremely difficult to make steamed desserts, but nothing could be simpler. All you need is a recipe, a covered mold, and any covered boiler large enough to hold the mold and the water to steam it. We bought our steamer for ten cents at a thrift shop, and new ones can be purchased for around two dollars. Served with whipped cream or a hard sauce, this dessert is one you simply can't beat for a cold winter evening.

Service with Charm. As you think about your menu, you should also be giving some thought to serving equipment. Any food tastes better if it is attractively served, so keep in mind your beautiful antique tureen and grandmother's "strawberry luster" cake plate. Build your menu around what you have. If this seems like backward planning to you, we guarantee that it is a successful system, tried and true. You will never find yourself scrambling around at the last moment trying to find a platter large enough for the meat that will harmonize with the dinner plates, or a dish the right shape for asparagus.

When setting the table in advance, we always arrange at the same time every single serving dish in its place. Then we can be sure that the correct container for each dish will fit well on the serving table. If you are planning a buffet luncheon or supper, give some thought to whether everything can be eaten easily with a fork, if you expect guests to use their laps. Knives are awkward and burdensome in this case.

Balance in Menu. Coordination is the key word of the entire party, and this carries right through to the food on the table. Some people have a natural talent for combining colors for a pleasing effect; others develop this through study and by trial and error; alas, some never acquire it. The same is true of combining foods for a palatable effect. There are certain foods which when eaten separately are delicious but when combined are revolting. Cheese fondue is superb with baked ham, but cheese fondue with roast beef—never! The sweet dishes—candied sweet potatoes, fruit salads, and the like—are appetizing with poultry, pork, or ham, but not with beef, which calls for greens and starches. This doesn't mean that you must have a staid, set, inflexible plan. Use your imagination and break the monotony with variations of the same vegetable from time to time. We'll give you some of our tricks a little later.

Color It Pretty. It is important to balance your menu both as to color and as to content. As we've said before, food always tastes better if it *looks* attractive. You may be wild about mashed potatoes and hominy grits, but please, not on the same plate. They are both much too colorless—and think of all that starch. There are enough green vegetables available for color contrasts. When you have too much green, add shredded red cabbage to your tossed green salad to vary the color scheme. Or use yellow wax beans instead of the green variety. Dark-green spinach leaves make a pretty contrast against other lighter salad greens. We can never resist that dash of paprika on the white sauce and a sprinkling of nutmeg or cinnamon on the whipped cream. A bit of chopped parsley or chopped chives adds color to a potato casserole or to buttered new potatoes.

Not Too Heavy, Not Too Light—Just Right. As you try to make the meal appealing in looks, make it equally appealing in character. Never fail to consider the effect on your guests. What a pity it would be if the only thing they remembered about your party was a bad case of heartburn. As the old saying goes, "Don't choke the cat with too much cream." If you serve a rich lobster à la Newburg as the entrée, go easy on dessert—perhaps a fruit ambrosia. But if the main course is not-so-rich baked ham or chicken, let yourself go with cheesecake or chocolate soufflé for dessert.

It is impossible to give a standard combination for any one meal, but generally speaking the following might serve as a guide: MEAT, STARCH, GREEN, SWEET, SOUR (or TART), HOT, and COLD.

Amounts to Plan On. Never let it be said of you, "Too late with too little!" Our motto is always "Better too much than not enough." Nothing is more embarrassing than to run short of food. That's worse than running short of money! Don't worry about how much is left over—just count your blessings if there is enough for tomorrow's dinner. You'll be grateful for leftovers after a day of cleaning up. If a recipe is proportioned for four people, don't believe it unless you've actually proved it on the family. Better to increase by a half, making it for six, or in reality four hungry people. If a recipe is for eight, play it safe and increase to twelve servings. Who said that women don't need arithmetic in school! You'll praise the teacher who taught fractions when you come to multiplying and dividing your recipes. And never forget to note on your recipe card or book how many you actually served. Next time you won't have to guess. And as we've said earlier, don't forget to increase preparation time if you increase the amount prepared.

There are many things that involve no guesswork at all. It's easy enough to see how many pieces of pie or cake you can cut, from the size of your pans. When it comes to meat, this is a different story. Sometimes it is difficult to know exactly, so we recommend that you consult your friend the butcher. He will be cooperative and glad to help you with your problems, and his advice is usually reliable. Allowing a half-pound of meat per person is a common rule. With the present-day custom of buying only the chicken parts you like, it's a simple matter to decide how many pieces to buy. We seldom bother with anything but chicken breasts and sometimes drumsticks. Wings seem like such a waste. Always cut the breasts in half, or ask the butcher to do so. You're fairly safe if you figure on two halves for each man and one for each lady, unless the girls take a devil-may-care attitude about their figures.

If you're making chicken salad or chicken Tetrazzini, one large whole chicken breast makes approximately one cup of chopped chicken. These are the things you learn through experience, but don't trust your memory. Note it on the recipe. Two large stalks of celery chopped usually fill a cup. If you're puzzled as to how much chopped food should go into a salad, such as potato or shrimp salad, be sure that the total number of cups of chopped ingredients will equal the number of guests. In other words, if you have eight people, keep chopping until you have eight cups of salad. Even then, we like to toss in a little extra for reassurance.

All those things that expand two or three times their original size—rice, noodles, spaghetti—can be baffling, and the directions on the box seldom let you in on the quantity it will make. Here are our discoveries to help you. These dry measurements will make approximately one individual serving of the product when cooked.

⅔ cup medium-width noodles
1 cup very fine noodles
½ cup large or small macaroni
¼ cup regular rice
⅓ cup pre-cooked dehydrated rice

One 8-ounce box of spaghetti will make four average servings. One cup of wild rice will serve six.

When serving rice, we believe that there's simply nothing like the wild variety. The Indian name for wild rice is Mah-No-Min, which translated means "good berry." Among the early Indians it was given as a token of friendship. Even though it's like buying champagne, it's worth every penny. One school of thought confines wild rice to being served with game, but we have found that it enhances any meat or menu. Use ordinary rice on the family for economy, but for guests, give them your token of friendship. It's not only superior in flavor, but also easy to prepare and keep. Preventing some rice from becoming gummy is tricky, but wild rice can be cooked a day ahead and reheated in a small amount of water or in a double boiler. There is absolutely no waste, because whatever is left over can be reheated many times without changing texture or flavor. You will find it's money well spent to buy it. Many cooks make it sound difficult, in the belief that it must be soaked or cooked in several different waters. No need to be frightened by these warnings, for we've never done anything other than cook it slowly in a small amount of salted water for 40 or 45 minutes, and it's consistently good.

When using white rice, we heartily recommend the ease and versatility of pre-cooked dehydrated rice. It's fluffy and ready to serve in a matter of minutes, and is practically failure-proof. You can prepare it in consommé, broth, or buttered water. You can steam special seasonings right in by mixing curry powder, saffron, or herbs with the dry rice before adding to the liquid. When rice is ready to serve, you can give an extra fillip by stirring in sliced cooked mushrooms, or slivered almonds that have been heated in a little butter.

Seasonal Savors.   Although some foods are good at any time of year, there are others that simply do not appeal to the taste buds in all seasons. For instance, we associate spicy desserts, such as pumpkin pie and plum pudding, with the cozy fireside of fall and winter. Although it may be purely mental, they simply don't taste the same in the middle of summer. Certain dishes aren't even possible the year round, because the ingredients are not available. Of course, there are always the frozen fruits and berries, but they never have the same zest as the fresh. Make the most of the berry season, which is all too short. Nothing is better than luscious red strawberries with a powdered-sugar dip or a bowl of fresh blueberries with cream—easy as can be, and enjoyed by almost everyone.

A DOZEN DON'TS IN MENU MAKING

1. DON'T stuff the guests with too many hors d'oeuvres, or the dinner will be an anticlimax.

2. DON'T have two pale or white servings on the same plate—such as white potatoes and pale squash—or two green vegetables such as green beans and green peas. Balance menu as to color.

3. DON'T serve fruit salad and fruit for dessert, or cheese soufflé and cheesecake. Balance the menu as to type of food.

4. DON'T serve all hot or all cold. Serve hot bouillon or hot coffee with an all-cold lunch. If you have a cold meat or meat salad, serve a hot vegetable.

5. DON'T serve lukewarm food. See that cold dishes are cold and hot dishes are hot—especially the coffee.

6. DON'T underestimate the appetite of the guests. Better too much than too little.

7. DON'T spend all your time in the kitchen. Plan your menu so that some things are prepared well in advance of guests' arrival.

8. DON'T serve hard-to-cut food at a buffet supper. Serve food that is easy to eat with only a fork, unless you have small tables for everyone.

9. DON'T attempt to serve a great variety of food without servants. Better to prepare a few things well. Makes for less confusion in serving, too.

10. DON'T buy everything ready-prepared or frozen. Make at least one thing with your own two hands.

11. DON'T serve what is strictly ladies' luncheon food when men are present.

12. DON'T try for "cute" disguises of food. There is enough interest and beauty in the food itself when it is served attractively. An upright banana inserted in a slice of pineapple is not a candle, so don't try to make it look like one.

Mix with Tricks

If you use a little imagination, you can do wonders with a very basic and simple menu to transform it into sheer eating delight. Poppy Cannon, well-known food authority, said in a radio interview that the great revolution in the kitchen is that the gourmet has now become the doer, not just the spectator, as in the past. Unfortunately, many would-be gourmets have the mistaken idea that epicurean cooking involves only the far-out and unusual. But a gourmet is defined as one who is a connoisseur of food and drink and is discriminating in taste. His taste may run to what is basically a simple dish, but one prepared and served with finesse. One restaurant on the West Coast advertises as a menu specialty a hamburger with two glasses of champagne—a perfect example of glamorizing the commonplace.

To prod your imagination, here are a few of our kitchen tricks:

❋ Wrap meat loaf in smoked bacon strips to enrich the flavor.

❋ Mix artichoke hearts with buttered green beans or peas.

❋ Serve sour cream with black caviar on baked potatoes.

❋ Mix toasted slivered almonds with buttered green beans or peas.

❋ Whip butter and your favorite herb with an electric beater; chill and serve on asparagus or broccoli.

❋ Chopped chives (you can get them frozen) add zest to buttered carrots, peas, beans, or Brussels sprouts.

❋ Combine lima beans, green beans, or peas with sliced water chestnuts.

❋ Top buttered asparagus, green beans, or Brussels sprouts with seasoned bread crumbs.

❋ Mix wax beans, green beans, and lima beans for a pretty mélange of beans. Good marinated, too.

❄ When a recipe calls for raisins, use half raisins and half currants.

❄ Add a generous daub of peanut butter to hot fudge sauce.

❄ Top a casserole of mashed sweet potatoes with chopped pecans and a sprinkling of cinnamon. To go a little more Southern, add marshmallows over the top and brown in oven.

❄ Surround ham with whole spiced apricots or spiced peaches, instead of the usual pineapple slices or crab apples.

❄ Use crushed Corn Flakes instead of cracker crumbs on top of casseroles.

❄ Sprinkle Parmesan cheese over a serving of vichyssoise.

❄ Grate egg yolk over the top of salads such as potato, chicken, or a green salad.

❄ Use half mayonnaise and half French dressing for fruit salad, or half mayonnaise and half sour cream.

❄ Scatter raw red onion rings over green vegetables for both color and added flavor.

❄ Put a pinch or two of dry mustard and a pinch of egg-cheese herb blend in white sauce or Welsh rabbit to improve the flavor.

❄ Pour claret over vanilla ice cream for a light dessert.

There are almost as many combinations for salads as there are number combinations. And it's not always necessary to combine fruit with fruit. Try grapefruit or orange sections with green salad, green seedless grapes with chicken salad, and ham or chicken slivers with fruit salad. Sliced avocados are an asset to any salad. Contrast often accents flavor. Serve a warm sauce on a cold dessert or a cold topping on a warm dessert.

We could go on and on with our tricks, but develop your own to suit *your* taste. First thing you know, you'll have a loyal following of fans and eager guests. However, it's a wise cook who knows when to curb her impulses. You know you've gone too far with your variations and improvisations when your husband says, "Can't we just have green beans that taste like green beans?" Of course, most husbands present a difficult problem when it comes to trying anything more original than steak and potatoes.

We make it a practice never to discuss the ingredients of an unusual dish before our husbands, because it's sure to contain something that they object to, such as sour cream, mushrooms, or just plain butter.

It's All in Good Seasoning

If you've never played around with herbs, spices, and wine in your cooking, you have a great deal of fun in store for you. Almost all spices and herbs are now on the shelves of supermarkets, even the ones that were formerly available only in exclusive food shops. Experimenting with these many flavors is a headily creative experience in cooking. It's possible to buy ready-mixed combinations for meat, for salads, and even for spaghetti sauce, but half the fun is in combining your own favorites. The more you work with them, the more adept you become. The proper way to release the full flavor of herbs is to pinch them between the fingers before adding to any dish.

The simplest sauce is improved by using a dash of the right seasoning. And old-fashioned beef stew develops a richer flavor with a bit of Burgundy wine. There are many booklets, free for the asking, provided by spice and wine companies telling how to use their products in cooking. It's even more fun if you have a charming spice shelf to work from. Somehow this helps to inspire you, and also makes the spices easy to find and readily available. But a word of advice: when cooking with either herbs or wine, don't be heavy-handed. If your recipe calls for one bay leaf, don't theorize that if one is good, a half dozen will be six times as good! They may look small, but some of these tiny leaves pack a mighty wallop. Same with the wine. A little sherry will greatly enhance the flavor, but in quantity it can leave your guests gasping. If you overdo either of these cooking accessories, it will overwhelm every other ingredient. You should work toward achieving a hint of exotic flavoring. Better to have your guests murmuring to each other, "I can't quite place that delicate flavor," instead of "Well, she certainly emptied the bottle in this." So beware! It's up to you whether you're wizard or witch in the kitchen.

Fine with Wine. There is often controversy over how much to pay for cooking wine. Some say to buy the cheapest, while others recommend the finest. We think the middle road is a safe one and suggest a medium-priced wine. With so many good American wines on the market, it is not difficult to find a variety in this price range. There are excellent medium-priced imported wines, too. We have found the advice of liquor dealers can be depended upon when we are in doubt.

Generally, the kind of wine you use in a dish is the kind you would drink with the same dish (see page 176): add white wines to recipes for chicken, fish, veal, cheese, and creamed dishes; add red wines to red meat dishes.

The Sauce Is Boss

As everyone knows, the secret of fine French cooking is in the delicacy of their sauces. After all, the chicken or veal is the same to start with, no matter what the country. So it's the sauce that makes the difference. It's almost impossible to find a meat or vegetable that wouldn't be good with the right sauce. We once took a gourmet course and found the entire series of lessons to be on the preparation of sauces and how to combine them with other foods. Interestingly, the course was not for the purpose of giving us recipes so much as it was to teach us how to develop, create, and season our own sauces.

First, the White Sauce. Since nothing is more basic than a basic white sauce, this is the first thing to conquer, for with it you can improvise all sorts of combinations. It's significant that this is the very first recipe we learned to make in junior high school cooking class. Actually, the only trick to white sauce is keeping it smooth and thick. Just stir, stir, stir, without stopping until it is thickened, and suddenly you have a creamy sauce. We don't understand the need for all the gadgets many people use to get lumps out of sauce; it's so easy to keep it smooth, if you'll just stay with it a few minutes. The new instant, all-purpose flour, which is the consistency of salt, is a great asset in making smooth sauces and gravies. You can't miss. As soon as the sauce is thick, don't push your luck by continuing to cook, for sometimes it separates. If you don't use it immediately, cover, but leave an escape for steam. Otherwise you'll be disappointed by a watery sauce from the accumulation of moisture.

Now, don't stop with this. Anybody can make white sauce, but you surely want to prove your individuality by other imaginative creations. This is the fun of cooking and entertaining. What is sauce for the goose is not necessarily sauce for the gander. One sauce may be sensational on veal, but not on ham. This is where the herbs, the seasonings, and the wines come in. Even though we have to serve the same meats and vegetables year in and year out, variations are endless. It's up to you.

Be sure to make your basic sauce thick enough so that any liquid addition, such as wine, won't thin it too much. And as we've cautioned you previously, use a gentle hand, because the seasonings can be potent. "Try and taste" is a good rule to follow.

Transform your basic mixture into a heavenly cheese sauce, after it is thickened, by adding cheddar cheese, a tablespoon or two of sherry (depending on amount you are making), a pinch of dry mustard, and a pinch of egg-cheese herb mixture. Don't be satisfied with plain old-fashioned gravy. With no more effort than a wave of a wand, it can become a brown sauce, subtly flavored with Burgundy and an herb blend for meat. Glorify chicken with a basic white sauce enhanced by chicken stock, a little cream, white wine, a bit of parsley, and some water chestnuts.

Then the Butter Sauces. Butter sauces are a cinch to make, and they give the finishing touch to fish or vegetables. With a mixture of butter, light brown sugar, crushed tarragon, salt, and freshly ground pepper, the lowly carrot can be very special indeed. A butter-and-lemon sauce goes with fish as naturally as bacon goes with eggs. Flavor can be varied by adding different herbs to melted butter.

Graduate to Egg Sauces. The egg sauces, such as Mornay, béarnaise, or hollandaise, are not only heavier and richer, but also trickier to make. These sauces appeal to a more sophisticated palate. While hollandaise requires skill to make, you will find among the wonders of modern entertaining aids a dehydrated hollandaise sauce, ready to be mixed with water, thickened over heat, and served within a few minutes.

Dessert Sauces. An ordinary piece of cake can be completely changed in flavor and become a delicious English trifle, if you use a sauce. An egg custard sauce is delicious on a strawberry soufflé or a charlotte russe, and even on fresh peaches. Instead of using routine whipped cream on desserts, vary it by adding cocoa and sugar, or a teaspoonful of powdered coffee, after it is whipped.

A superb sauce is made by beating an egg white with 1/4 cup of confectioner's sugar and the yolk with another 1/4 cup of confectioner's sugar. Combine the two mixtures and add to 1/2 pint of stiffly whipped cream. Then add 1/2 teaspoon vanilla extract and two or three drops of almond extract. This makes a delicious topping for steamed puddings and spicy desserts.

Fruitcake is good with hot lemon-butter sauce or a brandy hard sauce.

Beverages

The Coffee Cult. If a vote were taken on America's favorite beverage, we are certain that hot coffee would win by a landslide. If this country has a national drink, it is certainly "acuppacoffee." In fact, some coffee fans go so far as to suggest that the Boston Tea Party was planned over a cup of coffee! So you are generally safe in serving hot coffee for most occasions.

There are certain times when you should show special consideration to your guests and serve both coffee and tea, particularly when there are older people present, for they frequently prefer tea, or perhaps a caffein-free coffee. It goes wtihout saying that if young folk are present, milk or fruit juice should be provided. If you know your guests well, so much the better, for you will be familiar with their habits. It's customary at most afternoon affairs, such as a tea or a club meeting, to offer a choice of coffee or tea. Of course cream, sugar, and lemon should be on the serving tray for those who desire it, and have a few saccharin tablets, too.

After a lunch or dinner party, it's proper to serve coffee in demitasses. This is a help to the hostess because it requires much less coffeemaking. And if the coffee is served in the living room, the small cups are more easily handled. (Don't make the trite remark, "Let's go into the living room, where we'll be more comfortable." We like to think our guests have been comfortable in the dining room, too!) Although demitasse is served black, the sugar cubes should be provided. Both cream and sugar are too heavy a load for a demitasse. For an interesting taste variation, put a stick of cinnamon in each demitasse for stirring and flavoring.

For added interest at a morning coffee or an afternoon party, it's a nice change to serve hot coffee with whipped cream, Viennese style, for those who like it. A dollop of fluffy cream on top of the coffee makes a truly delicious drink, and even those who prefer their coffee black usually sneak a little.

It is customary to serve a beverage with dessert, or after, and this is the easiest arrangement for a hostess. There are always a few persons, usually men or those from the Deep South, who prefer coffee with their meals. If you're the kind of hostess who loves to cater to the guests' whims, give them coffee whenever they want it. However, if it's a large lunch or dinner party and you find it inconvenient, don't worry about pampering anyone. Don't *ask* when they want it, but simply serve it at the end of the meal, without any discussion. If you try to please everybody, you will probably end up not pleasing anybody—not even your-self!

To Each His Own.   A word should be said about making coffee. There are two schools of thought on this subject. Many people have the idea that the coffee must be made not more than five minutes before serving, but we believe this is a bit fanatical. In fact, we've found that coffee is actually better if it is allowed to stand for a few minutes, because there is always a certain amount of sediment, no matter what system you use. If you let this settle, you'll have a clearer, better coffee.

Everyone has her own preference as to method of making coffee. Some of our Scandinavian friends swear by coffee with an egg in it. Personally, we steer clear of this method because we can never remember whether to throw in the shell or the egg or both. We're afraid that when we pour the coffee, we might end up pouring a poached or hard-boiled egg!

A clean pot and a good brand of fresh coffee are essential. Keep coffee fresh by storing it in a tightly closed container in the refrigerator. Recently, we read in a Texas newspaper one male columnist's recommendation that the only way to make a good cup of coffee is *never* to wash the pot. Just rinse it and let it drain, he said, leaving the sediment from the old coffee clinging to the pot. His theory is that this enriches the coffee and gives it more character. Perhaps this is the way they prove that men are men in Texas, but we believe that it is merely the poor housekeeping of a helpless man. He needs a wife to take care of him and to wash his coffeepot.

It doesn't matter whether you use the percolator, drip, or vacuum method, but you must be sure to choose the proper grind. Coffee authorities recommend the drip method as easiest, most failure-proof, and best. This requires a medium grind through which the water drips slowly only once, for a perfect extraction of flavor and aroma. Although the percolator method is by far the most popular in America, it may over-extract and become bitter, since the water goes over and over the coffee. If you choose this method, use the coarser grind and be sure to "perk" only long enough to obtain a full-bodied brew. Vacuum pots take the finest grind of all, since a filter holds back the water and permits only brief contact with the coffee.

We suggest that instant coffee is for emergencies or family use only. It's a happy convenience at the proper time, but for a planned party, don't take the shortcut. In fact, we believe that most instant foods are great for a camping trip, but not for party fare.

There are many varieties of automatic coffeemakers on the market now, and these not only take the guesswork out of coffee-making, but also liberate you from the annoyance of the watched pot that never boils. Thirty-cup electric coffeemakers for large groups are now almost standard equipment in a home. If you're not fortunate enough to own one of these, or to own a friend who owns one, there is a practical solution to making those 30 cups of coffee. Stitch up a pair of small white muslin bags, approximately 5 by 8 inches, large enough to hold about 15 measures of coffee loosely (a coffee measure holds 2 level tablespoons). Tie bags tightly at the top with clean string. Fill two large boilers with 15 cups of water each. When the water is boiling, toss a bag of coffee in each boiler and allow to boil for 5 or 6 minutes after the bags have become well saturated. This may sound a bit primitive, but it does take care of quantity coffeemaking very nicely. And connoisseurs will compliment you on the flavor.

Coffee Foreign Style. In spite of their great love for coffee, Americans have always favored a mild coffee made from an American or regular roast. Now many are discovering the fun and flavor of foreign roasts and methods. Irish coffee, with a lacing of Irish whiskey and a topping of whipped cream, served in little footed glasses or special glass mugs, is good for an occasional after-dinner treat. For a more dramatic effect, there's the French café brûlot made famous in New Orleans. Since this is more complicated to make, we'll have to send you looking for the recipe in a cookbook.

The coffee that has won many devotees and is gaining new ones every day is the Italian caffè espresso. This is a stronger Italian dark-roast coffee made from the finest grind (pulverized) in an espresso maker, which converts the water to steam, drives it through the coffee, and condenses it into liquid again. It may also be made successfully in an Italian or American drip pot. It is served in demitasses with sugar and a twist of lemon peel, but never with cream. Using espresso as a base, you may easily make many delicious European variations, such as:

~~ *Caffè Cappuccino*—Equal parts of espresso and hot milk with cinnamon and nutmeg, served in demitasses with sugar.

~~ *Roman Espresso*—Espresso served in small wineglasses (that hold about the same amount as a demitasse) with a twist of lemon peel.

~~ *Caffè Borgia*—Equal amounts of espresso and hot chocolate served in demitasses with topping of whipped cream and grated orange peel.

~~ *Caffè Cioccolata*—Equal amounts of espresso and hot chocolate served in a taller cup (some have a little pedestal) and topped with shavings of French chocolate.

Tea for Some. As for tea, loose leaves are traditionally considered to make the best drink, but even British diehards are coming around to the American tea bag. Use one bag or a tea-

spoon of loose tea for two cups. Start with cold water and bring
it to a quick boil, but do not let it boil up. Warm a china or
earthenware teapot by rinsing it with some of the hot water.
Put in the tea or tea bags and pour in the hot water. Cover,
steep three to five minutes, and serve.

Always have sugar and a pot of hot water on the tea tray.
Although it is customary here to have thin slices of lemon on
the tray, too, the rule in England is lemon for China tea, but
milk with Ceylon or Indian tea.

The Cocktail Hour.   Ideas vary on the subject of pre-dinner
drinking according to each person's way of life, and there is
always a certain amount of controversy over how much time
should be spent before dinner on this phase of the party. It can
be said of any part of entertaining, "Don't overdo it," whether
it's decorations or the dessert, and this goes for the cocktail hour
as well. If you invite your guests for seven o'clock and don't
serve dinner till ten, you will completely spoil the evening for
everyone. Only a dipsomaniac would want to extend the cocktail hour that long. Our continual emphasis is on appropriateness, on good taste, and on the host's control of the party. Run
a *taut* ship, not a *"tight"* ship!

Plan to serve dinner within an hour after all guests have arrived, allowing enough time for two drinks around. This should
be adequate for any guest. Keep in mind that it is a *dinner* party
and *not* a cocktail party. If a guest seems to want to go on drinking, put on your most winning smile and say sweetly but *firmly*
that dinner is ready and the cocktail hour is over. If you know
of heavy drinkers in your crowd, it's unwise to set out soda and
alcohol where guests can mix their own drinks. And never,
never force a drink on a guest who has declined. For all you
know, he may be wrestling with a serious problem. Recently
when traveling on a historic road in New Jersey, we were star-
tled by a huge neon sign over a restaurant, "Bad Liquor, Good
Food." We don't suggest that you go to quite this extreme to

discourage over-imbibing—whatever you serve should be good—
but make the dinner the highlight of the evening.

It's easier and more efficient to limit the choice of drinks,
unless you have a professional caterer or bartender who will
provide and serve a wide variety. The host simply states what
he is serving and asks which the guest prefers, instead of saying,
"What would you like to drink?" Or serve only a good cocktail
sherry. Always have on hand non-alcoholic beverages for those
who prefer them. Serve only non-alcoholic drinks at teen-age
parties.

Some people don't wish to serve hard liquor, but do not object
to wines. If it is against your personal belief to serve liquor in
any form, DON'T. Have the courage of your convictions, and
don't be influenced by the Joneses. Everyone has the privilege
of running his own home the way he desires. To do something
just because the neighbors do is no reason at all. You will lose
your individuality as well as your principles. If your guests come
only to drink, or if they stay away because you don't, they're
freeloaders, not friends, so cross them off your list. You can
always serve either a fruit drink or tomato juice with a few
appetizers to replace cocktails. This breaks the ice and gives
guests a chance to get acquainted. Whatever you do, do it gracefully and graciously, without apology. Serve your drinks in an
attractive way, as though this were the finest champagne, and
no one will criticize.

Pre-Dinner Snacking. When guests have been invited to dinner, don't stuff them beforehand. The trend today is away from
huge assortments of rich, fancy hors d'oeuvres, although customs differ in various parts of the country. Most people we
know have become bored with them. Better to serve only a few
appetizers that are especially good and not too filling. For example, an assortment of cheese with rye bread rounds or crackers, hot fish balls with a dip, and stuffed celery. At a recent
elegant party the hostess served only two things with drinks—
an enormous platter piled high with oysters and clams in the

shells with big wedges of juicy lemons and another platter with giant shrimps and a dip. (See page 190 for other foods to serve with cocktails.) You can feel reasonably safe in allowing five or six individual hors d'oeuvres for each person.

If your household is not blessed with servants, the smoothest way to serve is to make an attractive arrangement on one large tray, using a number of small containers for the different appetizers, so that everything can be passed at once. The hostess can always refill the tray as the snacks diminish. Or serve an hors d'oeuvre "shish kebab" with everything on one 9-inch cocktail pick—cubes of ham and cheese, shrimp, tiny sausages, and olives.

Give each guest an individual cocktail tray or small plate for convenience. Nothing is more disconcerting to a glamorous guest than to have a shrimp plop into her lap right out of a red tomato-sauce dip. Nor will the hostess like it on her pale beige carpeting. Set bowls of nuts and some of the interesting crunchy cocktail snacks on tables at strategic points to simplify serving.

If you can make this first hour truly relaxed and enjoyable, you are off to a good start for a totally successful party. This is when the rapport between guests is established, and if it's a happy time, nothing can really ruin the party after that—not even a less than gourmet dinner.

Dine with Wine.   One of our more civilized drinking customs is serving wine with dinner. It has been said that food without wine is like romance without kisses. A beautiful glass of wine at a candlelight dinner always brings that special touch of elegance that everyone enjoys. Momentarily we live the life we'd all like to become accustomed to—even though it's back to the kitchen three hours later. Since the quality of less expensive American wines has steadily advanced and is beginning to rival French imports, many more hosts feel that they can afford to indulge in this luxury. Some of the Spanish and Portuguese wines are also comparatively inexpensive and have their own distinctive characteristics.

A familiar guide is to serve chilled white wines with white meats or those of delicate flavor, such as fish or chicken, and to serve red wines at room temperature with darker meats, such as roast beef, steak, or game. However, these are merely suggestions, not laws. There is great flexibility in these old rules, and people are now serving whatever wines particularly appeal to them. For example, a chilled rosé is delightful with chicken or fish and equally pleasant with beef, especially in summer. Favorite white wines are Chablis, sauterne, Rhine wine, and champagne. Popular red table wines are Burgundy, claret, sparkling Burgundy, and the lighter rosé.

You may serve golden or red wines from a decanter, but never decant a white wine or any of the effervescent wines. And don't allow wine to stand open for any length of time. If you have a bottle only partially used, recork it and store it in a cool place on its side to keep the cork moist. This will keep air, the enemy of wine, from getting into the bottle.

Dessert Wine.   Serving wine with desserts is a rapidly growing trend in this country and a delightful custom to establish in your home. Wine with dinner is optional in this case. Dessert wines are sweet and can be served either with dessert or after. Make your choice from port, tawny port, cream sherry, Tokay, muscatel, and Madeira. Sparkling Burgundy and chilled rosé are always appropriate at any dinner with any course. And you can never go wrong with a steady diet of champagne. Dom Pérignon, who reputedly perfected this heavenly drink, expressed it aptly when he remarked after his first sip, "I am drinking stars."

Nightcaps.   Serving alcoholic drinks after dinner is purely optional. Many people enjoy a liqueur as a final touch to a gourmet dinner, while others feel that enough is enough and prefer to let the dessert wine become a lingering memory.

If anything at all is served, the preference is for liqueurs and cordials, such as Drambuie, B and B, anisette, curaçao, crème de cacao, crème de menthe, and kümmel, or a good brandy. These are served in small portions in tiny stemmed glasses and are always sipped. There are several other after-dinner mixed drinks that are popular, such as a good stinger. Cocktails are never served after dinner, but some guests may want a highball.

Pre-Luncheon Spirits. We can't bring ourselves to sanction morning martinis, but we do suggest lifting the spirits of your lady luncheon guests with an apéritif or a cocktail sherry. Some of the light table wines, like chilled rosé or Chablis, are also popular. However, if your friends are the kind who insist on a very sweet wine, go ahead and give them the sticky cream sherry that they love. It's not necessary to serve appetizers with wine before luncheon. Some special little crackers or salted nuts are sufficient, if you feel it's wiser to keep the girls from getting giddy.

On Ice. When you plan to serve iced beverages of any kind, remember to lay in an extra ice supply. Too often a hostess forgets this necessity when making out her shopping list and ends up begging from neighbors. And this could become embarrassing, if you haven't invited them to the party!

Locate a grocery store or delicatessen near you that sells ice, so that you won't have to make a frantic search when you need it. Some cities have ice vending machines that are in operation 24 hours a day. Ice today is usually sold in cubes—either square or round—and it is perfectly proper to use it in this form. If you want crushed ice, there are electric or manual crushers—or the old reliable ice pick.

Ice should be stored in plastic bags in the freezing or storage compartment of your refrigerator. Or special insulated ice containers (that double for picnics) may be purchased. Failing all else, layers of newspapers may be used to store the ice (the layers act as a non-conductor of heat). The secret is not to let it start to melt before storing, as the cubes will then stick together.

If you have enough space in your refrigerator, it's easy enough to make your own ice supply if you start a day or two before a party. Fill the ice trays, and as they freeze, loosen the ice quickly and dump it into plastic bags before it starts to melt. Just as quickly pop them back into the freezing or storage compartment. Don't use water to loosen the ice, as it will freeze together when put back into the freezer—and you'll have a huge, hard block, when you take it out. Refill trays and keep repeating until you have an adequate supply.

How Much.   It is safer to have extra bottles on hand than to run out of potables. It's embarrassing for your husband or beau to have to sneak out the back door and make a run for the corner liquor store in the middle of a party. You can usually arrange to return for credit or exchange the next day any unopened bottles. As a general guide, a fifth (fifth of a gallon) of liquor is 25.6 ounces, a quart contains 32 ounces, and each drink is 1½ ounces. And here is a little guide to how many drinks to estimate from a bottle. The number varies for the same size bottle because the size of the drink varies with the type of drink.

PURCHASING GUIDE FOR DRINKS

Type of beverage	Size of bottle	No. of drinks
Champagne	One fifth	7 to 8 drinks
Table wine	One fifth	8 drinks
Dessert wine	One fifth	10 drinks
Whiskey, gin, vodka	One fifth	16 drinks (1½-oz. jigger)
Rum	One fifth	16 drinks (1½-oz. jigger)
Sherry	One fifth	10 to 12 drinks

How to Make Your Parties Fun to Go To

> Love sought is good, but given unsought, is better.
> —Shakespeare

CHAPTER

6

When most of us decide to give a party for the sheer pleasure of being with friends, we spontaneously think in terms of sharing our homes with our guests and of making the home an attractive and comfortable background for the party.

Aside from the most important consideration of sharing hearth and board with friends, the highest compliment you can pay them, there are many other reasons for giving parties at home. Your own individuality will prevail because your home is different from every other home in the world, even if you live in a cookie-cutter house in a "development." Your own furnishings and way of life make your house a personal thing. A party at home can be more intimate, more friendly.

Then there's the very practical side to having a party chez vous. It's much less expensive. *You* do the work, do the purchasing, and prepare the food and fun. Naturally, there's an economic advantage, if this is important to you. And if you entertain frequently, as we hope you do, it is important.

If you keep in mind a few basics of entertaining at home, you can sail through a party smoothly and emerge a party pro:

1. Plan the kind and size of party your house is suited for. If yours is an Early American décor with cobbler's benches and candle molds, keep your parties in kind. Don't try for "The Age of Elegance." By the same token, if you are chatelaine of a Louis XV setting, a barbecue in the marble fireplace won't make you the "hostess with the mostes'." The same rule goes for the number of guests. Plan to have your house "pleasingly full"—not too many, not too few.

2. Recognize the fact that, cultivated as your guests may be, someone is sure to *use* that needlepoint footstool. So expect normal wear and tear on furniture—and the occasional crash of a coveted cup. Unless you can be casual and debonair about your possessions, your guests will feel uncomfortable. The author remembers being the victim of one otherwise gracious hostess whose white rugs were just too pale and precious for human feet. The hostess herself always wore slippers, and she demanded that guests doff their shoes at the door and wear assorted pairs of her size 6 slippers, no matter how big or little their feet! The final straw came when my husband was made to jump around all one evening on a little throw rug because he didn't want cold feet and refused to take off his shoes. We never went back!

3. Arrange the elements of the party so that the guests are distributed around the area and are not clumped together in a football huddle. This means that the bar is not a bottleneck (no pun, please!), that the buffet table has space for movement around it, that games are set up or planned in an adequate area.

4. Naturally you will have your home looking as attractive as possible. The best and easiest plan is to keep it always ready to receive. Each week, whether entertaining or not, go over one area such as polishing the silver, checking linens, or washing and polishing infrequently used glassware and dishes.

When you're running the dishwasher after a regular meal, add a few dishes or glasses from the cupboard that need freshening. Better yet, if you rotate the dishes you use, so that none are ever left sitting on the shelf for months, they will always be clean and ready. Don't let household chores pile up until it takes an old-fashioned spring housecleaning before you can serve a cup of tea. If a slipcover is soiled, send it to be cleaned. Don't wait until the whole living room has to go out. If you follow this policy, you'll never have to duck when the doorbell rings!

Instant Hospitality

The moment your party gets under way via the arrival of the first guest at the door, your every thought and action as hostess should express love and care toward your guests. You are "giving" a party. Your guest is king—or queen! Make him or her feel "every inch a."

The party's beginning should reflect the excitement of the theater the moment the curtain goes up. We were once backstage near the director of a show and heard the charming signal for everyone to be ready for the curtain to rise—"It's magic time." That's how parties should start.

One of the basics of a good party is to *be ready* when party time comes. This means the house, the food, and you. Your husband, too, if it's a "co-ed" affair.

In most cases and places (except Washington), it's unusual for any guest to arrive on the dot, so hostess and host can avail themselves of the 5 to 15 minutes of grace before the first arrival to sit down for a little breather before the curtain goes up.

When the bell rings, the hostess or some designated member of the family opens the door and greets the guest with a word of welcome and a handshake. If one is lucky enough to have a maid—or even a butler—naturally the door is opened by the servant. Almost anybody can have this luxury once in a while, with servants easily "rentable" from part-time agencies (see

Chapter 7). If a maid answers the door, she takes the coats or shows the guests to the coatroom and then to the party room where the hostess is waiting.

If it is a party of all females, such as a luncheon, the guest is directed to the room where she may leave her coat and glance in a mirror—usually a bedroom with a bathroom nearby. She then proceeds to the room where the hostess is receiving. If the party is mixed, the host takes the male guest's coat and hat and puts them in a closet near the door, cleared for the purpose, or may put them on a rack in the hallway set up or rented for the occasion. The hostess takes or directs the female guest to the coatroom arranged for that purpose. In many homes where there are no servants, the host tends the door and handles the coats, so that the hostess is not continually excusing herself from the guests who have already arrived. Again, if a maid or butler answers the door, the man's coat and hat are taken and the lady is directed to her coatroom. Ladies may leave coats at the door, too, but they usually like a chance to peek in a mirror before appearing. The guests are then shown to the party room and the host and hostess.

The traffic must be worked out carefully to make the entrance of guests as easy and natural as possible. Sometimes you can't help having the escort join the party while the lady is taking off her coat, if your entrance door opens right into your living room. But let guests take off their coats and be ready to join the fun before introductions are made. Just be sure that all are welcomed and taken care of—and that no one is left at the door waiting to be discovered by the hosts. We have attended cocktail parties where by the midway point the host and hostess were gayer than the guests and hopelessly lost at their own party. New arrivals were left to wander in and take care of themselves.

The Comforts of the House. Be prepared to take care of coats and hats without their being heaped on a bed so that departing guests look like tramps in wrinkled rags—that is, if they can find them at all. Remember boots, rubbers, umbrellas, and dripping coats when the weather is bad. Guests will be happier, and you will be too, if there is a proper place where they can drain and dry. In the hostess's bedroom and bath, or wherever feminine guests leave their wraps, have emergency supplies such as needles and thread, tissues, emery boards, cotton pads, personal napkins and tampons, and even neutral-colored stockings in sizes 8-9-10 (or size 9 stretch stockings) for a guest in distress. She'll bless you forever!

Our nation's number one home, the White House, goes to no end of trouble to make its feminine guests comfortable. A maid is always on hand equipped to take a stitch or two in a guest's gown, repair a contrary zipper, or even to administer smelling salts or first aid. No need to go to that extreme, but do make a point of a pleasant room for the girls.

Gracious All the Way.   Several other thoughtful observances will assure a smooth-running function and a happy guest group:

- If parking is a problem, arrange for space, or let your guests know where they may leave their cars.

- While your guests are present, be self-effacing as far as household and hostess duties are concerned. Never flutter or hover so that guests are made to feel they are a burden and a hardship.

- Resolve never to make apologies to guests. Do your very best and let it go at that. The story is told of a hostess whose butler let the Thanksgiving turkey slip from platter to floor just as he entered the dining room. She calmly commanded, "Just take that one back to the kitchen, Smith, and bring the other one." Be thou as composed!

- When in your home, let your guests be guests. Treat them as special, so they may enjoy themselves and their fellow guests to the utmost. Don't impose on them as bartenders, cooks, or dishwashers. Make provision to handle all work with members of your family or with outside help. Your turn to enjoy the same privilege will come when you are the guest in someone else's home.

❧ Keep the cost of things your own secret. And also how you made the muffins the guests all admire. If someone asks or hints for the recipe of a dish, don't reenact the making of it before the guests. Send the recipe quietly the next day—if you want to divulge it.

❧ When you've done all you can to create a great party, relax and enjoy. Have a good time yourself. Worry not about an olive seed in a potted plant, ashes on your orientals, or a 200-pounder on your precious Louis XVI chair. Control each situation as best you can. But remember Bacon's observation that "Houses are built to live in, and not to look on."

May I Present

Introductions seem to confuse and constrict some hostesses—and. guests. Actually, introducing people is a matter of being thoughtful and natural. But if you must have rules, it's very simple:

1. Men are *always* presented *to* ladies, no matter what the ages of the persons involved.
2. When introducing persons of the same sex—man to man or woman to woman—present the younger person *to* the older person. If they're about the same age, just make the introduction in the simplest and most natural way.

Introductions can be very short and to the point:

Mrs. Johnson, may I present Mr. Kingsley? (more formal)

or

Mrs. Johnson, may I introduce Mr. Kingsley? (less formal)

or

Mrs. Johnson, Mr. Kingsley.

The acknowledgments are equally simple: "How do you do?" or a more informal "Hello."

The host and hostess shake hands with each arriving guest. As for the guests themselves, men always shake hands with each other when meeting or being introduced, no matter what the situation; women do not usually shake hands when introductions are made at a party (except in New York or Europe, where the custom is quite common)—they just smile and nod.

If you are entertaining twelve persons or fewer, you will want to be sure that everyone meets everyone else. This usually calls for group introductions after the first few guests arrive. If all of the guests are in one conversational group, repeat all of their names and then the names of the newly arrived guests. If the guests have broken up into smaller groups, take the new arrivals to each for introductions.

If your party is a large one, it is very awkward to try to introduce each arriving guest to all others. In this case, after greeting the guest, lead him to the nearest conversational group and make introductions—or take him to a group you believe he might especially enjoy.

When there is a receiving line, as at a tea or reception, the hostess at the head of the line greets each guest with a few words of welcome—"I'm so glad you could come," or "I was so eager to have you meet . . ." She then introduces the guest to the next person in line, and so on to the end of the line, with all shaking hands. (This is one time when ladies must shake hands.) If the guest is a stranger to the hostess, she introduces and identifies herself first as she enters, saying something like, "I'm Gayle Gibson, Mary's cousin." As the guest goes through the line she simply says "How do you do?" and may add to some of the members of the line that she's especially happy to see them again or to meet them.

If the party is given in honor of someone, *every* guest must meet the guest of honor, because that's obviously the point of the party. If feasible, the hostess makes this introduction when each new guest arrives.

Whether to introduce by first names or by using titles depends on where you live and the customs, and also on the degree of formality of the party. You must use your judgment and gauge the situation. At a casual or very informal party such as a cookout, it is appropriate and quite natural to introduce a couple as Eunice and Gregory Todman. At a party with more dignity, you might find it more appropriate to introduce a couple as Mr. and Mrs. Todman. However, there is a trend everywhere toward more use of first names in every age group.

The subject of identifying guests to each other is a touchy one. Certainly, you don't want to reel off everyone's occupation or station in life! But a clue or two when introducing people will help them start the conversation on the right foot. If you have been clever enough to snare a celebrity, certainly everyone will want to know it—and if we know celebrities, most of them like to be made known. This will prevent embarrassments such as happened to a friend of ours. She didn't quite catch the name of an attractive man introduced to her at a party. In conversation she spent a full 15 minutes describing her new one-room apartment and how she was decorating it. Not till the next day did she find out that she had regaled with tales of her simple apartment the country's most famous interior designer, whose name was literally a household word!

So it's perfectly proper—and helpful to the conversation—to add a starting word, such as "The Millers have just returned from a fabulous trip around the world." This is sure to start anybody who has ever been anywhere on a lively chat with the Millers. Just avoid such crass remarks as, "Mr. Miller is president of the Central National Bank, you know."

Dinner Is Served

When the time comes to serve—whether dinner, lunch, supper, or whatever—the hostess announces, "Dinner [or whatever the occasion] is served. Won't you come in, please?" If there is a servant, he or she announces to the hostess, "Dinner is served," and the hostess may add to her guests, "Shall we go in?" Sometimes it takes a firm hand to get the guests on the way, if they are enjoying chatting and drinking. So have your husband posted to flush out any lagging males. No need to delay serving more than a maximum of 15 minutes for any tardy guests. After a cocktail hour of 45 minutes to an hour, you need not wait any longer for anyone who has not arrived.

At an informal party the hostess leads the way to the dining room with the other ladies and men following, the host coming last. The hostess indicates where each is to sit, whether or not there are place cards, and each man seats the lady to his right.

It's a little pointless to have place cards for six or fewer, unless it's a special occasion and you want to carry out a theme, such as for a birthday. But for eight persons on up, we highly recommend them. Sometimes in the excitement of a party and trying to handle all details, a hostess forgets how she planned to divide the Joneses. With place cards, she can really forget it. (See page 138.)

Be sure to break up couples at the dinner table. At a rectangular table the hostess sits at one end and the host at the other (he heads the table) if the count comes out right. If not, the host heads the table, and the hostess sits one place to the right or left of the other end of the table, with a man sitting at the foot. The most important lady present (she may be guest of honor) sits at the host's right, while the most important man takes the hostess's right. Second most important lady sits at the host's left, and second man on the hostess's left. Others are ranged in between. At a round table, this same order can easily be followed, with host and hostess on opposite sides of the table. If a woman is entertaining alone, she heads the table, and a man who may be a close friend or member of family sits at the other end—or if the count comes out the other way, another woman sits there. The woman guest of honor is either at the foot of the table or at the right of the gentleman of honor, who always sits on the hostess's right.

At a really formal dinner, rare today in a home, each gentleman picks up a small card in an envelope bearing his name, arranged on a table near the door. The card shows the name of the lady he is to escort into the dining room, while a chart nearby shows where they will sit. Before dinner he makes a point of meeting the lady, if he does not know her. At a dinner of this formality, the host leads the way to the dining room with the lady guest of honor. All other guests follow, paired off as the hostess has indicated on the cards. The hostess is last with the most important male guest. At a party of this consequence, you would want to have place cards—plain white cards (not folded) that may have a gold or silver beveled edge.

Contrary to what many believe and practice, the hostess should *never* be served first. This custom began when hosts invited guests to dinner for the sole purpose of poisoning them. The host who dared to serve himself first was only trying to prove his innocence. We think of ourselves as being more civilized, but if we follow this barbaric lead, we are displaying not only lack of manners, but ignorance as well.

If there is a servant to serve the meal, the serving dishes are presented first to the hostess for a nod of approval. Then the lady guest of honor is served first. The service proceeds around the table counter-clockwise, with the host being last. The old-fashioned idea of waiting for the hostess to take the first bite is passé. Practically, the guests may begin to eat after several have been served, so that the food won't cool. Food is always served to the left of the guest for a very simple reason that's easy to remember: most people are right-handed and can thus help themselves more gracefully this way. When dishes are removed from the table, they may be removed from either the left or right, whichever is more practical. Or to speed the service, the maid may remove two at a time—one from the left and one from the right, naturally picking up one at a time.

Serve Alone and Like It. We're sure the majority of parties, including our own, take place without any outside help. This is one of the great talents and accomplishments of American women, in our estimation. So let's consider how the hostess can most gracefully and graciously handle the whole show alone, or with her husband's help if it's a mixed party.

First step toward tranquillity for the hostess is to make the first course an extension or part of the cocktail hour. This can be as simple as serving a big bowl of shrimp on ice with a piquant sauce for guests to spear and dip. Or it may be a hearty bowl of iced carrot sticks, celery spears, olives, and cauliflower nibs with an interesting dip (good for dieters). Trays of tomato juice may be offered. Or even a piping hot tureen of soup ladled up in cups or mugs, accompanied by hot cheese straws. Or skip this course entirely, and let the cocktails and hors d'oeuvres suffice.

At the table, limit the courses to two or three: main meat course, salad, and dessert; or combine the salad with the main course, and finish with dessert. Offer coffee or demitasses back in the living room. All of this can be managed quite nicely by placing the main course on the table in serving dishes just before dinner is announced. We think it's nice for the man of the house to take over here to carve and serve. This can be handled in one of two ways. If you like the look of a plate at every place as the guests sit down, set the table that way (it is the only correct way, traditionally). As the host serves the plate in front of him, he passes it to the lady at his right and she exchanges her plate. Next he serves the lady to his left and so on, serving himself last. Other dishes may be served by the host at the same time, or they may be passed around the table, each guest helping himself. The other method of serving is to omit the plates at each place and set the entire stack in front of the host. He serves and passes from this stack. Although we dislike the look of the pile of dishes, this has two advantages: the plates may be warmed, and it eliminates a lot of passing back and forth.

Another smooth idea we like is to set the dining room table as formally and prettily as possible with everything except the dinner plates. These are placed on a sideboard or buffet where the dinner is set out in serving dishes. Guests serve themselves and find their places at the table.

Then there's always the tried and true buffet, from which guests serve themselves. Card tables or other small tables with places set as attractively as for a dining room table will give the party a special air.

At the end of the main course, the hostess may rise, quickly remove the plates to the kitchen, and clear the table; or guests may pass the used plates along to the host to place on a nearby table provided for the purpose. Personally we think it's much neater for the hostess to handle the used dishes and to get them out of the dining room. Or easiest yet, guests may pass their plates to the host, who puts them on a waiting cart to be quickly wheeled out of sight by the hostess.

The salad course should be ready and waiting on a small table beside the hostess—or the host, if he is a salad specialist. This is served on salad plates and passed along as the first course was. It should also be cleared away in the same manner.

Now it's nice to bring the dessert out from the kitchen as the surprise and climax. The dishes for serving it can be standing by on the same table the salad was on, or on a shelf of the same table. The hostess should serve and pass the dessert. A thoughtful finale is cigarettes and a dish of mints.

If wine is served with the meal or with the dessert—and this is becoming almost basic in some areas—the host should officiate. The wineglasses would have been a part of the table setting. He can open the bottles from a small table by his place, but will have to rise from his seat to circle the table and pour. This is much more gracious than passing the bottle around. When the host opens the bottle, he pours a tiny bit into his glass to taste for quality and in case any particles of cork should float in it. Then he serves the guests, filling his own glass last. Glasses should be only partially filled, in order to retain the bouquet within the glass. Avoid making a big production of serving wine, and don't clutter the table with ice buckets or towels wrapped around bottles. Use a handsome wine coaster to hold the bottle between pourings.

At the end of the meal, the hostess rises and asks the guests back to the living room for coffee, which she brings in on a tray with cups and saucers. At this point the host may want to offer a spot of brandy or liqueur. At a formal dinner the gentlemen may remain in the dining room for cigars and liqueurs with their coffee, while the ladies go to the living room for demitasses.

The Toast. A European custom that tends to baffle the uninitiated in this country is the proposing of a toast. A toast is simply a good wish expressed toward someone and sealed with a drink. Aside from the everyday "Cheers" or "Skoal" expressed among friends with a cocktail, a toast is usually given upon some ceremonial occasion—a christening, announcement of engagement, bachelor dinner, wedding party, anniversary, or birthday. Champage is the classic toasting drink, but wine or punch is equally appropriate. For the ceremonies connected with engagements and marriages, though, it should be champagne. If budget must be considered, use the good domestic brands; the best of them can be superb.

While anyone may propose an appropriate toast at a regular party, tradition specifies the toaster at more ceremonial occasions. At a christening, the godfather toasts the baby. If an engagement is announced at a dinner, the bride's father breaks the good news with a toast to the betrothed. The groom-to-be toasts "To the bride" at his bachelor dinner, while the best man proposes the toast "To the bride and groom" at the wedding party. At these two occasions everyone stands to drink the toast, except at the wedding party, when the bride and groom remain seated.

The persons toasted *never* drink with the others, as this would be drinking to themselves. Guests of honor wait until all of the beverage is drunk by others, if it is one that is traditionally taken all at once. If it is the kind that is sipped, they wait until everyone has taken a bit before drinking. A nod of thanks and appreciation is given by the guest of honor when the toast is proposed.

For ceremonies, traditions also prescribes *when* the toast is drunk. Baby's toast is proposed at a christening party as soon as everyone's drink has been poured. An engagement toast is usually proposed at the end of a dinner as a sort of climax, as is the groom's toast at the bachelor dinner. At a wedding party or anniversary party, it is the reverse, with the toast being drunk at the beginning, as soon as everyone has been served.

Single Blessedness

The woman alone—unmarried, widowed, or divorced—does have certain problems peculiar to her state. On the other hand, she probably imagines more problems than she actually has. It's in her own mind if she feels like a fifth wheel—that is, unless she acts like a fifth wheel when she is with others.

The first hurdle is the decision to entertain. The emergence of the single girl as a hostess of note is now history. Unmarried women of any age may and do give any kind of party they choose. The divorcee or widow, however, faces a problem when suddenly deprived of the security of a husband. She must make the decision to go it alone again and must make the effort to integrate anew into a social group—either her old set or a new one. The quicker the step is taken, the easier it is. The divorcee may immediately take steps toward a new social life, but the widow naturally wants to wait out a respectable period of time. The important point in either situation is that the woman shouldn't go into a shell from which she never emerges.

While the unmarried girl or woman may get away with a dash of daring now and then, it is essential that the widow or divorcee follow the pattern of exemplary and impeccable conduct at all times. Certainly they must never be accused of desperately "eyeing" other women's husbands!

The first step toward creating a new social world for the

woman who is suddenly without husband is to force yourself to
"get out and go." Aside from the fact that it is needed escape
from too many memories in the home and from too much
thinking about a former life, it will expose you to new people
and new ideas. Travel affords the greatest possible break from
your former pattern of life. Try to take a trip with a friend or
relative so that you will have someone to share experiences and
lonely moments with. If a traveling companion isn't available,
go alone. You will undoubtedly experience loneliness at times,
but you would feel this more deeply at home. There are even
advantages to traveling solo, as it makes you more approachable
to other travelers and forces you to make friendly overtures to
them. Jean Baer in *Follow Me*, her book for women traveling
alone, counsels that unless a woman travels with a man she
should strike out by herself. This author assures us that "She
travels fastest, most happily, and most productively who travels
alone."

If you must make your readjustment nearer home, this is the
time to cultivate other women as companions for attending concerts, the theater, or just the movies. In every city there are
lovely restaurants where women dining together may feel perfectly comfortable. Just guard against becoming so engrossed in
female friends that you shut out the possibility of another man
in your life some day.

Churches and social service organizations are forever seeking
volunteer workers. This is the time to offer your help for any
good cause. It can lead to meeting both women and men. Some
of the committee meetings and activities even take on a semi-
social nature and can be most pleasant.

Neighborhood mixing is another easy way to make your way
alone. Whenever you are invited, accept. Just be sure that you
contribute to the occasion and don't become a rock around the
hostess's neck. Take care of yourself, and don't be a clinging
vine to anyone. Make yourself an interesting part of the group
by having something to say and by participating in whatever
the entertainment is. Then begin to entertain in your home by

inviting compatible neighbors and other friends, and those who have entertained you.

One widow we know has solved her problem of entertaining in a community of married couples by always entertaining with a couple as co-hosts—in her home or in theirs. She's the recipient of many invitations as the result. She always accepts—and she goes alone.

It's a good idea to maintain your membership in any clubs or groups to which you belonged as a married woman, if it is permitted. Unfortunately some clubs, such as many country clubs, do not permit women who no longer have husbands to maintain membership, for the simple reason that they do not want to become havens for lonely women. If you want to entertain in a club to which you can no longer belong, it is sometimes possible to do so through a brother or other family member who may belong.

Managing the Ménage.   One mechanical problem of the woman alone is the size of her abode—usually smaller than that of a family. The answer is very simply to fit the function into the frame. Concentrate on the number of guests whom you can make comfortable.

If you have no maid to answer the door and help with the coats, ask a friend, a relative, or a couple to assist you. It is perfectly proper to ask a male friend to help, if you wish. Just be sure his attitude is not too proprietary. We must confess we've been left wondering a few times, when a male friend played the role of host almost too well!

The hostess entertaining alone leads the way to the dining room and directs the guests to their places. If there is no servant, she can choose between serving the guests or asking a male family member or friend to take over. The hostess would then serve the dessert and coffee as usual.

When the guests are leaving, the lone hostess may need a bit of help with coats and the door, if the party is large, so she can call on the same person who has helped her throughout the party.

The whole secret is to be as natural and unselfconscious as possible. There's really no reason at all to feel otherwise. We're living in probably the most casual and understanding period of all time.

Double Entendre

Some time or other, you will find yourself a co-hostess with another woman, either in your home or in hers. A mutual understanding of cooperation, respect, and thoughtfulness must prevail between you if the occasion is to be a happy experience for both of you. You must agree *together* on all arrangements, from the guest list to how much to spend on the food. There's a rocky road ahead if one of you insists on overriding the other or goes off on her own. We remember sharing an apartment in our single days with a well-salaried young woman who was secretary to Texas's richest oil man. Whenever there were guests, she insisted on overspending extravagantly on the food, which finally forced us to seek another abode.

One of our good friends had an equally disheartening experience when she agreed to co-hostess a party with a casual acquaintance to honor a departing mutual friend. Our friend graciously offered her beautiful home as the setting, only to find herself the victim of a selfish and thoughtless co-hostess who proceeded to turn the occasion into her own private party by inviting a horde of people unknown not only to our friend, but to the guest of honor as well.

After you have agreed to co-hostess a party, and have fairly and squarely laid the plans together, then you are honor bound to carry through to the end, bitter or not. If for any reason of emergency you cannot carry out your part, you do not just walk away with your excuse. You must agree to a postponement or cancellation of the party, or make arrangements for your share of the responsibility—and the expenses.

We lunched one day with a friend who was still completely shattered from an unbelievable co-hosting experience the evening before. She had agreed to the use of her apartment for a party to be given by two young women. Several days before the party, one of the hostesses called to say she had been summoned out of town by a family emergency. Our friend suggested canceling the party, only to be told, "Oh no, Alice has everything organized—and besides, only twenty-five are coming!" When party time came, Alice had never been heard from—and a hundred people turned up. In the midst of the confusion, when our friend was still frantically trying to order in more food, drink, and dishes, there came a long-distance call from the absent hostess to ask, "How's the party going? Having fun?"

Carrying the Conversation

No matter how entertaining some of your guests may be as raconteurs, it's the responsibility of the host and hostess to keep the conversation going all during the party, and to keep it from ever getting unpleasant in any way.

Rarely do you find a family in which both husband and wife are tongue-tied. If both are not ebullient, usually one of the two can effervesce. For several decades we have been in a trend where conversation at parties was the preferred pastime, and games took a back seat. Though this is beginning to change, there's still nothing more pleasant and stimulating than good conversation among interesting people. There are just a few cautions we'd like to make:

❊ Personal acquaintances (not present, of course) are very poor subjects for conversation. So steer clear of talking about friends or acquaintances, unless it's about a recent outstanding accomplishment of some kind. Otherwise, it tends to get gossipy and unkind.

❊ It's thoughtless, and even rude, for the host or hostess to carry on an "inside" conversation, with each other or with any of the guests, which leaves the others wondering what it's all about.

❋ The host and hostess should de-emphasize the "I" and "we" in their conversation. Instead, concentrate on the "you."

❋ Your children and pets are not nearly as interesting to others as they are to you. Neither are your aches and pains! So skim over these subjects lightly.

❋ Always have in the back of your mind as the hostess several current topics that you can launch if a sudden lull falls over the talk. Front-page news, if not hotly controversial, is always good for a whirl. A new book, a good movie or play, a new record album, a new restaurant—all can be provocative and generally discussed.

❋ Never let a guest get dictatorial or argumentative on a touchy subject such as politics or religion. This is the time to jump in with one of your subjects-in-reserve.

❋ If one guest hogs the conversation, watch for an opening to bring someone else into the discussion, or change the subject to something that will bring in the others. If a guest is silent, attempt to include him by asking a question or addressing a remark to him. If he is still noncommittal, don't embarrass him by pressing the point.

The Game's the Thing

A gamier era in entertaining has emerged in the Sixties, and many groups now like a bit of after-dinner competition instead of conversation. This has actually gone so far that one designer originated a rug woven for hopscotch games that guests play indoors in stocking, or even bare, feet!

Of course, *bridge* goes on and on as probably the best all-round game of all time. It's a regular with many groups. If you have slipped out of the habit, try it again. Brush up on the latest rules, or even invite a bridge expert to come to your party and give everyone a refresher lesson. Always be sure to have attractive and fresh cards on hand. For a poolside or outdoor game, use the marvelous magnetic cards and boards, and you'll never lose a trick!

Word Games such as Scrabble and Royalty have a great following and are good for parties. You can set up a card table or two and let those who want to, play. Or everyone can participate and compete for prizes.

Jigsaw Puzzles have staged a big comeback. Most sophisticated and most difficult are the abstract ones—just a square or circle of color, or an abstract painting reproduction jigsawed into bits. Better put a time limit on these, though, or you might find yourself with guests for breakfast, too. In some cities, jigsaw puzzles may be rented at libraries or party rental agencies.

Then there are many amusing *paper-and-pencil word games* that the whole group plays together. These may be played according to the original rules, or may be easily improvised by the hostess to fit the theme of her own party occasion. They can be played individually, or by couples working on one sheet of paper as a team. Here is a starter on what we hope may be many challenging evenings:

1. *Categories*—Probably the best-known and most popular is Categories, said to have been President Kennedy's favorite word game. Basically, each guest draws a diagram on a sheet of paper—five squares across and five squares down. The hostess or the guests may decide on one subject for the game, such as food. Each guest then writes FOODS or another five-letter word that pertains to the subject (such as LEMON) down the left side. Across the top are written five categories of foods, such as: Soups, Desserts, Drinks, Meats, Vegetables. Or the subject could be MUSIC written down the left side, with five musical categories across the top, and so on. Gauge the game by the sophistication of your guests.

Within a given time limit, each player fills in the squares with appropriate words. For FOODS, each word in the first row must start with "F" and be in the category listed above the square; the second row words must start with "O" and so on. Time decided on depends on the difficulty of the game. Foods are easy; music is more difficult. If one person succeeds in completing his diagram before the time limit, he shouts "Category" and wins. If no one has finished by the end of the game, score four poins for each square filled (game totals 100). Where words are duplicated among players, score only half—two points. Highest score wins.

Sometimes Categories is played with any set of five letters down the left side and any miscellaneous categories at all across the top. For example, down the left side: S O T U L. And across the top: Artists, Countries, Politicians, Battles, Boats.

2. *Alphabet*—Guests are provided with pads and pencils. The host has predetermined a set of letters that may spell something that has to do with the party, such as "MERRY CHRISTMAS," or he may list about 15 unrelated letters. Using a watch with a second hand, he calls the first letter, and guests list as many words as they can think of in 60 seconds that start with that letter. The next letter is called, and so on to the end of the game, which should last only about 15 to 20 minutes. Winner is the one with the largest number of words.

3. *Quotations.* Before the party the hostess looks up a list of about five quotations and writes them down. They may all pertain to the theme of the party, such as lines from love poems for a Valentine or wedding anniversary party. Or they may all be humorous, or famous quotes from history such as "Fifty-four forty or fight."

As the hostess reads the quotation, each guest or team writes it down. At the word "Go" they then make as many words as possible using only the letters in the quotation.

Within a single word, letters may be used only as many times as they are shown in the quote. Then hostess reads next quotation, and so on until all have been used. Allow about 3 minutes for the play on each quote. Person or team with most words wins. As an extra fillip, give an extra 10 points if the player can identify the source of the quotation.

4. *ID*—This game involves the identification of names, songs, pictures, ads, or whatever your imagination may dream up. The hostess reads a list of names who may be any kind of celebrity; or she may play on a record player or piano a line from a series of songs; or she may hold up a series of magazine ads (with identification covered); or may read advertising slogans. About 20 make a good game. The guests try to identify the hostess's list. Winner is the one with all or most correct ID's.

5. *Character*—A guest is chosen or volunteers to be "It." He decides on a character whose identity he assumes. Or he may draw a name from a "kitty" provided by the hostess. The name may be a historical person, fictional, live celebrity, local wonder, or anyone who could be known to the group—even one of them.

   Guests now take turns asking the "character" one question each that is answered only "yes" or "no." Object is to guess who the character is. The winner then becomes the next character—and the game proceeds as long as you want to play. A time limit of about 10 minutes should be put on each game.

6. There are *word games* that the whole group plays orally that are fun and lively. An example of this type is "Chain of Words." Here again a subject category may be chosen and all words have to pertain, or the game may be general, with any word counting. The latter is easier and more exciting. One player is designated to start. If the classification is to be the theater, he might say "Stage." The next player within five seconds must shout another theatrical word that starts with

the last letter of the word "Stage." If the game is wide open, any word may be shouted as long as it starts with the last letter of the preceding word. Anyone who breaks the chain by not being able to give a word drops out. Words can't be repeated after being used by one player. Player who stays in longest wins—or limit the game to 15 minutes, and all remaining players are winners.

7. *Charades* or *The Game*, as it has come to be called, is one of the most popular group party games where everybody is brought into one game. For our money, it's for the robust and the athletically inclined. But it is exciting and lively if your group will drop its inhibitions and let go.

Guests divide into two teams in two separate rooms. Each team writes on slips of paper phrases, song titles, quotations, proverbs, or whatever they may decide, composing enough for each member of the other team. The teams meet, and a member of one team draws a slip from the other team and proceeds to act out the phrase for his own team, usually word by word. They try to guess the phrase within a period of time, about 3 to 5 minutes. Score each time is the number of minutes it takes the team to guess the phrase. The play alternates back and forth between the two teams until everyone has had a turn. Winning team has the lowest score.

8. *Equipment games* are wonderful if you have the equipment and the space:

❊ Games of *billiards* have returned in a big way. Since the tables are fairly large and costly, not every home can boast a setup. But you can take your party to a nearby billiard "parlor" for an evening of "shooting." Many of the posh bowling lanes have lavish billiard rooms.

❊ *Darts* are an English favorite that can give life to a party. The equipment is small and easy to store. It's best played in a game room or outdoors unless you don't mind taking a chance on having your most valued painting darted!

❦ *Games of chance* can be played in good fun. Most famous is roulette, and play sets may be purchased. We recommend playing for chips or "play" money.

We Have with Us Tonight

Consider for special occasions the possibility of special entertainment, or even paid entertainers.

A surgeon friend of ours is an amateur violinist and forms a quartet with three other musicians of like accomplishment. They regularly inspire musical evenings in the home of one or another of the group. Another friend is an amateur numerologist and often enjoys charting the future for guests at her own or another's party. Magicians, palmists, and handwriting analysts are guaranteed to hook any group of guests at a party.

So if you are able to snare a talented friend—or a new act in town—try it for variety. Be very careful, though, not to impose on a friend. Don't invite someone with the hope he or she will entertain. Instead, tell your friend that you would like to plan a party around his talent, be specific about what you want him to do, and make plans together. If it is someone who is usually paid for his services, discuss the fee frankly.

Movies shown at home as entertainment at parties are a new rage. Those who can afford it are harking back to the good old days of Hollywood, when every movie mogul had an elaborate screening room in his mansion. Most of us can be just as happy with a simpler arrangement. If you haven't a projector and screen, rent one for an evening. The 16mm size with sound equipment is perfect for any film you would be likely to show at home. As for what to show, we're not talking about the record of your last trip to Yellowstone! We're talking about a real treat of a professional movie that you can rent for a surprisingly reasonable amount from companies in the film rental business. Both full-length feature films and shorts are available. Invite friends to an after-dinner Flicks Party. Be sure there are plenty of small tables in the room for bowls of popcorn, cigarettes, and ashtrays. Serve demitasses at intermission. The evening will provide a nice change from the usual showing of amateur movies.

To locate movies available locally, check the yellow pages of your telephone directory under the heading "Motion Picture Film Libraries." If you don't find any listed in your city, go to the library or telephone company office and check their New York or other big city telephone listings. (Though some telephone directories do not have classified sections, those that do are very helpful in locating services and merchandise. We will refer to these listings wherever appropriate. If they are not available to you locally, try the directory of the nearest large city.)

On the subject of movies, there's another new entertainment kick you could try on your crowd with a little planning and effort. It's the "underground" movie where a group of amateurs plan plot, players, and shooting. This could be a whole day's or evening's amusement. But don't take the movie too seriously —spoof it up for fun. The result can be a good reason for another party.

Dance All Night

The return of dancing as a social pacesetter is just about the most exciting happening of the Sixties. Those lively ones—the teen-agers—rediscovered, revived, and revamped dancing with their own beat. They started with the twist, which set off vibrations all over the world with all ages. They continued with a whole brace of gyrations that they perform like tribal rites.

As in so many other areas, adults who had forgotten that social life could be anything but sedentary suddenly caught the beat, and dancing is back—in homes, hotels, and clubs. Discothèques where disc jockeys preside over the turntable have become meccas for the most devoted. One of the nicest developments of the return of dancing is the small dance in the home. It doesn't require much more than pushed-back furniture, a rolled-up rug, and a well-polished floor. Pile the records on the player, and pick a partner! Cool drink on the sideboard, a hot supper dish in the oven—and you're stepping! If your group hasn't caught up with the new dances, hire a dance instructor for the evening, and have a ball.

Seen But Not Heard

That's the old view of the part children should play in the social life of their elders. Personally, we believe this is a little severe, and we fear a few antisocial individuals may have been created along the way by such pigeonholing of the small fry. This is not to say that we're not opposed to little terrors turned loose on helpless guests.

As in all other things in life, moderation and appropriateness should be your policy regarding the appearance of small children at a party. If they are really well behaved, they are a joy to spend a few minutes with, and they can be a charming opening to a party. Our own godchild at age six is one of those joys. With great little-girl dignity and charm she can greet guests, direct them about her mother's house, and even pass small dishes of hors d'oeuvres. At the witching hour of her early bedtime, she says good-night and disappears without a tear. No, she's not a saint—just well trained.

At the opposite end, we can remember an almost murderous evening spent in the suburban home of a couple with three absolute fiends as children. We were screamed at, jumped at, and even shot at with a toy gun, until we fled to the station at an early hour with a case of acute indigestion and the excuse that we had a very early appointment first thing next morning!

Children can cause their share of embarrassing moments, too. Kay's husband, Tom, when six years old made his mother wonder why she ever let him put in an appearance at a big party for 50 that she and her husband were giving with the help of caterers. At the first lull in the conversation, Tom shrieked to all the guests, "All the dishes and chairs are rented!"

Pets can be a hazard at parties, too. It's variety that makes the world go 'round, so some guests will cringe at a cat, defect at a dog, or pass right out at a pet mouse. So best feed and put pets to bed early, too. They're really no good at all at passing hors d'oeuvres!

Emergency Squad

It is as inevitable as the first snowfall that occasionally an emergency or a catastrophe of some sort is going to occur at a party. So don't break up. Handle any unexpected unpleasantry in the quietest, most inconspicuous manner possible.

❋ If key guests don't appear at the last minute, call on close friends or family to fill in, and tell them why. Or reset the table, turn the music on a little louder, and make the drinks a little stronger.

❋ If a sudden storm blows up, and nobody can get through to your castle on a hill, put everything on ice and tell them all to come the next day, same time. If it's a real blooper of a storm, freeze the food and live off it for the next month. You won't have to cook for a while.

❋ If your *spécialité du jour* goes flop, try to pump it up with kitchen first aid and save the dish—and the day. Some of the most exciting dishes have been the result of such necessity. If it can't be revived, put it away for the family next day— or the dog—and take out a canned or frozen dish from your emergency supply reserved for just such an occasion.

❋ If a guest breaks, spills, or otherwise makes a mess of one of your treasures, just adopt an existentialist philosophy—*che sera sera*. People are always more important than things. Things can be easily replaced—friends can't.

Good-night, Ladies

When your wonderful, successful, memorable party comes to a happy ending, let it end quickly. If there is a guest of honor, he or she may make the first move to leave, but this rule isn't always strictly observed today. When the first guests start to depart, don't go into a false plea for them to stay longer. They apparently feel they have stayed long enough. Tell them what a pleasure it has been to have them, and help them with their coats.

It's thoughtful for the host to remain at the door of the house until a guest has started his car safely. If you live in an apartment, keep the door open until the guests are in the elevator—but remember your neighbors on the floor, and keep voices low. If a lady leaves a party alone at night, the host should ask someone to see her into a taxi. If you live in an apartment that has a doorman, call down and ask him to be sure to obtain a cab for a lady.

After the door has closed on the last guest, sit down and have a quiet little reprise of the evening. Savor mentally the pleasures of friends and sociability shared. Then if somebody rushes back for a pair of forgotten gloves, you won't have to answer the door in your pajamas—as has happened to us when we have shut up shop too soon!

$\mathcal{F}$irst $\mathcal{A}$id for $\mathcal{E}$ntertaining: $\mathcal{S}$ervices $\mathcal{Y}$ou $\mathcal{C}$an $\mathcal{C}$all $\mathcal{O}$n

Work consists of whatever a body is *obliged* to do....
Play consists of whatever a body is not obliged to do.

—Mark Twain

CHAPTER

7

A party can be play all the way for a "body" these days. During the past few years, services of all kinds have become a major business. In no area are services more welcome than for parties. A hostess can rent a potted palm or a lace tablecloth, gold ballroom chairs or a coatrack. She can have the food cooked by specialists who will deliver it piping hot at party time, or she can hire caterers to come in and take over every last detail.

A friend of ours wanted to have a series of early summer parties in the garden of her town house before going to the country for the summer. Planting the garden would have been an extravagance, as it would have withered away during her

208

absence. So she rented a bower of potted greenery for the party period—and sent it all back before departing.

Another friend, wife of an internationally known surgeon, constantly entertains guests from all over the world, always without servants. Her dinners are frequently prepared by a professional kitchen and delivered just before the guests arrive. Yet another friend, a young magazine editor, seeks out unusual or foreign restaurants and cons them into preparing party specialties for her that she picks up on the way home and she never tells!

Our favorite story of a clever hostess who called on outside help was told us by the fashion director of a big store. A helpless Southern belle, she got carried away by a sale of frozen Rock Cornish hens when she stopped at the supermarket for a loaf of bread. She bought 10, found they crammed her refrigerator, so invited 10 for dinner the following night. The next morning, suddenly realizing she had no idea how to prepare dinner for 10, much less cook 10 Rock Cornish hens in a pint-sized oven, she loaded the lot in her car and drove them down to the store restaurant. To the manager she instructed, "Cook them by six o'clock, and trim their feet with ruffles so they'll look Southern!" Next she called the best restaurant in town and persuaded the owner to whip up a bottle of his famous salad dressing to be picked up at 6:15. Calls to all the florists in town couldn't turn up yellow gladiolas to match her apartment, so she telephoned a rich friend with a greenhouse, who insisted on contributing 6 dozen. When the guests arrived, they entered a candlelit room filled with yellow gladiolas and feasted on a gourmet dinner. Small wonder this helpless but sly young woman now has an enviable reputation as a hostess.

Guests can use rental services to advantage, too. It is rumored that at many of the biggest balls in New York the furs that aren't borrowed are rented. For ski and skating parties, clothing and equipment are frequently rented.

Help! Help!

Extra help of one kind or another is the most common outside aid for a harried hostess. If you can manage to have help,
from both the budget and the availability standpoints, by all
means do it. A hostess who is preparing and serving dinner for
as many as eight persons has a much busier time than the proverbial one-armed paperhanger. We all do it, but on occasion
a pair of paid helping hands would make it ever so much easier.
Not the least of the advantages is that it enables you to concentrate your attention on the pleasure of the guests and to
have some fun yourself. Whenever you can, give yourself the
extravagance of being a glamorous and enchanting hostess by
letting someone else tend to some of the less glamorous duties.

There are many ways of having help for a party. The simplest and least expensive is to have a teen-age high school girl
come in and take complete charge of your children, if you have
any—feed them, entertain them, and put them to bed, freeing
you for other duties. Or such a girl could serve nicely, if you
school her a bit beforehand in how you want the serving handled. Be sure to ask her to wear a simple solid-color cotton or
linen dress and a little white tie-around apron. There's scarcely
a teen-age girl who doesn't have to help Mother with the dishes,
so this is another way such help can function. Their charges
shouldn't be much more than their baby-sitting rates, if any
more. This varies from about 50¢ to $1 an hour. Just be sure
you provide transportation home for a young girl after an evening party.

The next source of an extra helper is your "cleaning lady,"
who often can be quite useful because she is familiar with your
house. If you are lucky enough to have good help of this kind,
train her in all the aspects of your entertaining and you'll never
have to worry. Teach her to receive guests at the door and take
coats, to make drinks, to serve, and to clean up. Some are even
good cooks. Of course, one woman can't do everything, but if
she knows how to do everything, you can shift her responsibili-

ties about for different parties. For example, if she knows how to make and serve drinks, she can function quite adequately at a cocktail party, while you tend to other chores—or she can do the serving and cleanup at a dinner party for which you have done the cooking. If you use your "cleaning lady" as a waitress at parties, be sure she has the proper uniform. It might be worth your while to buy a serving uniform for her—a black dress with below-elbow sleeves and white collar and cuffs. Over this she ties a white apron that may or may not have over-shoulder straps. If yours is an informal ménage, you can get away with a beige or simple blue short-sleeved uniform, which is less expensive, with a white tie-around apron, though it is not truly correct. Don't use a white uniform for parties.

You will probably have to pay such help a little more per hour for entertaining aid than you do for cleaning, but this is still relatively inexpensive. For example, if you pay $10 for a day's cleaning, the going rate in New York, your helper may want $10 or $12 for four or five hours of extra work, especially if it is at night.

Another source of sometime help might be students from a local college or university. In New York, there are student agencies for party help at both Columbia and New York University. If your local university doesn't have such a program, why not suggest it?

Then there are professional part-time servants—maids, butlers, waitresses, bartenders—who may work individually on a free-lance basis—if you can find them. For example, one of the handymen in our mother's apartment building works as a butler and bartender on the side and comes neatly packaged in an appropriate uniform. So ask around among your friends, if you are looking for such help. Someone will undoubtedly know someone.

In cities, there are agencies through which part-time bonded servants may be booked. ("Bonded" means that you don't have to worry about their walking off with the silver service Aunt Sadie willed you. The insurance company that furnishes the bond will pay for any missing object, provided you can prove the theft.) These helpers, of course, cost a little more, as the agency must make a fee, but in most cases the persons engaged are worth it, as they are highly skilled, can work more efficiently, and are always properly uniformed. Rates depend on the kind of help you engage, the length of time you book them, and naturally on where you live. (Everything in New York seems higher!)

Wages for these servants booked through an agency are handled in one of two different ways. They may expect to be paid directly by you, and they in turn pay a percentage to the agency that referred them. Or they may be on the regular payroll of the agency, which will bill you for the services. Tipping is usually expected (we fully expect to have to tip St. Peter at the pearly gate!) and may be given directly to the help or added to your bill.

To locate a part-time agency, check the classified ads in your local newspaper, or the yellow pages of the telephone directory, where they are listed under the heading "Employment Agencies" or "Employment Contractors—Temporary Help." The latter classification covers those who work as employees on the payroll of an agency.

The Party Was Catered

For a party of any size or a special party that you want to have in your home, which you can't handle in the ordinary way, calling on caterers can be your answer. Though services vary among caterers, a good one can take every shred of work off your hands and can supply all kinds of equipment that you may not have. They thrive on big parties, one in New York advertising that they can handle all the way from 25 to 25,000 guests! Your only responsibility is to make clear to them exactly what you want in the way of food and service.

Aside from working in private homes, caterers can create a party almost anywhere—on boats, in schools, in museums, in theaters, in stores—or in the middle of Main Street, if called for, we're sure! Some will even travel out of town, so if you can't find good local ones in a smaller city, try the nearest big city. Simply look under "Caterers" in the yellow pages of the phone book. If you are based in a smaller city where there are no catering concerns, try a good delicatessen. Some of them cater food regularly, even though they may not have any or all of the usual services a good caterer offers.

Caterers know how to plan and serve anything from a lunch to a luau. And clean up afterwards! In large cities, there are frequently caterers who specialize in a certain kind of cuisine, such as Italian, Chinese, Hawaiian. For a party with a foreign accent, they can provide the food and even special equipment such as big spoons for twirling spaghetti or chopsticks for dining à la Chinese. Again, these specialists can be located under "Caterers" in the telephone book.

A caterer's charges are based on how much you demand of him. Food and drink charges depend on the elaborateness of the menu and the number of persons to be served. You can usually save money by buying your own alcoholic beverages, wines, and champagnes, even if they serve them for you. Then each additional thing you ask them to supply, such as dishes, serving pieces, chairs, coatracks, etc., is charged for. So you will save money by using as much of your own equipment as you can. Naturally, it is expensive to have dishes brought in, uncrated, and recrated, and to have large pieces delivered, such as chairs and tables. So don't be shy about discussing all of this with your caterer. One word of caution: if you use his equipment, ask to see what you are getting. His taste may not be your taste!

The help that the caterer sends you is charged for on the basis of the kind of help, the time of day or night (you expect to pay more at night), and the length of time they work. Discuss with the caterer exactly what help you need and how you can get it at the least price. Also ask whether his help is bonded.

The caterer will write up all of your instructions and the fees. Be sure to check over this list carefully and see that everything is covered, because they will not be equipped at the last minute to handle extra services that you forgot. You may be asked to sign this list as a contract—and it obligates you to pay for everything listed—or your verbal order may be accepted. When food is involved, expect to advance a deposit that could range up to 50 percent of the cost of the food. This is a natural protection for the caterer, who must make a commitment for the food. You will be expected to tip the servants provided by the caterer. Ask him whether he adds service to his bill, or whether you are to give tips to his people directly. We can't tell you how much to tip, because this depends on the customs where you live, on how long the servants work, and on what they do.

Here is a list of services you can expect caterers to offer, each one priced separately:

> Cooked food
> Beverages
> Ice
> Flowers and centerpieces
> Linens
> China
> Glassware
> Silver flatware
> Silver serving pieces
> Chairs
> Tables
> Portable bars
> Coat and hat racks
> Coffeemakers
> Waiters and waitresses
> Coat checkers
> Bartenders
> Butlers
> Kitchen help
> Dishwashers (the human kind!)

For Rent

The "For Rent" sign in a window today doesn't necessarily signify the availability of an abode. It may mean something quite different—the availability of any and all kinds of items that may be rented for a few hours or for a longer period of time. Equipment for parties makes up one of the major rental classifications—whether it's a silver tea service with which to impress your future in-laws or a tent under which to throw a ball. There are even agencies that handle rentals of party equipment exclusively.

With smaller rooms and pint-size closets the order of the day, a rental agency can be a boon in many ways. It saves storage space in your home or apartment, saves you from having to invest money in many items that you use only infrequently, and makes your party-giving much more flexible. The agency may even pick up the dirty dishes and wash them for you. In fact, a visit to one of these agencies will start your imagination to climbing with new entertaining ideas.

A friend of ours recently decided to surprise her dinner guests with a completely new look in her dining room. So she removed her regular chairs and rectangular table to another room and replaced them with three smaller round tables skirted with cloths to the floor and red-velvet-cushioned gold ballroom chairs—all delivered by a rental agent and picked up the next day. The guests voted it a VIP—very important party.

Among the myriad things you can rent for a party are:

Big equipment—

> Booths for bazaars and fairs
> Stages
> Tents of all sizes and types
> Dance floors
> Air conditioners
> Furniture for indoors or out
> Color TV sets

Big equipment—

    Rugs and runners
    Paintings
    Tables and chairs .
    Steam tables
    Bars
    Coatracks
    Outdoor grills

Smaller equipment—

    Electric appliances
    China, silver, glassware
    Linens
    Coffeemakers
    Tea services
    Punch bowls and cups
    Trays
    Chafing dishes
    Wine coolers
    Decorative pieces, such as candelabra

And of course there's the grand idea of renting a fleet of chauffeur-driven limousines to transport guests to or from the theater, to a ball park, or for a progressive dinner. We once hired seven Rolls-Royces to transport guests from cocktails to dinner at a fashion-industry party—and they're still impressed.

We must caution you that for the most part *you* are responsible for any equipment rented and must pay for any breakage or loss. You can expect the rental company to take care of any repairs on "maintenance" items such as an air conditioner or TV set that doesn't work—or a tick in the Rolls-Royce! But for the most part, you are responsible for the property from the time it is delivered to you until it is picked up by its owner.

Rental charges are based on what the particular item is and the length of time you want to keep it. In some cities, there is a minimum charge, so your order must total at least that amount. If you have a credit rating or an appropriate credit card, the rental company will bill you later. Some department stores act as agents for rental companies and will charge the service on your regular account. If you prefer to pay cash, the delivery man can collect when he brings the items.

There's no stigma whatsoever attached to "hiring" anything that strikes your fancy and that will give your party a fillip. Quite the contrary, it's quite chic. So browse around and pull a social coup, next party you give, with some rented extras. You'll find local rental services under the heading "Party Supplies" in your trusty telephone directory—the yellow pages, of course.

Social Security

If you are planning a large party such as a debut or Golden Anniversary, or are chairman of a party for an organization, or are just plain lazy, or awfully rich, consider the complete party services that are offered by social secretaries, party service organizations, and party designers. With these specialists at the social helm, you can be sure of an impeccable setting and service.

The profession of social secretary is a diminishing one in this age of do-it-yourself. However, a few still exist, mostly in large cities. They are frequently women of excellent social background themselves and thus experienced in all phases of handling a party. They can suggest the place and book it, they can issue the invitations and receive the replies, they can book entertainment and orchestras, they can plan the food and drink. However you want to entertain, whether at home or not, these talented women can manage the party as if it were their own and they were hostess. Fee for their services is naturally based on how much responsibility they take on. To ferret them out, ask the local society editor of the paper, or the finest engraver of invitations, or check the yellow pages under "Parties Arranged" or "Party Planning Service."

A newer profession than social secretary, but also available mostly in larger cities, is party arranger or party service organization. One group of these party professionals stems from the decorating or display world. In many cases the artist has become involved in planning and decorating for parties through a client who has wanted some special décor designed for a debut or other big affair. One assignment leads to another, and pretty soon there's a new party designer in vogue. Though their service stems from their artistry at decorations, they may go all the way through food and entertainment. Usually you learn of these professionals through society-page publicity or by word of mouth. If you are seeking such a service for a smashing party, try the yellow pages under "Parties Arranged," "Party Supplies," or "Decoration Contractors."

More practical for most of us is the store or service that offers a dream world of party supplies. These can be found almost everywhere. Some of the department stores now even have very extensive party supply departments. You can prowl through these stores and departments and come out with a horde of ideas to try out on your next set of guests.

You will find invitations galore, from engraved formal bids to the gayest informals . . . every paper item imaginable for your more casual events . . . fantastic favors . . . decorative papers and ribbons in a kaleidoscope of colors . . . artificial flowers and other decorative items . . . a myriad of miscellany such as dance programs, raffle tickets, matchbooks. New York's biggest party store boasts a variety of 47,000 different items!

Some party stores specialize in decorations and favors for children's parties. They may also be equipped to book children's entertainment, such as clowns, ventriloquists, puppets, ponies.

Since the salespeople in these stores live with party merchandise all day long, they are frequently wonderful sources of ideas for themes and decorations. They may be able to suggest decorations and centerpieces that you can easily assemble and make yourself. They are experienced, too, in estimating the amount of supplies you will need. Or there may be one or two persons in the store who act as party advisers to the customers. Take advantage of this special service by asking questions.

All of these party specialty stores are most easily found in the classified telephone directory under "Party Supplies." You can telephone your favorite local department store to ask whether it has a party department.

Favorite Favors

The party "favor" or little gift given to each guest as a memento of the occasion was absolutely *de rigueur* from the first part of the century through the Twenties. Some very wealthy hosts and hostesses spent thousands of dollars on the most elaborate gifting of guests. Debutante parties, particularly, were occasions for extravagant favors. Then came a period when the lavish favors went out of fashion and the usual little party favors were considered naive and unsophisticated. Now the party favor emerges again as a new compliment to your guests. It's a surprise that gives a party a lift. While the favor should be small, it can be attractive and useful, such as a Christmas-tree bauble at holiday time, or a pretty paper fan for a prom. It goes without saying that you should always have some little favors at a children's party.

Charming favors can be picked up almost anywhere—department stores, party stores, gift shops, ten-cent stores, florists, even drugstores. So always keep an eye open for clever little goodies that will lend luster to your next party. In her *White House Diary,* Henrietta Nesbitt recorded Eleanor Roosevelt's love of unusual party favors and told how she collected them wherever she went in her travels.

If your imagination bogs down, there are specialists in party favors listed under "Party Supplies" or "Favors and Souvenirs" in the yellow pages. At these same stores you will find many other items that make a party fun—confetti, serpentine, snappers, horns, hats, noisemakers, balloons, fans, streamers, parasols, to name a few.

Flowers Do Tell

It pays to cultivate a favorite florist, because nothing gives a party more beauty and elegance than flowers. They are present somewhere at practically every party. In fact, we can't quite imagine any social function without the softness, beauty, and "friendliness" of nature present in flowers and greens.

Before setting your heart on a special floral decorative idea, consult your florist. His free advice is an invaluable service that will make the flowers you order more effective and economical. He is a specialist and can tell you what is seasonal and thus the best buy, what will arrange best for your purposes, and what will stay fresh longest. Without charge, he will give you an estimate of the cost of your job, whether it's only a bowl of spring flowers for a centerpiece or a carload of carnations for a ball. If you ask for extra service, such as sketches of arrangements or installations, he will probably have to make a service charge, as it may necessitate extra expense on his part. So ask the specifics, if your problem goes beyond the usual services of a florist.

All good florists have access to nurseries and flower growers all over the country and in many parts of the world. So if you have a big idea—and a big budget to match—there's no limit to what your florist can accomplish for you at any time of year. Jet planes can rush flowers and plants to us still dewy-fresh from halfway around the world. All it takes is money!

Catch the Act

Even though you may live ten miles from nowhere, today it's possible and popular to plan professional entertainment or music for a special treat now and then. Music can do much to accent whatever theme you wish to carry through a party: Hawaiian songs at a luau, Spanish music at a fiesta, or country music at a Western barbecue.

For a little dance at home, it's just as desirable to have live music as it is at a prom or a ball. So consider booking a local combo as a surprise coup. If nothing else is available, there are high school combos almost everywhere now, and these talented teen-agers will furnish enough music to wear you down for a nominal fee.

If you prefer the record route for dancing, you can expand on your own record player by renting a professional jukebox or one of the newer Scopitones (music and movies) for a special fillip.

Other entertainers who can make a party special are handwriting experts, magicians, quick-sketch artists, accordionists, guitarists, strolling singers, fortune-tellers, pianists, and folk singers. Be careful how you stage your entertainment, so that the effect will be more charming than alarming. We have a friend who carefully plotted a musical surprise for dinner guests when she hired a folk singer. Her home is unique in design, with a tiny stairway at one end of the dining room that leads directly up to a balcony bedroom set apart from the rest of the house. A perfect spot to conceal the musician and her guitar. When guests sat down to dinner and began the first course, the door at the top of the stairs suddenly flew open, and a crashing cadenza was struck on the guitar. Guests reacted with shrieks of terror. Was it an ancestral ghost returning, an angel dropped from heaven, or a bandit to relieve them of their jewels? For a brief period, it looked as though the doctor-host might have to revive his guests.

For children's parties, there are other appealing forms of entertainment you can engage. They love clowns and magicians, a musician who can lead them in singing and marching, or a pony to ride. They adore cartoon films and animal acts.

There are agencies in all larger cities that specialize in handling talent of many kinds. So look under "Entertainers" or "Orchestras and Bands" in the classified pages to locate them. Though they may handle animal acts, a pony is best located through a nearby pony riding ring—or maybe you even grow your own.

You don't have to have pros to make a party. Ask around about local amateur talent, which can usually be engaged very reasonably. And they will love the limelight.

Say Cheese!

Photographic services are available for parties absolutely everywhere, even if you have to resort to Junior and his Brownie! Every town or city has a coterie of flash experts who can record a party in pictures, and sometimes it's very appropriate. A photographer is as essential as the minister for weddings and receptions these days. And they can add to many other occasions as well, such as:

❊ Provide publicity pictures for the newspapers (although papers will sometimes send their own photographer, if the occasion or the hosts or guests, are important).

❊ Make a "memory book" for the guest of honor at a party.

❊ Form a gimmick at a carnival or bazaar party where guests are snapped in a photographer's booth.

Most photographers of this type make a charge per picture taken, for which they will deliver one print each. Additional prints cost extra. Naturally there will be a pre-determined minimum set on the number of pictures he is to shoot, as you couldn't expect a professional to come with equipment to take only a few shots.

Names Make News

The society columns of the country's newspapers exist for the purpose of printing names of local residents and their doings, because everybody likes to read about people. Many hostesses want to be reported often and accurately, and the editors welcome their news to fill their pages. Without it, they couldn't exist.

You will get more and better "press" if you know how to go about reporting your parties and other goings and comings. Much society news is handled on the telephone, because news must be new and immediate. But advance notice of parties can be handled more accurately and efficiently in writing.

Publicity agents exist to handle such news for organizations, businesses, celebrities, and very active society women. Your husband's company undoubtedly has a publicity or public relations department that might be called on for very special events, such as civic or charity functions, that you are chairing. These freelance agents and company representatives know how to write a story, or "release" as it is called in business, for the society editor. It is written in the third person, shows a date when the story may be printed, and gives the name, address, and telephone number of a contact for more information.

As a layman, you aren't expected to send your news in this way, but you can write it clearly and briefly in a letter to the society editor. If you don't know her name, simply telephone the newspaper and ask it of the operator who answers. In writing such a letter, remember what the journalistic world calls "the five W's"—Who, What, When, Where, Why. Such a letter, written as soon as your party is scheduled, might follow this pattern:

March 2, 1965

Dear Miss Bennett:

My husband and I are giving a dinner party [What] that I thought you might like to know about for your society page. Here is the first information:

Hosts [Who]: Mr. and Mrs. Harold John Simmons
1275 Fairway Road
Old Oaks, Illinois

Date [When]: Tuesday, March 21st, at 7:00 P.M.

Place [Where]: The Empire Room, Silver Brook Country Club

Guests of Honor [Why]: Mr. and Mrs. Gerald Francis
Boston, Massachusetts

Dinner will be followed by dancing in the Gold Room with the Stanley Smith Orchestra playing.

If you need more information now, my telephone number is Oak 3254. I will call you the day of the party to give you final details.

> Sincerely,
> [Signed]   Belle Simmons
> (Mrs. Harold John Simmons)

Miss Alice Bennett
Society Editor
The Daily Gazette
Old Oaks, Illinois

When Mrs. Simmons telephones the editor later, she should be prepared to give her this information:

> theme of party, if any
> color scheme
> flowers and decorations
> guest list

Papers in smaller cities and towns tend to describe parties in more detail than those in big cities and may want additional facts.

Of course, all of this information may be given over the telephone. But be sure you are prepared when you call to give complete and accurate information. The editor may have three more calls waiting, so give your story as quickly and briefly as possible. Don't offer your own opinion, such as, "Everybody said it was the best party they ever attended," or "My tables really looked pretty." Give the *facts.* Be careful about spelling all names, as this is a touchy subject with everyone. Marye Johnston won't thank you if you report her name as Mary Johnson! If you submit a photograph, be sure all persons are identified from left to right on a slip of paper attached to the picture (don't write on the back).

One more important point—there is *no charge* by the newspaper for the services of the society editor or for a story printed, so don't offer to pay for any story or mention on the society page.

Classified for Convenience

While one of the best ways to locate help or services of any kind is through friends, sometimes they act more like the Secret Service and balk at revealing how they racked up a social success. We've mentioned other sources in this chapter, but one of the best is the classified section, or yellow pages, of the telephone directory. Usually, the larger the city and directory, the more services you will find listed. Here are the headings to look for:

Amusement Devices
Artificial Flowers and Plants
Artificial Fruits and Foods
Automobile Renting
Awnings and Canopies
Boat Renting
Boats—Excursion
Canopy Rental (See Awnings and Canopies)
Caterers
Caterers—Equipment and Supplies
Chairs—Renting
Check Room Equipment
Dance Floors, Portable
Decoration Contractors, Party, Convention, Etc.
Electric Contractors
Employment Agencies
Employment Contractors—Temporary Help
Entertainers
Favors and Souvenirs
Flameproofing
Floors—Portable
Formal Wear—Rental
Fur Renting

Furniture Renting
Limousine Service
Motion Picture Equipment and Supplies—Renting
Musical Instruments—Dealers
Orchestras and Bands
Parties Arranged
Party Planning Service
Party Supplies—Retail and Rental
Phonographs—Leasing and Renting
Photographers—Commercial
Public Relations Counselors
Publicity Service
Recorders—Sound—Equipment and Supplies
Sound Systems and Equipment
Television Renting

*E*ntertaining *A*way

from *H*ome

Why, then the world's mine oyster.
—Shakespeare

CHAPTER

8

Sooner or later, there does come a time when it seems desirable to entertain outside the home. It's necessary to have a large party, and you haven't enough space. Or you just don't have the physical stamina to undertake a party at home without a staff of servants. Or maybe you're the greatest party girl at heart, but you don't like to cook and prepare. You're a fussbudget, which we seriously inveigh against, and you want to shift the wear and tear on furniture and rugs to another place. Or it's that once-in-a-lifetime Silver or Golden Anniversary, and you want to go all out. Although you have some responsibility when you entertain away from home, you can be a guest at your own party. And best of all, you escape the *un*-creative task of cleaning up, taking down decorations, and putting away.

In selecting the scene for a party, all the rules of appropriateness apply. Go where you and your guests will feel comfortable, and where you will be welcome. If you've never frequented an

227

elegant restaurant or hotel, don't aim to impress your friends
by trying to give a party there. It will only end in embarrassment for all. Always try out a place where you plan to entertain others. Look for a place with a home or social atmosphere,
rather than a commercial one. We know of an elderly couple
who feel that they can no longer undertake entertaining at
home, but who cherish their friends and want to share hospitality with them. So they have arranged with their favorite restaurant to have an expandable private dining room on the same
evening every week. They are at home at dinner there on that
night, and all their friends know they are wanted and welcome
whenever they want to come. It's a gracious custom they have
established, and by selecting one restaurant they are assured of
good and understanding service.

The scene of the party is limited only by the imagination of
the host or hostess. Some of the more usual places are:

The Private Club.   Entertaining in your own private club is
the nearest thing to entertaining in your own home. Naturally,
you are well-known there. The captains, waiters, and other service people are almost like your own staff, because it is a part of
their jobs to know each member's likes and dislikes.

A private club is open to members only, and so it follows that
if you don't belong, you cannot entertain there. Clubs that
usually fall into this private category are country, golf, athletic,
downtown, tennis, bath, beach, women's, and college clubs.
However, if you are visiting another city, some clubs have short-
term memberships or limited guest privileges for out-of-towners.
This is especially true in a resort area or when a country club
is host of a golf tournament. In these cases you usually have to
be recommended by a member or have member references. But
be sure of what your rights are in such cases, as they may be
limited. Don't plan to hold a family reunion there unless you're
sure your relatives will be welcome.

Making arrangements to entertain at your own club is easy.

Through the manager or banquet manager you may book private rooms or tables in members' dining rooms for a party. In some clubs you are also permitted to book a party for an organization you belong to. Just always be sure you know the membership rules and rights.

A few clubs are semiprivate. That is, they have memberships, but also will rent their facilities for a fee to nonmembers; these are of a nonexclusive nature, such as women's clubs. If you are in doubt about whether a certain club to which you don't belong will permit you to book a party there, telephone the manager's office and ask.

Then there are "clubs" that are not really clubs, but just use that title. There are numerous public golf and country clubs that can take private parties. There are nightclubs that aren't clubs. Again, if you are in doubt, telephone and ask.

A club, private or otherwise, will usually charge a fee for the use of a private room. This is to be expected, since it means giving special attention and engaging extra help. Naturally, if you are just entertaining a table of guests in one of the regular dining rooms of the club, there is no extra charge for this.

Hotel. Many different facilities are available in hotels, and the bigger the hotel, the more services there are. You may book all the way from a private living room and bedroom suite, which gives the feeling of a private home or apartment, to a presidential suite, to a grand ballroom that may hold 2000 people. There are various kinds of suites for parties of different sizes and types, so shop around until you find the one just right for you. Consult frankly with the banquet managers, and take their experience-backed advice.

Sometimes a party is given in a public dining room, with an appropriately sized table reserved. We wouldn't recommend this, though, for more than about a dozen persons. In this case you can have your own centerpiece (although the hotel may provide one), place cards, and even specially ordered food. But it would be unpleasantly conspicuous to go beyond that. Also, what you and your guests wear must be compatible with the tenor of the room and the dress of others in the dining room.

If it's a birthday party, you can arrange to have a cake brought on at the proper moment—and the whole room just might join in "Happy Birthday."

A rental fee over and above the cost of the food is usually charged for private accommodations. However, whether or not a fee is charged often depends on the kind of party and the room—so again, ask. Naturally, there is no extra charge for reserving tables in a regular public dining room, although there may be a cover charge for each person.

Restaurant.   A good restaurant is a perfectly acceptable and pleasant place to give a party. While all do not have private dining rooms for parties, many do have. Or you can reserve a table or tables in the main room. Sometimes one part of the restaurant may be made more private. And sometimes, for a very important party, you may book the entire restaurant, and it will be closed to the public. Another alternative is to book the restaurant for a party at a time when it is not open to the public. For example, a breakfast party may be given in a restaurant that doesn't open until lunchtime, or a cocktail party in a nightclub. Restaurants may or may not make an extra charge for a private room. As we've said before—don't be afraid to ask, if you don't know.

Hall.   Many public halls exist across the country for the sole purpose of party bookings. If you are unfamiliar with whether there are any in your city, check the classified section of the telephone directory, where you will find them listed under "Halls and Amphitheaters."

Theater, Opera, Concerts.   Special parties at the theater, opera, or a concert are a great treat and may be planned by purchasing a block of seats for your guests. To make it a real party, a before or after get-together should be included in the plans. Most the-aters in this country do not have food and bar facilities as they do in England, so this means starting or ending the evening in your home, or in another place of your choice. A theater evening is excellent for a club or for a "Dutch" progressive evening, starting with the dinner and ending with the supper. Naturally you should provide the best possible seats! And the party shouldn't be too big. Purchase the tickets early enough, and be sure you have them in hand before inviting any guests (you can always invite substitute guests if someone falls out).

Nightclubs. The reason for going to a nightclub is to enjoy the music, dancing, and entertainment. So taking a party to a night-club means that in all probability you will not have a private room, but will simply reserve a table or tables for the party. The maître d'hôtel (pronounced mĕtra dōtell—so don't call him the "māter-dee") should be called or visited to make arrangements. Remember the economics of a nightclub—that there may be a tax when there is music and entertainment, and that there may be a cover charge per person. Ask about all of this when you make the reservation.

Other Outside Places. There are many other spots outside the home that can be used for attractive party settings. There are beaches for clambakes, such as the one that was given on the beach at the Lido in Venice, complete with grand piano! There are boats for sailing and fishing parties. There are fancy ice cream parlors for teen-agers, and traveling circuses for children. Bowl-ing lanes and the new billiard lounges provide party settings for good sports. Sometimes such places will close to the public to permit a private party on an evening, or if they are regularly closed one day or night a week, they may open for a private party on that day. Frequently it is possible to book a boat or ship for a party, if you live near water.

Alan King, the comedian, is said to have given a party in a chartered bus that drove the guests around Miami to the tune

of music provided by mobile musicians. Mike Todd once engaged the cavernous Madison Square Garden in New York for
one of the biggest parties ever. One of the most unusual places
ever selected for a party was Grand Central Terminal in New
York, where a New Year's Eve ball was given for a charity. The
utter extreme in entertaining away from home is the "Be My
Guest" service offered by one of the big worldwide travel agencies. Via this ingenious setup you can arrange to entertain
guests in any one of 850 restaurants without leaving your
own home and without even being present yourself. A good idea
if you prefer not to see your guests!

So test your imagination next time you want a new look for
your party. However mad your idea may seem, go ahead and try.
You may be surprised at how the proprietor of the particular
place you choose may be captivated with your idea and go all
out to help.

How to Arrange a Party Away From Home

Though you may be relieved of the actual work when you
plan a party away from home, the planning may prove to be
even more important than that for a home party. You will be
counting on others to prepare your party for you—so you must
plan every last detail with them. But be unperturbed about this
responsibility because, as we said before, the planning stage of
a party is the creative stage and can be half the fun.

Making the Reservation. Almost all hotels have banquet or
sales departments that handle bookings and arrangements for
private parties. It is best to telephone this department and make
an appointment to go see them. (It is perfectly all right to go
without an appointment, but you may have to wait your turn.)
A banquet or sales representative will be assigned to you and
will thenceforth handle everything in connection with your
party. Tell him what kind and size your party will be. He will
then describe what the hotel can offer you. Ask to see the sug-

gested rooms, and frankly ask any questions that trouble you. Ask whether there is a rental fee for the room, over and above the food and beverage charges. Ask the price range of the menus, beverages, hors d'oeuvres, or whatever. Find out what the tipping percentage is, and how it is handled, and what the coat-handling and washroom situation is.

When you have decided on the room and the date, you may make a definite reservation or ask the hotel to hold it as a tentative reservation until a certain date. When the final decision is made on your part, the hotel will send you a letter or contract that you must sign and return to them. *This becomes binding on you, and you are liable for the room rental if you should cancel your plans.* There may be certain circumstances under which a hotel may permit you to cancel a firm reservation without penalty, such as a family death or illness, if there is still a reasonable amount of time within which to book another party. So if it becomes necessary for you to cancel for some reason, get in touch with your representative immediately. Naturally, the hotel will appreciate having as much time as possible to re-rent the room; the earlier you cancel, the better are your chances of having the contract dissolved without penalty. These contract rules apply to almost any place where you book private rooms.

If your party in a hotel will be in a public dining room, simply telephone the captain in that room and tell him you want to reserve a table at a particular time for a certain number of persons. He will write it in his reservation book, and that is all there is to it. If you should change your plans, just telephone and tell the captain that you want to cancel the reservation previously made. There will be no obligation to pay anything unless you have made special arrangements of some kind—flowers, menu, or strawberries flown in from France! If you find that your party is going to be delayed and will not arrive at the specified time, telephone the captain as soon as you know this, or you are likely to arrive and find that he has given your table away.

Reserving a private room in a restaurant is easier than it is in a hotel. In the first place, restaurants usually have only one or two private rooms, if any at all. Just telephone the preferred restaurant and ask whether a private room is available at the time you want. If so, ask that it be reserved for you for the number of guests you expect. Be sure to ask whether there is a rental charge and what the food and beverage prices are. Also ask about tipping. You can visit the restaurant later to make definite arrangements. If you are not familiar with the private rooms, be sure to go to see them before definitely reserving. You may or may not be asked to sign a contract or a letter. But if you do, remember that this is a legal and binding agreement.

You reserve tables in the public dining rooms of a restaurant exactly as you would in a hotel, and you may cancel as easily, if no special arrangements have been made.

To make a reservation for a party in a private club you belong to, telephone for an appointment with the manager or banquet manager, whichever handles bookings. Look at the rooms and inquire about the food prices, if you are not familiar with them. They may or may not charge for a private room, depending on the size and kind of party. If it is a big party with elaborate food and drink, there may be no charge. If it is an inexpensive luncheon without a bar, they would probably have to charge a fee for use of the private room. This is understandable, as a club must operate in a businesslike way and at least break even. If you should have to cancel your plans for some reason, expect to have to pay a fee if your notice is short, if it is the busy social season, or if the club has already purchased food and ordered extra help.

To entertain guests in a regular dining room of a club, reserve as you would in a hotel or restaurant. Your obligations would be exactly the same.

To make a reservation in a nightclub, just telephone. The person who answers the phone is probably in charge of reservations, so simply give your name and ask for a table for a certain number at the time you want to go. If you want a special table or a table in a specific part of the nightclub, make that request clear when you telephone. If it is a popular place and a busy night such as Saturday, better call a day or two before and re-confirm the day of the party. There is no obligation if you want to cancel.

Whenever a change of plans is made, whatever the place and accommodations, be sure to call and cancel. Don't just fail to show, or next time you may find yourself persona non grata.

When you reserve any kind of unusual facility, such as a hall or boat, you must check every detail with the manager:

ॐ Do they serve food, or must you hire caterers or do it yourself?

ॐ Do they have bar facilities, or must you handle it?

ॐ Are there waiters?

ॐ Are dishes, glassware, and linens furnished?

ॐ Do they clean up afterwards, or do you?

The Preliminary Arrangements. About ten days to two weeks before the party, call the representative at the hotel, restaurant, or other place and make an appointment to come in and make the specific arrangements for the function:

ॐ Confirm the time of day or evening.

ॐ Give estimated number of guests as accurately as possible.

ॐ Select beverages, hors d'oeuvres, menu, etc.

ॐ Specify whether cigarettes and cigars are to be provided and billed to you, or whether you will provide them.

ॐ Specify whether flowers are to be provided and billed, or whether you will handle.

ॐ Give instructions about how coats and hats are to be checked.

ॐ Give instructions about washroom tips.

ॐ Give instructions about any special decorations you are planning to bring in (and be sure you will be permitted to bring in).

❧   Order piano and music stands if there is to be music (usually no charge is made for these), and find out whether union musicians must be used.

Ask that all of these arrangements be confirmed to you in writing, so that there will be no misunderstanding. A hotel will probably do this automatically and may ask you to sign one copy and return it to them, so that no slip-up can possibly occur.

The Sound of Music.   If you plan to have music of any kind, either for entertainment or for dancing, book as early as possible, in order not to be disappointed about getting the musicians you want. If you do not know any musicians, ask the manager of the place where your party will be held. He may even give your name to musicians who frequently work in his establishment, so don't be surprised to receive a phone call. But you are under no obligation to use the suggested musicians. You will probably find the better-known ones of your city under the heading "Musicians" in the classified section of the telephone directory. Telephone the musician or leader and discuss your party. If union musicians are necessary, ask whether this individual or group is. Ask what the musicians will wear. You wouldn't want checked jackets at a formal dinner dance, for example. Musicians usually expect to be paid promptly—so frankly check arrangements for that.

A Menu Fit for a King.   You naturally want to serve the best possible food and drink to your guests. Therefore, it's wise to lean heavily on the maître d'hôtel or manager for advice. After all, entertaining is his business, and he's hosting parties every day. He knows both the likes and the dislikes of the majority of people, and he knows what foods combine happily in a menu. So give him an idea of how much you want to spend per person and let him suggest to you. Tell him frankly whether you want a minimum menu or whether you want to go all out on a gourmet feast.

Remember to take into consideration dietary religious laws that some of your guests may observe. For a party on Friday, it is always well to make provision for guests who may not eat meat, unless you are absolutely sure there are none. And then there's that problem of no alcoholic beverages on election days in many states, so you may want to hold your election party at home or in a private club where beverages may be served. Several of our friends have unwittingly planned parties in hotels only to discover too late that it happened to be a minor election day of which they weren't aware. One overcame the problem by planning a grand march of waiters carrying bottles of champagne at the exact moment the polls closed and the bars opened. But this didn't help the party an hour earlier!

On Sundays, many states permit alcoholic beverages to be served only after morning church hours, or not at all. If this is the case in your city or state, plan your Sunday brunches, lunches, or suppers in private quarters—your home or private club—if you want to offer your guests a cup of cheer.

When you are hosting a party or group of friends in the public dining room of a hotel, restaurant, or nightclub, consider planning the menu with the maître d'hôtel or captain and ordering ahead of time, so that the meal will be served smoothly and graciously, without confusion and commotion. This will also insure that you can control the amount you spend. All of us must have attended one of those affairs where a dozen guests were left to order as they pleased, and chaos resulted. The waiters tend to forget their usual quality of service and resort to calling out, "Who ordered the beef stew?" or "How many want coffee, and how many want tea—raise your hands!"

If your party is small and you feel individual ordering would give added pleasure to your guests, by all means do it. But *you*, as host or hostess, should take the orders from the guests and transmit them to the captain or waiter. If the group is too large for this, or if you haven't mastered a memory course, it is perfectly proper for each guest to give his or her order directly, but make sure that it is done without confusion.

The problem of controlling the amount of alcoholic beverages served at a party outside the home is an old and difficult one. For a party in a private room, it is usual to order that a bar be set up and stocked with the most popular drinks, including some soft ones for those who do not drink anything stronger. The amount of drinks served may be handled in one of three ways: 1) The host may give instructions to serve as many drinks as his guests order, and he simply tells the bar when to shut down at the end of the party. This is putting no limit on the amount served—or charged for. 2) The host may specify exactly how many bottles of liquor to use, and serving is stopped when this limit is reached. Of course, at this point he may order more if he wishes. 3) He may specify to the maître d'hôtel or manager that he expects his guests to drink an average of two drinks each, or three, or whatever. He will then receive a bill for approximately that number. When we asked one of the most important hotels in the world how to solve this problem, the answer was, "The host must have full confidence in the management responsible for the engagement."

The Comfort of Your Guests.   There are two facilities that you must be sure are provided adequately and nicely for your guests. There must be checkroom service for men and women alike. Even if it's midsummer and no one is likely to wear a hat or a coat, there's always the chance of a sudden rainstorm, which necessitates raincoats, umbrellas, and overshoes. It is proper and desirable to arrange to have the checkroom gratuities included in your bill, so that your guests do not have to tip the attendants. In this case the management usually sets up a special checkroom of sufficient size for your party, or has racks with attendants outside the door. They will display a small sign that tells the guests that their host or hostess has taken care of the gratuities.

The other comfort that you owe your guests is washroom facilities. There are usually washrooms for men and women adjacent to private dining rooms or ballrooms. If attendants are on hand who must be tipped, again it is more gracious for you to take care of this and have the same little sign displayed. Naturally, if your party is a small one in the public dining room, guests would use the same cloakroom and washrooms as everyone else. You can ask the manager to let you take care of the coatroom tips, but you may want to let any guests using the washrooms leave their own tips.

Say It with Flowers.   It's hard to imagine giving any party anywhere without carefully planned flowers in the rooms and on the tables. The responsibility of planning and purchasing the flowers when you entertain outside the home is yours. The only time a hotel or restaurant ever provides flowers without charge is occasionally when you are entertaining a small group in a public dining room. Then, if flowers are provided for all tables, the management may arrange something a little extra for your table. But you'd better be sure!

You are free to order whatever flowers you wish from your own florist. Be sure to explain carefully and completely to the florist the size of the tables, the color scheme, and the time when you wish the flowers delivered.

Hotels, restaurants, and clubs usually have a florist with whom they work regularly. It's a good idea to consider using this florist, as he knows all of the rooms and can make suggestions about size and color scheme of the floral pieces used. He will also often come and arrange the flowers in the room and on the tables. This extra service solved a problem for us when an organization we belong to gave a big party in a hotel grand ballroom. There were a hundred tables, which made it impossible for the committee personally to arrange the centerpieces on the tables. The waiters couldn't do it because their union rules wouldn't permit it. So by using the hotel's preferred florist, the problem was solved, as he sent adequate help and very quickly had all the tables looking pretty.

The manager of your party will handle the floral arrangements for you if you prefer. He will have the florist bill you, or it may be added to your party bill.

The flowers you have ordered belong to you, and you may take them with you after the party. Some establishments have special waterproof bags in which you may put them—so ask. Sometimes at club luncheons the guests at each table draw for the centerpiece. Today most florists use inexpensive containers that they do not pick up or expect to have returned to them, so the flower arrangement may be removed exactly as it is.

The Table Appointments. Just as you would at home, try to make your tables away from home as attractive as you possibly can. Sometimes there is a choice of color in the linens used. Ask about this, and select a color that you can carry out in flowers, place cards, and any other table decorations. Remember that most guests like a cigarette or two during and after dinner, so bring them or ask that they be provided and added to your bill. They look much nicer if placed in little glass cigarette urns, rather than on the table in their packages. Again, it is likely that the urns are available, but ask. You may want to offer cigars to the men at the end of the meal, if it is a dinner party. These may be included in your bill, or you may bring them.

Discuss with the establishment how the tables will be arranged, taking into consideration the size of the party and the shape of the room. You may want individual round tables of six, eight, or ten, which make conversation easy. Or you may want a long rectangular table for all guests, or a T shape, or a U shape. If it is an organization party, you may want a head table. If there is to be a speaker, a microphone must be ordered, and there may be a small charge for the electrician's services.

One word of caution: At a hotel, restaurant, or club, you are practically never permitted to bring in any food or beverages. This is what they are in business to sell, so you must order everything you wish to serve. The one exception is in states where it is illegal to serve liquor. In these cases, members of private clubs may be permitted to bring in liquor or keep it in lockers provided. If there is anything else you want to bring in, ask the representative who is handling your party whether it is permitted.

The Guarantee. Any establishment in business to handle parties must operate in a businesslike way. Thus one or two days before your party, you will be required to give the final "guaranteed" number of guests you are expecting. This is for your protection, as well as theirs. They must be sure to have adequate food and drink for all of your guests, they must provide ample service, and they must have the room set up to handle the number you are expecting. Also, they should not be expected to prepare for more guests than you really expect. So the final count that you give becomes the guarantee. They provide for that number—and you pay for that number. Usually, they are able to accommodate a few additional persons at the last minute, if you let them know. At the time of the guarantee, you can also give any last-minute instructions you want carried out.

The Big Day. This is the time when having a party away from home really pays off. All of the heavy work necessitated on party day at home is shifted to someone else. If you have planned wisely and well, you have no worries. Have a beauty nap, go to the hairdresser, look and feel divine.

For a really big party, you should arrive at the hotel about an hour before party time to be sure all arrangements have been carried out as you wished, to give the tables a final check, and to arrange the place cards. If it is a smaller party, half an hour or 45 minutes beforehand should do the trick. The captain or headwaiter who has been placed in charge of your service will introduce himself to you and will be available at all times to carry out any of your wishes.

At the end of the party, the hosts must remain at the place

of the party until all of the guests have taken their leave. If
lingerers stay beyond the time you have reserved the room,
politely say, "Won't you have another drink before the bar is
closed?" or if there is no bar, "I'm afraid we must say good-by,
as the hotel [or club or restaurant] has another party booked in
the room."

If your party is a small one in a restaurant or public dining
room of a hotel, be sure to be there yourself about 20 minutes
before your guests are expected. Check the reservation and the
table, and be sure everything is as you like it. Then wait for
your guests inside the entrance, if it is spacious enough. Greet
the first arrivals, and then let the captain seat the party. He
will direct the remaining guests to the table. You yourself should
be seated where you can easily rise and welcome them. If there
is no place at all to receive the first guests, wait for them at the
table, instructing the captain to conduct them to the table. Rise
and greet each one, and indicate where you would like him or
her to sit. Make introductions if necessary.

Unlike the procedure for a party in a private room, at the
end of the party you must make the first gesture to leave.

The Check-In System.

If your party is a large one, or if it is a teen-age party and
"crashers" are likely to appear, or if it is a business party, you
may want a checking or control system at the door. Socially, it
is usually assumed that only invitees will show up at a party,
and thus no formalities are required at the door. Each guest is
welcomed warmly. However, there are occasional parties given
by celebrities or prominent socialites or by teen-agers in certain
locales that may anticipate uninvited guests. It is best to handle
this by having someone receiving at the door who personally
knows each invited guest. Any unexpected person should be
told firmly but politely, "The party is a private one, so we know
you will understand why only invited guests will be admitted."
Of course, if the crasher is brought by an invited guest, you can
only be gracious and accept the situation. It is unthinkable

that a guest would bring someone uninvited to a seated dinner. If it should happen, do let the guest know later that next time you will expect to be asked whether it is convenient to include an additional person.

Occasionally, for a very large formal party or for a big wedding to which formal invitations are issued, guests are asked to present a card that is enclosed with the invitation. Two ways of wording these engraved cards are:

M   [fill in name]
will please present this card at the door
Monday, the sixth of March

or

M   [fill in name]
will please present this card for
Mr. and Mrs. Field's dance
on Monday, the sixth of March
at half after ten o'clock

Tickets are usually issued for a charity ball and are collected at the door. Also, for a business party, tickets may be mailed to all guests who have accepted the invitation. Or a secretary may be seated at a small table at the door with a checklist. Either way, the company is able to obtain a record of who attended the party. For a large seated party, a printed or mimeographed alphabetical seating list with table numbers may be distributed at the door. This provides a good guide for table-hopping, too.

The host and/or hostess should remain near the door to greet guests until they are sure all have arrived. As in their own home, they should see that each guest is introduced to several other guests, so that no one is stranded alone.

Paying the Piper. Arrangements must be made prior to your party for handling the bill. You may establish credit by giving the usual credit references and ask that a bill be mailed to you afterward. Or you may simply pay by cash or check after the guests have left. It's always wise to inquire beforehand whether they will accept a check. If the affair is given in a private club to which you belong, you will automatically be billed, since private clubs rarely handle cash.

At this point comes the problem of tipping. In some places the union specifies the amount, and the hotel, restaurant, or club is required to add it to your bill. Actually, this is the easiest way. If it is not handled this way, you may ask that a percentage be added to your bill for the gratuities—usually 15 percent (up to 20 percent in a *very* posh place). If the captain has given you exceptional service, or service beyond the usual requirements, you may wish to show your appreciation with an extra tip to him (he usually shares in the general 15 percent). The representative who handled your booking and arrangements is usually not tipped, unless you feel he has taken unusual interest in making your party a success. In this case, he would be grateful if you remember him. The amount of these extra tips depends on the kind of facilities—average or de luxe. The custom in the place where you live or are entertaining also determines the tipping scale. For the captain, or captains, $5 to $10 each is sufficient—again, it can vary, depending on all the circumstances. If you want to include the banquet manager who handled your party, give him whatever you feel it was worth to you. In the major cities, such as New York, Chicago, Los Angeles, San Francisco, and the like, everything should be upped a bit in a first-class place.

If yours is a small party in a restaurant or public room of a hotel, try to handle the check as unobtrusively as possible. You can pay in advance, if you have ordered the dinner ahead. However, this leaves no provision for special beverages or wines that can't be computed in advance. So it's usually best to pay and tip as quickly and quietly as possible (but do take time to check the check), or if you have a charge account to sign and add the tip to the bill. To avoid having to do quick mental gymnastics, simply write on the face of the check, "Add 15 percent for gratuities." You can slip the captain a folded bill as you leave, the amount depending on the size of your party and the size of the bill. This tip would range from $1 to $10 or more.

The State of the Union. In highly unionized areas, be sure to check to see where you must use union members, or what union rules you must observe. In the first place, as we said above, there may be a union tipping requirement that you must meet, which is added to your bill. In the second place, the musicians in most places are required to be members of the musicians' union. Thus you must be sure that any musicians you engage fill this requirement, or else every employee in the place may walk out on your party and everybody else's. If there is to be a fashion show, special entertainment, or an exhibit, it may be that union members must be used. Also any special equipment or decorations may have to be union-made and delivered and unloaded by union members.

The hotel, restaurant, club, or whatever can tell you exactly what the union story is. If you are having a small, simple party, it is unlikely that you would run into any problems at all. But for a big affair, an organization party, or a business function, check out any union questions with the management.

Extra Curricular. For club or organization functions, you may want a photographer to snap candids or to take a formal picture. The manager of your party can give you the name of one equipped to do this kind of work, or you may find one under "Photographers" in the classified section of the telephone directory.

Fire laws in most places require that any fabrics used for decoration be flameproofed, and that any other inflammable decorations be treated against fire. In some cities, the fire department will do this for you. If not, companies equipped to do this are listed under "Flameproofing" in the classified telephone directory.

Check-off for Entertaining Away from Home

To insure that you won't overlook even the tiniest detail that might make or break your party away from home, here is a checklist to follow. Each time you entertain outside, type or write out this list to follow, and check off as you proceed. Here are the basics:

( ) Reserve room or tables and verify time; specify room arrangement.
( ) Select hors d'oeuvres, beverages, menu; verify prices and tips.
( ) Choose color of linens (if there is a choice).
( ) Check any union requirements.
( ) Decide on table arrangement.
( ) Select and order flowers.
( ) Arrange for coatroom or checking facilities.
( ) Arrange for washroom facilities.
( ) Decide about music, engage musicians, order piano and music stands if needed.
( ) Plan decorations and purchase place cards.
( ) Arrange for cigarettes and cigars.
( ) Establish credit, or make arrangements for handling the check.
( ) Engage photographer, if you want pictures.
( ) Give guaranteed number of guests.

Of course, if you are having a party in a place where you must bring in food, dishes, silver, and everything, you must add these requirements to your checklist:

( ) Arrange for food, beverages, and ice.
( ) Arrange for china, glassware, silver, serving dishes, linens.
( ) Provide service.
( ) Provide cleanup service and waste disposal.
( ) Provide for removal of all equipment carried in.

There comes a time in every hostess's life when she must arrange a party away from home, whether for herself or for an organization to which she belongs. We haven't intended to frighten you with so many cautions—only to remind you. Entertaining at home is wonderful, it goes without saying. A party away from home can be exciting, interesting, different, and a hit, too. So try it sometime.

 Part Two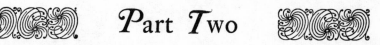

Instant Party Guide:
A Dictionary of Ideas
and Plans for Parties

All parties are variations on a few basic themes. Here we give you in capsule form, alphabetically, the essential ingredients of the major types of parties. Many of them are interchangeable as to purpose and menu. Specific party ideas appear at the end of each section to stimulate your imagination to dream up your own original versions. We hope your ideas will snowball into creating parties that will mark you as a distinguished hostess.

After-Dinner Party

The Party. Any time after 8 P.M. Presents the minimum in problems. You have all day to put the house in order, and young children should be in bed by the time guests arrive. An after-dinner affair can provide the same informality as a morning coffee, with a bonus of having husbands on hand. Invite whatever number you wish, from 6 to 60, depending on the purpose of the occasion. Entertain teen-agers on a Friday or Saturday night and during holidays; get a neighborhood group together for an evening; honor departing friends. A practical solution to entertaining houseguests when daily routine is upset. Invite a couple to dinner on their anniversary, and ask other friends to drop in later. At Christmastime invite a group of friends to decorate the tree.

Have an evening of complete relaxation and chatter, or a game night for a group that thrives on activity. (See page 197 and pages 198 to 203.) It can be a simple party for a busy hostess, or elaborate for those who dote on giving their all to any party. This can also be an inexpensive way to entertain, and it requires no special decorating, although any desired theme can be carried out.

The Menu. Serve simple but appetizing refreshments. Heavy food is taboo.

❋ A simple dessert with nuts, mints, and coffee when guests arrive or later in the evening.

❋ A very special dessert with champagne, a chance to make a recipe that is too time-consuming for a dinner party.

❋ Chilled punch with tiny open-faced sandwiches and cookies.

❋ Highballs with snacks when guests arrive (substitute non-alcoholic drinks for teen-agers), and later a tray of sandwiches with coffee and cake.

An after-dinner party is a perfect excuse for pursuing today's coffee craze. Serve one type or give guests a choice among several (see page 173). Don't forget to provide caffeine-free coffee for insomniacs. Since preparation for an after-dinner party is comparatively easy, do try to serve attractively. It takes very little extra effort and gives a lift to any party. At least have a few flowers and candlelight. Serve buffet from either dining table or sideboard, and provide individual snack tables. Or serve from a cart that has been attractively arranged and wheeled into the party room. At this hour of day, most people want to sit down, so provide comfortable chairs unless it's a drop-in-and-out affair.

The Ideas.

❅ Get music lovers together to spend an evening listening to favorite records, either jazz or longhair. You could give opera buffs who will really listen, not talk, a musical treat. Select an album of a complete opera. Before beginning the music, review the story and announce who the featured musicians are. Afterwards serve refreshments or a very light supper.

❅ Since many persons prefer cheese in place of a sweet dessert, have an after-dinner Cheese Tasting Party. Serve red wine such as Burgundy, a medium or sweet sherry, or port, and set out trays of different varieties of cheese, each with a little flag giving its name and type, such as "CAMEMBERT—MILD." Have an assortment of biscuits, crackers, and miniature loaves of sliced French bread, and a crock of butter. As an accompaniment, provide a tray of fresh fruits, such as pears, apples, and grapes, which are good with cheese. Serve demitasses. As decoration, use some of the attractive cheeseboxes found in antiques shops. These can be filled with flowers or fruit; or why not serve cheese from them?

❅ All ages love to sing, whether their vocalizing is on key or off. An after-dinner sing-along party will give those a chance who would be intimidated by the town glee club or the church choir. Ask a friend who is an amateur singer, or book a professional musician or group, to start the ball bouncing. Then let all join in. Hand out typewritten words to some of the favorite old songs. Caroling would be appropriate during December. Home organs have become popular and provide the perfect background for Christmas singing. Our neighborhood organist has established a custom of inviting all families on the block to come for caroling on Christmas Eve. No matter how deep the snow, the doors and windows are thrown open at a certain hour, and organ music peals forth. This is the signal for all neighbors to dash over and join in singing on an open porch. After caroling, everyone is invited inside for hot cider and cookies. There is ice cream for the small fry.

❋ With interest in foreign travel at an all-time high, organize a group for a series of after-dinner Fractured French (or whatever language you choose) parties. Engage a professional teacher to instruct in conversation. After the serious session, specify a 15- or 20-minute period when everyone must speak nothing but the foreign language. Each participant must forfeit a penny for every English word spoken. Pennies go toward paying the teacher. Serve simple refreshments of a sweet and coffee of the country involved.

❋ For an after-dinner movie party, see pages 203-204.

Anniversary Party

The Party. An anniversary party is usually an intimate celebration that includes members of the wedding party and other close friends and family, but only guests who are important to the anniversary couple. You may give the party for another couple, or you may invite friends to help you celebrate your own anniversary. When honoring another couple, gifts are optional and are generally given only on special anniversaries such as the 25th or 50th. (Of course, the anniversary of special events in one's life other than marriage may also be feted.)

The party could appropriately be a dinner, supper, open house, sherry, cocktail buffet, or after-dinner party. Anything reminiscent of the wedding day can be used in decorating, especially flowers. If you wish to carry one theme throughout, use the traditional symbol for the particular anniversary year in invitations, centerpiece, color scheme (an all-gold party for a 50th anniversary), and in gifts. The following is a traditional list of symbols along with an updated one. We favor the sentimentality of the old list over the commercial overtones of the new, but make your own choice.

Year	Old List	New List
1st	Paper	Clocks
2nd	Cotton	China
3rd	Leather	Crystal and glass
4th	Fruits and flowers	Electrical appliances
5th	Wood	Silver
6th	Sugar and candy	Wood
7th	Wool or copper and brass	Desk, pen and pencil sets
8th	Bronze or pottery	Linen and lace
9th	Pottery or willow	Leather
10th	Tin	Diamond jewelry
11th	Steel	Fashion jewelry and accessories
12th	Silk and linen	Pearls or colored gems
13th	Lace	Textiles, furs
14th	Ivory	Gold jewelry
15th	Crystal	Watches
20th	China	Platinum
25th	Silver	Sterling
30th	Pearl	Diamond
35th	Coral	Jade
40th	Ruby	Ruby
45th	Sapphire	Sapphire
50th	Golden	Golden
55th	Emerald	Emerald
60th		Diamond jubilee
75th	Diamond jubilee	

In keeping with the year, gifts might be engraved stationery, a leather album, a wooden tray or bowl, additions to china, a copper chafing dish, crystal candlesticks, or a silver photograph frame.

Have a guest book for all to sign as a permanent record of friends who participated in the celebration. Later, paste pictures

taken at the party in the book and send it to the couple you
honored.

The Menu. What is served depends on the type of party given,
but climax the celebration with a beautiful cake. It can be a
reproduction of the wedding cake, complete with bride and
groom and the year lettered on it, or it can be an entirely different shape. A cake baked in a ring-shaped mold, representing
the wedding band with proper inscription, could also serve as
centerpiece. Circle it with flowers, or make an arrangement in
the center of the ring. A bell-shaped cake would also be pretty.
Champagne to toast the honored couple, of course.

The Ideas.

❋ Give a Silver Anniversary dinner or buffet supper. This is
the time to use as much gleaming silver as possible without
appearing ostentatious. Make it a party to remember—second
only to the wedding celebration itself. Don't stint on flowers
and candlelight. Have a large heart-shaped cake decorated
with cherubs and flowers. As favors, give each guest a piece
of cake in a small silver-paper box tied with ribbon to take
home. Hire a musician to play and sing songs from the year
the couple were married. During the evening, show any
available home movies or stills that include the anniversary
couple, especially during the period the bride was being
wooed and won.

Since party rentals make almost anything possible, you can
rent whatever you need—additional silver equipment to add
to the splendor, a movie projector and screen, and even a
limousine to transport the honored guests. (See Chapter 7.)

❋ Select a year that is meaningful to you for a That-Wonderful-
Year-Party—the year you were born, graduated, engaged, or
married. Ask everyone to dress in styles of that year, have
music that was popular then, and use as decorations fake
headlines of big events that occurred that year. Great fun for
an anniversary or class reunion. As another version of this

party, ask each guest to come representing his own Wonderful Year. Let guests guess which year each represents.

Birthday Party

The Party. The fun of a birthday party shouldn't be the exclusive privilege of children. Everyone, including both sexes, enjoys special notice of his special day. Only children need tell the year! A birthday can be celebrated with any type of party. Just be sure it's the kind the birthday person enjoys. You can be safe in choosing a particular interest of the one celebrating —a bowling party, tennis, golf, swimming, "antique-ing," theater, or whatever. Lunch, tea, sherry, or dinner could follow. Gifts are optional, but packages always make it seem more like a real birthday party. Unless it's family or very close friends, specify inexpensive, amusing gifts, not more than $1, and the gift from the hostess should be in the same price range so that guests will not be embarrassed at their own. Or the hostess may ask guests not to bring presents at all, and she can present one nice gift to the guest of honor. Joint gifts with guests contributing to the cost should ordinarily be restricted to families and clubs, although there are special situations when it is permissible. Consider the person's hobby for possibilities when selecting gifts—stamps for a philatelist, sewing items for one who sews, recipes or a cookbook for the gourmet. Carry out interest theme in table decorations also, or simply use any pretty centerpiece. It could be the birthday cake.

Set the color scheme by the color of the birthstone for the particular month, and use flowers that are symbolic for that month in decorations.

Month	*Birthstone*	*Flower*
January	Garnet	Carnation or Snowdrop
February	Amethyst	Violet or Primrose
March	Aquamarine	Jonquil

Continued on page 258.

Month	Birthstone	Flower
April	Diamond	Sweet Pea or Daisy
May	Emerald	Lily of Valley or Hawthorne
June	Pearl or Moonstone	Rose or Honeysuckle
July	Ruby	Larkspur or Water Lily
August	Sardonyx or Peridot	Poppy or Gladiolus
September	Sapphire	Aster or Morning Glory
October	Opal or Tourmaline	Calendula or Cosmos
November	Topaz	Chrysanthemum
December	Turquoise or Lapis Lazuli	Narcissus or Holly

Purchase fake birthstone rings at a novelty store and tie to place cards. If you know the birth month of each guest, select individual rings with the appropriate stone for each. A theme can also be carried out with zodiac signs.

Period	Zodiac Sign
January 20–February 18	Aquarius
February 19–March 20	Pisces
March 21–April 20	Aries
April 21–May 20	Taurus
May 21–June 20	Gemini
June 21–July 22	Cancer
July 23–August 22	Leo
August 23–September 22	Virgo
September 23–October 22	Libra
October 23–November 22	Scorpio
November 23–December 21	Sagittarius
December 22–January 19	Capricorn

The Menu. Suit the menu to the type of party, but do have a cake, or at least a reasonable facsimile. We've seen such improvisations as birthday baked Alaska, birthday cheesecake, and even a big crusty apple pie properly adorned with candles. However, only the traditional decorated cake will do for children. If it

is an adult party, serve champagne with dessert, and toast the
honored guest.

The Ideas.

❊ Since packages are synonymous with birthdays, give a package
party and ask each guest to bring a "white elephant" wrapped
in gift paper. (One man's trinket is another man's treasure!)
As guests arrive, number the packages and pile them in an
attractive container such as picnic basket, tray, pretty wastebasket, wooden or copper bowl. If you are located near a
Mexican or party store, perhaps you could purchase (or order
in advance) an elephant piñata to hold the gifts. Have slips
of paper numbered to correspond with the packages. After
the birthday cake is served, let everybody draw a number that
tells him which package is his. After all packages are opened,
present a special gift or the container that held the packages
to the guest of honor.

❊ For a girl's sixteenth birthday, it's fun for a small group of
her closest friends to conspire with her mother for a surprise
Kidnap Party. The friends swoop down on her room early in
the morning, get her out of bed, dress her, blindfold her, and
drive to another girl's home for an all-day party. Have breakfast, play games, do nails and hair, talk, swim, or whatever the
girls like. Have a sandwich lunch followed by more loafing.
Dates come in late in the afternoon for a picnic supper.

❊ Also for a Sweet Sixteen Party, invite the birthday child's
closest friends to a luncheon in a particularly elegant restaurant, or one with special atmosphere that would be a treat
for all the girls. Start the lunch with nonalcoholic punch as
an icebreaker, follow with a menu girls would like (they're
usually dieting, but starved), and climax with a great birthday cake. Fairly lavish gifts are customary in some areas and
are opened after lunch. Engage a photographer to record the
important milestone.

Breakfast

The Party.   If you sparkle with the sunrise (and your friends do, too!), a breakfast party is perfect for certain occasions and a pleasant way to start the day. Think of it as the answer for such situations as these:

- for out-of-town guests and bridesmaids before a wedding
- for a group leaving on a motor trip
- for weekend houseguests
- for a group before early morning sports such as golf, sailing, riding
- for a morning committee meeting
- for wives of husbands attending a convention or other business meeting

Issue your invitations for as early as you dare, or any time up to 10 A.M. Make it a small party for 4 to 12 persons because of the early hour and lack of preparation time before the guests arrive—unless it is a large business breakfast to be held outside the home. Naturally, adequate seating must be provided, even if the meal is served buffet fashion. Flowers, leaves, or other very simple decoration will suffice. If the breakfast precedes some special activity, such as a trip or sailing, you may use as centerpiece something that relates to it—such as a doll's trunk brimming over with small items for the honoree's trip, or a ship model beside an informal bouquet of flowers before a sail.

The Menu.   Remember two requisites: plan dishes that may be partially prepared ahead; select foods that are quickly cooked. The two basics of a good breakfast are good *hot coffee* and good *hot bread*. The variables are fruit or juice, eggs, and a light breakfast meat. The best possible butter and a special jam or jelly top it off.

The Idea.

❊ To entertain wives from out of town attending a convention, plan a gala fashion breakfast. Schedule it in a private room of the convention hotel for convenience of the guests. Invite a local store to provide a fashion show. The store may ask the company or organization sponsoring the convention to pay the models' fees. Or local wives may be used as the models. Ask the store whether it can provide any little favors such as perfume samples. End the party with a drawing for a glamorous hat that you have purchased from the store (or give a gift certificate for the hat). If the store has a restaurant or tearoom, you may be able to book the breakfast there, so that the guests can shop afterwards. In this event, transport them from the hotel to the store in a caravan of buses.

Bridge and Other Games

The Party. Games are sure party mixers for getting guests acquainted and making them circulate. A game party can introduce a houseguest to friends or a newcomer to the neighborhood ... combine groups who don't know each other ... repay a large number of social obligations at one time.

When giving a large card party, hosts may play it safe by counting themselves out of the game. This leaves them free to fill in for any last-minute regrets. If not called upon to play, they can busy themselves with emptying ashtrays, refilling glasses, and generally circulating about.

If you want to play serious bridge, a small party is best, with only guests who enjoy the art of playing a good game. This, however, serves a different purpose and is not the fun kind of party you want to honor a special guest or to get friends acquainted. When it's a purely social affair, keep the mood carefree. Most players are good sports, but if you have friends who are poor losers and play for keeps, invite them to some other type of party. It's bad manners, of course, to call attention to someone else's mistakes—even trumping a partner's ace—but there are always a few who feel compelled to tell others how it's done. Such a competitive spirit should be curbed at parties and reserved for tournaments only.

To keep the atmosphere light and gay, have one or two traveling prizes that are strictly for laughs. Set up rules in advance, such as giving a prize to anyone who takes a trick with the nine of clubs, and another for whoever has seven hearts in his hand. Prizes remain wrapped until the end of the party, when holders are keepers. Other possible prizes could be:

❊ One inexpensive prize at each table that guests cut for at the end of game.

❊ One high-score prize that costs several dollars, suitable for man or woman, if it is a mixed group.

❊ One high-score prize suitable for a woman and another for a man.

❊ One high-score and one second-high suitable for either sex.

❊ Low-score prize is optional, but can be an amusing consolation for the consistent loser.

If it's a large party, there should be more than one prize. It's unwise to play for money unless it's a group that plays regularly for a quarter or fifty cents a corner instead of prizes. Some guests might be opposed to or offended by the idea. And besides, it's not very courteous to ask guests to contribute money in any way after they arrive at a party.

Many women prefer combination luncheon or dessert card parties in the afternoon while children are in school. Some of them like to play in the evening, when husbands can baby-sit. If men are invited, have a dinner-bridge, dessert-bridge, or bridge-supper. At an evening party, don't insist on guests playing so late they're exhausted. Most players prefer to quit at a reasonable hour, especially if they are not cardsharps.

A card party can be any size from a foursome to as many tables as you have space for comfortably. Better to have tables already set up with card table covers on them, if table tops are not in good condition. (A cover is nicer to play on, anyway, and is easier on hands.) For card games have on each table two decks of cards, score pad, a sharp pencil, and small ashtrays. Empty ashtrays often. If there are bowls of nuts or mints, use small ones and keep tables free of clutter. Use straight chairs and fill in with folding chairs if needed.

Tallies can be passed or used as place cards. Purchase printed ones or make your own from old greeting cards, wallpaper, or fancy wrapping papers. If you're an artist, sketch something personal and appropriate for each guest individually. If lunch or refreshments are served first, have card tables already set with linens and silver. Tables look pretty with a single large flower or a bouquet of small flowers on each. No particular theme is needed, but if the party has a special purpose, follow through with appropriate decorations. This might be travel, bridal, anniversary, birthday, or baby shower theme.

The Menu. Keep the menu light, if guests are to sit for two or three hours playing cards. Follow suggestions given for luncheon, buffet, after-dinner, and dessert parties in this chapter. It is important to select dishes that can be served quickly and easily, to allow plenty of time for playing. During the game have water, ginger ale, or other cold drinks available. You may want highballs at an after-dinner party for couples. It's easiest for guests to eat on card tables and easiest for the hostess if they serve themselves from a buffet. However, the hostess can serve each table if she prefers.

The Idea.

❦ Invite a large group to a "something-for-everyone" game night. Send invitations cut in several jigsaw pieces that must be fitted together in order to read the message. Set up as many tables as you can and have a choice of games—bridge, canasta, Scrabble, jigsaw puzzles, and Mah-Jongg. Bridge could be divided into serious bridge and conversation bridge to keep everyone happy. Have a prize for each table, since scoring will vary. Jigsaw-puzzle buffs can cut for theirs. This type of party is particularly adaptable to an office party because of the wide range of ages and tastes. Guests will feel more at ease doing what comes naturally.

❋ Invite a group of couples who are true bridge enthusiasts to an evening party. Surprise them by providing a professional bridge teacher who will give an hour's instruction before you start the play. When you make advance arrangements with the teacher, ask him to include in the lesson helpful pointers to improve the game of already experienced players.

❋ Use a flower theme for an afternoon dessert card party or a luncheon-bridge. Have card tables set before guests arrive, with centerpieces of different kinds of flowers. Before serving, distribute flower tallies that correspond with the table decorations. For example, there might be four tulip tallies, four daffodil tallies, and four rose tallies. Guests find their places by matching the tally flowers to the table flowers. To carry the theme further, linens could also match the flower colors. Dessert might be flower ice cream molds.

❋ To prevent guests from taking their cards too seriously, play a game of Table-Hopping Bridge. Break up the game at 10- or 15-minute intervals by ringing a bell. At that point the four players at each table put their cards face down on the table and move to the next table to continue the game in progress there. If there are three tables, Table No. 1 players move to Table No. 2, Table No. 2 players move to Table No. 3, and Table No. 3 players move to Table No. 1. Otherwise, the game is played as regular bridge. For each table, provide small blank cards on which the bid and trump should always be written, so that if players have to change in the middle of a hand, the next group will know how to pick up and carry on that game. Exposed dummy indicates which couple has the bid. Scores are listed on individual tallies at the completion of each hand, wherever the player is at that moment and whatever hand he has just played. If any players are between hands when the bell rings, the next foursome at the table deals the cards and starts anew. Since the same two partners continue to play together, have two prizes for the winning couple. If only a brief part of the evening is to be spent at cards after dinner, this is an ideal cure for after-meal lethargy. If you have planned to spend the entire evening at bridge, play Table-Hopping Bridge for the first 30 or 40 minutes as a mood-setter. Then continue the party with regular bridge.

❋ Plan a Bridge Tournament for four successive Saturday nights among a group of close friends who like to play. Let the girls play against the boys and take turns as hostess. Serve a buffet supper, either before or after the game. Total the girls' scoring and the boys' scoring separately each week. At the end of the month, compile grand totals for each side. Losers pay off by arranging and financing a night out in honor of the winning team. Make it dinner in a choice restaurant, the theater, a nightclub, or whatever appeals most to the group.

Brunch

The Party. Whoever thought of combining late breakfast with early lunch into "brunch" made a contribution to the social life of the century! Great for a group of 4 to 20, and a party husbands enjoy if you start off with a tasty bracer. It's an economical way to entertain because of the light food and drink required. You'll find it ideal for ladies before an early afternoon function such as a matinee or meeting. Especially good for mixed groups on Saturdays, holidays, Easter Sunday, or after church any Sunday. Schedule the party any time between 11 and 1 on a week day, or 11 and 2 on a weekend. No need for fancy décor, because of the early hour. Service may be seated or very casual, with buffet and little tables or buffet and casual seating. Just be sure everyone has a place to sit. Set the table or buffet the night before.

The Menu. If you have a mixed crowd, start with a special drink such as whiskey sours, bloody Marys, or a milk punch. Plan the rest of the menu around quickly prepared dishes or one that can be made in advance. A heavy menu at brunch is taboo. The main course is more important that it is for a breakfast, but a little lighter than for a lunch. It should contain meat or a meat dish. Casseroles or chafing dishes are perfect. Pivot your menu around something like creamed chipped beef and eggs, eggs Benedict, creamed chicken on biscuits, or cheese soufflé with Canadian bacon. Include sweet breads, and end with fresh fruits in season, a compote of stewed fruits, or an ambrosia. Gallons of hot coffee throughout!

The Ideas.

❃ Invite guests to a Lazy Sunday Brunch between 1 and 4 P.M. Have hot coffee and drinks ready as guests arrive. Arrange two buffets set up for guests to serve themselves—one with a hot egg dish and an assortment of cold meats and caviar, the other with coffee and a selection of fruit and sweet breads. Have little tables or card tables for guests to sit where they please. Later clear the tables and set out Sunday papers, jigsaw puzzles, and crossword puzzles for a quiet, relaxed Sunday afternoon.

❃ The revived interest in pancakes has reached epidemic proportions, and a Pancake Flip gives guests the fun of improvising with varied toppings and sauces. Especially appropriate for a brunch or near Shrove Tuesday. If you have one or two extra-large griddles, guests can cook and flip their own. Why not give a prize to the best flipper? On the buffet table have bowls of whipped or melted butter, blueberry sauce, sweetened crushed strawberries, honey, syrups of different flavors, whipped cream cheese. There are different kinds of pancake batter, too: plain, buttermilk, buckwheat, potato, and even chocolate. Have one kind, or a choice of batters. Serve fruit first. Accompanying meat can be sausages, ham, bacon, or creamed chicken.

❋ Gather all of your picture-taking friends for a brunch to be followed by a Camera Carnival. Plan it for good weather time, so they may work indoors and out. Plan backgrounds of furniture groupings; have some costumes on hand; select some out-of-doors spots. Invite several pretty girls in their teens or twenties as models. Number each location site. Each guest must try his prowess at each site, using models as he wishes. The following week, invite the guests back for an Exhibition. Arrange all photos around the rooms and award prizes (you can purchase award ribbons at a party store). Serve champagne punch with canapés, as at most openings of exhibitions.

Buffet Party

The Party. The word "buffet" is usually followed by the word "supper." But it doesn't necessarily have to be so. There are many parties for which buffet service is pleasant and appropriate —breakfasts, brunches, lunches, cocktail parties, dinners, picnics, late suppers. The beauties of a buffet party are many:

❋ You can entertain a larger number, since it doesn't have to be a seated party.

❋ Guests serve themselves, which minimizes the problem of extra help for serving.

❋ Serving is easy for the hostess and takes much less time.

❋ Fewer dishes are used, so there is less cleaning up afterward.

❋ A buffet is an ideal party to give if your equipment is limited.

Your home can be decorated in any way that ties in with the occasion. The buffet table is the focal point, so should have special attention. You may want to push your dining room table against the wall to provide space to set up small dining tables. Or it can be left in the center of the room so that guests can circulate around the table, which expedites service if you have a large group. This is one time when you can use a centerpiece or table decoration more elaborate than usual, because you have more room on the table and you don't have to worry about guests' craning to see over it. Organize the service so that guests serve themselves in the proper order—plates should be at the most accessible spot and the logical place to start; silver and napkins may be arranged in an attractive manner on the buffet (if you have tables for guests to sit at, set them as prettily as you would for a seated party); then progress from the main dish to relishes and salad. Salad may be served at the tables as a separate course, if you wish. Wine should be served to the guests wherever they are seated. The dessert may be put out on the buffet so that guests return and serve themselves, or it may be served to them from a cart, followed by coffee.

The Menu.   First consideration is to plan dishes that can stand without deteriorating in quality and appearance. You should have enough large and handsome serving dishes. If guests are to perch with their plates just anywhere, you need to plan "lap" food that doesn't require cutting, such as dishes with meat sauce, or something like chicken Tetrazzini. It is customary now to serve the first course in the living room with whatever beverages are served. This could be eggs *en gelée* or *à la russe,* a fish mousse, or even a soup. Or the first course may be skipped and just hors d'oeuvres served with the beverages. As a general rule you need at least one hot dish at a buffet party. If you are set up to handle an elaborate buffet, you may want a hot section and a cold section.

The Ideas.

❋ Plan a buffet picnic to open your garden for the summer season as soon as it is primped and presentable. Set up individual tables with chairs. Cover tables with green-and-white-striped cotton denim cloths that you can make yourself to harmonize with the green of the trees and shrubbery. Decorate tables with attractive outdoor candles or hurricane lamps. Mark each lady's place with a small basket of garden flowers. Instead of the usual cookout, set up the prettiest possible buffet table covered with pink-and-white denim with a denim canopy (if your husband is handy) and centered with a basket or tub of leaves and mixed flowers. Prepare some of the most elegant dishes in your repertoire. Include at least one hot dish and a good wine.

❋ Wine-tasting parties to discover favorite wines became popular as this country gradually learned to like and drink wine. But a wine-tasting buffet is a good way to entertain, even if your palate is sophisticated. Call it a Wine and Roses Party and strive for elegance with a wealth of roses and your prettiest wineglasses. Provide a selection of several white wines and several red wines. Don't decant any of them, as guests will want to see the labels and note their favorites. As at dinner, white wines should be tasted first, then red. Have trays of cheese, crackers, and thinly sliced rye or pumpernickel. Finish with a light, fruity dessert such as a strawberry mousse, coffee, and perhaps champagne, the greatest wine of all. Give guests little note pads covered with rose-printed paper and small pencils attached for notations.

Charity Benefit

The Party. The openhearted generosity of Americans gives reason to the now-popular party to benefit a charity or good cause. The benefit has many advantages: it's a way to have a good time while doing a good deed; it's a direct way for a person

to become a part of a new neighborhood; and it's an easy party
for a not-too-well-acquainted group, as the cause itself is an
icebreaker and conversation-starter. The type of party really
doesn't matter. It can go all the way from a neighborhood morning coffee to a glittering ball for a thousand persons. Now
routine are benefit bridges and fashion shows for ladies, and
charity balls with husbands participating and paying. So when
you are involved in a benefit, look hard for an appealing theme
or a new idea. You might consider:

   Open House—In someone's home, with guests paying a
subscription to attend, or with a silver bowl at the door for
voluntary contributions.

   Open Gardens or Open Homes—In the spring have about
five or six beautiful gardens open for viewing. At the last
stop, have a refreshment tent and a flower cart filled with
potted plants and seeds to sell. Or at any time of year select
several noted houses for the tour. Sell tickets for either tour.

   Dinner Dance or Supper Dance—Sell tickets or tables. In
addition to dancing, various kinds of raffles, games, and auctions make additional money.

   Bazaar—Plan an indoor or outdoor bazaar. Specialize in
one kind of merchandise, or have a variety—"white elephants,"
handwork, books, flowers and plants, pictures, bakery goods.

   Boat Party—Charter a boat (if you are near water) for an
evening cruise. Sell tickets, box suppers, and beverages. Have
music for dancing—either live or records.

   Carnival—In a club, hall, church, or garden, arrange all
kinds of games for adults and children—darts, beanbags, horseshoes, pin the tail, and the like. Set up an ice cream parlor
or counter for refreshments. Sell tickets of admission, and
charge for games and food.

   Antiques Show—In a church, clubhouse, or garden, measure off booths for rental to local antiques dealers to exhibit

and sell their wares. Charge an entrance fee (75¢ or more), and sell refreshments, lunch, or dinner.

~~ *Art Show or Opening*—Tie in with a local art gallery and have a benefit opening for a new exhibition. Or exhibit pictures of local "Sunday painters." Admission by subscription.

~~ *Theater Party*—Reserve a block of seats at a special movie, concert, play, or musical. Charge a subscription over and above the regular admission.

~~ *Decoration and Design Exhibit*—Enlist local interior designers, a furniture store, or the furniture department of a department store to have a private opening of a group of newly decorated rooms. Or socialites or celebrities could be asked to decorate the rooms. Charge a subscription.

Everyone loves to dress up for a ball, but give your charity ball a thematic idea that makes it distinctive. For example, the most famous charity ball in New York is the annual April in Paris Ball originated by Elsa Maxwell and Claudius C. Philippe. Décor varies each year but is always French, fashions are flown over from the couture for a lavish show, French champagne is served, French perfumes are given as prizes, and frequently a French celebrity is imported for an appearance. Tickets are $150 each, and as much as $20,000 is raised in one evening. Another famous charity ball in New York is the Junior League's Mardi Gras Ball given on Shrove Tuesday. Climax of the evening is a pageant of costumes worn by members and the crowning of a queen who has distinguished herself by her service to the community. Costumes are designed and provided by various businesses that pay a fee to participate.

If you do sponsor a ball, try to have the expenses underwritten by one or more business organizations. They do it for the publicity, and it frees all receipts for the charity. In fact, for any kind of charity benefit, many items and services may be obtained in return for publicity in the program and elsewhere.

For a benefit bridge party, tables of four players are sold for a certain amount. Some parties are held in private homes, with the hostess providing refreshments. Prizes may be donated by sponsors or by local businesses. To arrange a charity fashion show, invite a local store to show their clothes. If members of the organization are young, with fairly good figures, the store may let members model. If professional models must be engaged, you may be asked to pay for these. Most large stores have a policy against taking clothes out of the store for a show, but many of them have clubrooms or tearooms that may be booked for the party, with the store providing the fashion show there. Tickets are sold to cover the refreshments served and a donation.

The souvenir journal or program is a vehicle that many balls use for raising additional money. Advertisements are sold by a committee to local businesses. Interspersed with the ads are names of chairman and committee members who organized the ball, patrons and patronesses, credits for donations of decorations, prizes and the like, name of orchestra, and possibly a menu. If you plan one, go to a good printer and ask him to advise you on how to put such a brochure together.

A strong chairman and good committees are essential for a successful benefit of any kind. These are the usual committees needed:

> Administrative (assists Chairman)
> Publicity
> Tickets
> Plans and Arrangements
> Entertainment
> Program
> Decoration
> Prizes

The Menu.   For casual charity affairs the food may be relatively simple, in order to earn as much money for the cause as possible. However, for a dinner or ball, the subscription should be high enough to allow for fine food. For some events you may be able to have food and food services donated.

The Ideas.

❋ At Christmastime plan a benefit tour of private homes or private clubs that are known for their seasonal decorations, including table settings. Serve hot mulled cider, Swedish glogg, or other hot drink at the last stop. Sell Christmas decorations and wrappings at one of the stops.

❋ Since everyone is fascinated by somebody else's cast-offs, "white elephants" and auctions hold equal interest. Combine the two by inviting friends to a Silent Auction as a benefit for your favorite charity. Ask each guest to bring along one or more unwrapped "white elephants." Appoint the least-inhibited guest as auctioneer. Give small pads of paper and pencils to bidders, and as items are put up for auction, those interested write down their names and bids. After bids are collected, highest bidder pays his money and takes home his choice. After all items have been sold, serve refreshments while happy customers compare bargains. Have a verbal auction if you prefer. Either can be very remunerative if guests have a competitive spirit.

❋ Next time you are on a committee to plan a charity dance, make it a Taxi Dance. Male guests must buy tickets to dance with the female guests. The girls sell drink and raffle tickets to the boys as they dance with them. All for the benefit of a favorite good cause.

❋ Combine forces within a group to give a progressive lunch in several homes to raise money for your church, temple, or favorite charity. Make soup course the first stop, main course the second, dessert and coffee the last. Stagger the beginning hour on the tickets so that all the people won't arrive at each home at the same time.

❋ Plan a Night on the Moon Ball as a charity event or to make money for your club. Ask female guests to wear their versions of moon headdresses. Drape the ceiling of the ballroom with deep-blue theatrical gauze—or a sheer fabric or net—sprinkled with silver stars. Cover tables with blue gauze over silver metallic fabric, and lay cutout silver stars on top. Center tables with silver candelabra holding blue candles. Award prizes for the most original and most beautiful headdresses. Make extra money by selling Deeds of Sale for land in Moonbeam Acres on the Moon (for fun, of course).

❋ Plan a Flea Market on a Saturday. Rent space to antiques dealers for their station wagons. Sales are all out-of-doors from wagon tailgates. An alternate date in case of rain is important. Market should be held in an enclosed area, if possible, so that admission may be charged. To make additional money, sell baked goods, ice cream, and cold drinks. Hang a sign at entrance, "MARCHÉ AUX PUCES" and dot other signs around, "BON MARCHÉ" (cheap or a bargain) and "SOLDE" (sale). Bookstalls, prints, and odd dishes would make good bargain tables. Glasses sell especially well.

❋ A Beaux Arts Ball will always capture the imagination of guests. This is traditionally an artists' ball, with no limitation on the type of costume—daring, lavish, or whatever. (Some French versions are little more than a coat of paint!) Have a grand march of the guests, with judges to award prizes for the most beautiful, most amusing, and most original costumes. Provide good music, and dance till dawn. Have a photographer on hand to take pictures of guests for a fee—or a quick-sketch artist.

❋ A teen-age group could make money for school or hospital by having a Cookie Cook-Off at holiday time. Hostesses should prepare ahead of time a large quantity of a basic cookie recipe —or several recipes. At a counter or table in the kitchen set out an array of trimmings: chocolate bits or kisses, gumdrops, colored sugar, chocolate shot, candy sprinkles, sesame seeds, cinnamon, raisins, nuts, currants, dates. Let couples compete as teams in originating cookies. Bake in relays on cookie sheets (borrow some). Give awards made from big cookies and ribbons. Have a cookie sale the following day at a public spot such as school or a local shop.

Children's Party

The Party. 2:30 to 4:30 or 3 to 5 P.M.; a noon lunch; or a 5 or 5:30 supper. For a successful children's party, it's important to plan carefully and follow a few basic rules. Don't invite more children than you can handle, or it will end up in bedlam. Also, keep the party small enough for all children to participate in the games. Twenty to 25 youngsters should be the maximum; much easier with 8 to 10. Young guests should be within the same age group, not more than a year or two apart. Afternoon is usually the best time for the party, unless it's lunch or supper, but you might also plan a Saturday morning party and give Father a chance to help. Birthdays are the most popular excuse for children's parties, but other reasons to celebrate might be:

the end of school
a visiting friend
decorating a Christmas tree
an Easter egg hunt
Valentine's Day
St. Patrick's Day
Halloween

Invitations in the mail not only delight children, but also inform the mothers where, when, and how long. Purchase printed invitations or make something original yourself. You can write invitations on inflated balloons with felt-tipped markers, which come in all colors, or with brush and India ink. Then deflate the balloons before the rubber becomes stretched, enclose in an envelope, and mail to guests. The children find the message when they blow up the balloons.

Plan a time schedule for activities to keep children from getting bored and restless, but without regimenting them. Allow only short periods for each activity, and have quiet games as well as lively ones to keep things on an even keel. For a little girl's party, a doll beauty contest appeals to their maternal instincts. Let them bring a favorite doll to parade. Avoid tears by having enough awards so that each child wins something for her doll—prettiest, largest, smallest, cutest, blondest.

Costume parties are usually popular because children like to dress up. And they love to hunt for almost anything, indoors or out—Easter eggs, pennies, peanuts, candy coins in foil, or small gifts. For a quiet game, wrap a prize in a small box. Put that box inside a larger one; wrap, and continue with larger and larger boxes, until there are 6 or 8 boxes within one big package. Ask the children to sit in a circle and pass the box from one to another while you play music, sing, or hum. When music stops, the child holding the package is allowed to unwrap the outer paper and open and remove the outer box. When music begins, guests start passing the package again and continue the same procedure till they are down to the prize itself. The last child to unwrap the final box finds and keeps the prize. Or the box could contain favors for all.

Always have lots of favors and prizes, because children love to take home loot. It is customary to provide gay paper bags that you can buy for this purpose, but you might give small tin pails to the sandbox set.

Children enjoy novel entertainment such as a puppeteer, clown, magician, cartoonist, accordionist, silhouettist, or an artist to sketch their pictures. Movie parties are fun if Mother has the composure to sit out a children's matinee. And if it's a movie that is unquestionably for youngsters. Or you could rent a short movie or cartoons to show at home (see pages 203-204).

It wouldn't be a party for a child without lots of decoration. The more festive it is, the more exciting the party. This is the time to forget understatement and restraint. The party area, whether inside or out, should be pretty and colorful, and should *look* like a party, with paper hats and horns and bright balloons. Anything that appeals to children can be used as a theme: fairy tales and favorite stories such as Snow White, circus, carnival, spacemen, cowboys, Indians, pets, or typical decorations for special holidays.

The Menu. Since children like only familiar foods, keep the menu simple. The same old things may seem unimaginative to you, but if you try the exotic, it won't be eaten. At a birthday party, a cake with candles is the highlight of the day. And the cake wouldn't be complete without ice cream, too. It can be served in balls, sliced from a brick, or in special ice cream molds shaped like animals or flowers. You might have at each place a small plastic bag or a box filled with homemade animal cookies and tied with ribbon, for the children to take home. When the party is lunch or supper, again, the familiar is safest—hamburgers, hot dogs, milk or soft drinks, cookies, ice cream. If it's an outdoor picnic, let them toast marshmallows over a grill. A box lunch or supper is an easy way to serve. Give each child a bright-colored tin lunch box to be taken home later. Don't stuff children with so many sweets they go home ill. Small portions are adequate. Always serve on a table; buffet service is for adults only. Use a paper tablecloth that carries out the party theme, or an inexpensive cotton one that can be easily laundered. For little girls, purchase bright-colored plastic bracelets from the 10-cent store as favors and use them for napkin rings. Several in different colors would be pretty on each napkin. For small children provide the paper bibs that adults use for eating lobster.

The Ideas.

* The interest in bowling that has swept the country has now reached down to the small fry. Some bowling lanes are equipped with lighter balls for children. A bowling party would be the answer to getting the children out of the house in bad weather. Let parents know the plan in advance, so that children won't be dressed in fancy party clothes. Send invitations in the shape of a bowling ball or pin. Plan to stay a

specific length of time, without overdoing it. Have prizes for best bowlers. If the bowling lane has a nice restaurant, as some do, let them have lunch, supper, or refreshments there. If it's a birthday party, take them back home for cake, and have a soda fountain set up with an assortment of ice cream and all the fixings for sodas and sundaes. Children love the extras—chocolate shot, colored sprinkles, cherries, and marshmallow topping. A counter or bar can be converted to make it as much like the real McCoy as possible. Set up one or two card tables if you haven't a more convincing counter. Give prizes for the gooiest and the prettiest, and a booby prize for the messiest sundae or soda.

❊ Children like to keep moving, so hire a school bus and driver for a "Bus Stop" party. Invite kiddies to meet at your house at a certain hour. Load them into the bus, with an extra mother or two to assist, and take off on a tour of several stops of interest to the particular age group. Make about three stops such as a zoo, a museum, and a place of local historical interest. Other ideas are amusement parks, fairs, pony ring, carrousels, city parks, art galleries, sightseeing points. During the bus rides between stops, distribute little favors. The last stop should be a favorite eating place for refreshments or a meal.

❊ Since most children's parties are M.C.'d by Mother, turn the table and have a children's party with dads taking over as hosts. Make it an Indians and Chiefs Party, with your husband and one or two other fathers as the Chiefs. You might go so far as to have paper headbands with a feather or two for each to wear. This is a perfect occasion for an outdoor party such as a hike through the woods, returning to your house for hearty refreshments. On the hike the children might watch for birds, search for pretty rocks, or gather leaves or flowers.

❊ The love of every child is his pet. Next children's party you give, make it a Pet Show. Dogs must be leashed, cats leashed or in carrying cases. Other pets children might bring are fish, birds, turtles, hamsters, lizards—even snakes! Have each child "show" his pet before judges (three mothers) and give prizes for the biggest, smallest, most unusual, prettiest. You can obtain prize ribbons at a party store, or make them yourself. Before serving the children their refreshments, set out all kinds of pet food and let them feed their pets. Then feed the small fry—and pack them off. Need we say, this party is best in summer out-of-doors!

Christening Party

The Party. A christening celebration calls for a certain amount of dignity and discrimination, since it is a sacramental day. Parents of the christened child like to make it a memorable occasion by sharing the day with relatives, the child's godparents, and close friends. Include the minister and his wife, if they are personal friends. The hour of the party can be any time after the ceremony. Since most guests want to see the baby, pick an hour that isn't nap time. A brunch or buffet luncheon immediately following the service is appropriate, or invite guests for tea, coffee, or punch in late afternoon. Decoration is simple— flowers or potted plants that can later be set out in the yard as a reminder of the occasion.

The Menu. Pick your menu according to the time of day and type of party. Any simple brunch or luncheon is appropriate, and for late afternoon small sandwiches, cake, cookies, nuts and mints with tea, coffee, punch, or sherry. You may want to have champagne for a toast to Baby, usually given by the godfather. If you have a cake, a white one is traditional.

The Idea.

❋ Take pictures (snapshots, movies, or stills) of guests, table decorations, and the baby, to keep for later years when the one christened will appreciate and treasure them. Take Polaroid pictures of the baby so that each guest can take one home.

Club Meeting

The Party. This might be a bridge or canasta group . . . sewing club . . . church, charity, or civic organization . . . a study or book-review group. Seating depends on what you plan to do, but be sure everyone has a seat, even if you have to rent folding chairs. If it's a sewing or study club, use little individual tables for the convenience of guests to hold scissors and thread or pencil and paper. For sewing, it's a help to have containers for scraps. Why not buy a few paper buckets such as house painters use and decorate them? If you're entertaining a card club, this usually means eager players, so have tables set up in advance. (See section on Bridge and Other Games, page 261.) Good lighting is important for cards or for sewing. If cold drinks are served, have plenty of coasters. A pitcher of water and glasses can be put on a sideboard.

At a lunch or dinner and card club, members usually enjoy eating and chatting as much as playing. For a small group, you can set up tables after eating, unless you plan to serve on them. Or set up tables in advance in a recreation room where they will be out of the way. If it's a large club, you'll save time and confusion by having tables ready in advance.

For the type of club that has a formal business meeting, see that the president or chairman has a place to sit where everyone can see her and that she has a small table for her notes, pencil, and gavel. The secretary will appreciate a table, too, since she must take minutes.

Decoration can tie in with the theme of the meeting if there is a definite objective; it can follow a holiday theme; or it can be nothing more than flowers. If you plan buffet service, have the dining table looking pretty.

The Menu. Clubs that have only refreshments should keep the menu simple and easy to serve. What you serve depends on the time of day. A morning meeting calls for coffee and something sweet. In the afternoon there is usually a choice of coffee or tea. In warm weather serve a cold punch, and in autumn vary the regular routine with mulled cider. Refreshments can include any of the following: nuts, mints, small sandwiches, nut bread, tea cakes, layer cakes, shortbread, cookies, petits fours, miniature cream puffs, small pastries, cheese straws, brownies, and date bars. Pie is all right for an early afternoon dessert meeting, but be sure it isn't the runny kind. Whatever you serve should be easy to handle, especially if guests must stand while eating. If the meeting is lunch or dinner, select a menu that will require the least amount of time for serving, in order to leave adequate time for the meeting to follow—unless yours is strictly an eating club!

The Ideas.

❋ In a small club of 8 to 16 members, draw names several months before the Christmas meeting for an exchange of gifts and specify that members must make, not buy, the gift. Hidden talents heretofore uncovered will become evident. Do whatever strikes your fancy, whether it's sewing, knitting, cooking, needlepoint, Christmas decorations, or ceramics. It's more fun without too many restrictions. Keep all gifts secret until the Christmas party. Open them at beginning of party and display the handiwork on a table for all to see and admire throughout the afternoon. Let this become an annual challenge to your group.

❋ In a large club (woman's club, church organization, etc.) have a Christmas lunch at your regular meeting place. Draw names in advance, or ask for volunteers to act as hostesses. Let each hostess design and set her table, making it as original and pretty as possible with linens and decorations from her own home. Ask a committee to serve as judges and award prize or ribbon to the best. Guests can circulate among tables before lunch and take notes on ideas to use in their homes. Hostesses also head the tables at lunch and help with serving. This gives a more personal touch to a large club party that might otherwise appear commercial.

❊ Organize a gourmet club of couples to meet periodically for a very special dinner. Plan a series of "An Evening in..." (Greece, Scotland, Italy, Portugal, or whatever countries interest you). Use décor and menu of the country. Let husbands bone up on the drinks of the countries for their contribution. The hostess at each meeting might type the foreign recipes for guests to take home.

❊ For a club of couples, schedule a Ladies' Night Party with the men taking over as hosts and the girls as guests. Let the men plan, shop for, and prepare the dinner—which may be a steak-and-potatoes feast indoors, or a cookout in summer. Give each host a man's cooking apron and a chef's hat. Let them work out their own assignments—bartender, saladmaker, etc. Be sure to appoint a cleanup committee!

Cocktail Party and Cocktail-Buffet

The Party.   We know we don't have to describe the all-American stand-up function, the cocktail party. Though it still serves a purpose as a strictly business party, socially it has become almost an outcast in many places. David Yunich, president of Macy's in New York, amusingly described a cocktail party as one to which the bright are invited and the dull come. So many hostesses have resorted to it as a kind of mass payoff of social obligations that many guests have become rebellious and simply stopped going. They tired of being jammed into a room so full of people that it rivaled a rush-hour subway, and they tired of being jostled against dripping drinks and smoldering cigarettes. However, the hostess who still likes to give cocktail parties can avoid this crush by following one simple rule. Invite only the number of people who can move about your home comfortably, leaving sufficient elbow room for all. Don't be tempted to stretch your guest list just because the house is clean, you've ordered flowers, and the silver and brass are polished. You'll end up with a clean slate as far as obligations are concerned, but you will have failed to give your guests a memorable evening with a chance for a pleasant interchange of conversation. And don't invite problem drinkers to a cocktail party. Put them on your guest list for dinner parties only.

Some couples have been known to send invitations to a large group for cocktails from 5 to 7 P.M. and then invite a selected small group to stay for a later supper. This is risky and can only lead to awkward and embarrassing situations. If some of the cocktails-only guests are caught in the party shift, they are uncertain whether to go or stay. It happened to us once, and we still don't know what was expected of us. Walking out on the buffet appeared rude, but eating it seemed worse, without invitation!

The cocktail-buffet now outshines the cocktail party in popularity and has become a pleasant kind of party. Guests are invited for a little later than the usual cocktail hour, from about 6 or 7 to 9 or 10. Cocktails and hors d'oeuvres are served first, followed by a buffet supper that may be quite simple or very elaborate. Or the buffet may be set up during the entire period of the party. Guests serve themselves and perch somewhere to eat. Because of the additional service of a supper, hostesses tend to cut guest lists to normal size and to be more selective than for a regular cocktail party, where the tendency is to squeeze in just one more. The cocktail-buffet differs from a regular buffet supper in that its menu is simpler, it may end considerably earlier, and it is a drop-in affair. If there is entertainment, it is only music. At a buffet supper all guests are served at the same time and are expected to stay the greater part of the evening, which may be devoted to games or other entertainment, or just talk. The only things needed in the way of decoration are flowers, leaves, and candles. If the party is on a special holiday or to celebrate a special occasion, decorations may tie in, as at Christmastime.

The Menu. One of the most important considerations at a cocktail party or a cocktail-buffet is a good bar. You don't have to have every kind and brand of liquor, but what you have should be good quality, and there should be plenty. (See purchasing guide, page 179.) The most popular drinks vary across the country, so have a selection of what your crowd likes. Then add a cocktail sherry, ginger ale, and another soft drink for those who prefer. Have a nice bar set up on a table or sideboard if you don't have a regular bar. Don't try to run back and forth to the kitchen mixing drinks. Remember to order or make plenty of ice, to cut some lemon peel, and to have soda, quinine water, and other mixers popular with your crowd. You will need several types of glasses—stemmed cocktails, double old-fashioned glasses that serve for both on-the-rocks drinks and highballs (we love old cut-glass water tumblers for this purpose), and sherry glasses.

When budget or limited help requires the simplest drink of all, serve a punch made of wine, champagne, or rum. At holiday time a wassail bowl or eggnog is a happy and festive solution for large groups. In England there are both sherry and champagne parties in addition to cocktail parties, and these are easy to handle, since there is no mixing of drinks. (See Sherry Party, page 315.)

Cocktail party food can be very simple. At one party the only food served with the drinks was long loaves of French bread, butter, cheese, and black olives. Dips are popular and easy to make, but tend to be a bit messy. Big bowls of icy-cold raw vegetables are delicious and calorie-low—carrot slivers, celery sticks, cauliflower buds, and green olives. It's nice to have both hot and cold hors d'oeuvres. It used to be a chore to make hot ones, but there are many frozen ones now that you just pop in the oven or broiler for a few minutes.

Most men prefer a platter of meat, such as cold sliced ham or turkey. With deboned meat easily available, the slicing no longer presents a problem. Near the meat platter place a tray of assorted breads, small slices that can be easily managed. Guests can make little sandwiches if they wish. One or two large cheese balls, with plenty of crackers for spreading, and hot meat balls could round out this menu. Or fill in with bowls of sautéed pecan halves, a pâté, and some of the special tidbits that can be purchased in jars and cans in every conceivable flavor. All of these things can be prepared by the least experienced hostess. Among the easiest and most delicious hot hors d'oeuvres are *quiche Lorraine* and *tarte à l'oignons*. See also "The Cocktail Hour," page 174, and "Pre-Dinner Snacking," page 175.

If you turn your next cocktail party into a cocktail-buffet, see page 268 for menu suggestions.

The Ideas.

❋ Add zest to your next cocktail party by making it a cocktail-buffet dansant. Invite guests from 7 to 10 P.M. Give the party all the elements of the cocktail-buffet, with a good bar and delectable food throughout. Clear one or more rooms of furniture and rugs, and polish up the floors so your guests can have a dance or two when they drop in. A small local combo or a well-edited stack of records provides the inspiration. If you have teen-agers in the house, bribe them to be on hand to coach guests in the newer dances. You'll probably have to play "Good Night, Ladies" to get your guests to go home!

❋ If you are moving to another neighborhood or another city and want to say farewell and thank-you to old neighbors and friends, plan a Housecooling—the opposite of a housewarming. After you are packed and crated, engage a bartender for the night before the move and have a bash. Cover boxes and crates with paper tablecloths, and use paper plates and napkins—the smartest you can find.

❋ Invite friends to a cocktail-buffet and arrange a Do-It-Yourself Sandwich Buffet. Provide a lavish assortment of sandwich makings and a variety of breads in baskets. Selection might include roast beef, corned beef, chicken, ham, sliced smoked turkey or other cold sandwich meats, cole slaw, pickles, cheese,

condiments, lettuce, and an assortment of mustards and dressings. With dessert and coffee, it's an easy menu for a large
guest list, and one an inexperienced hostess can handle.

❋ A Cocktail-Buffet "Happening" could be an amusing evening for your crowd. Set up a "studio" in one room (a game
room is a good place) or in a convenient corner. On a large
easel or against the wall stand a large blank canvas that has
been mounted on a stretcher (purchase from an art supply
store). With a pencil lightly divide the canvas into the same
number of squares as there are guests. Provide oil or poster
paints, long-handled brushes, a pair of artist's smocks, and
turpentine with gay cotton cloths for cleaning hands. During
the cocktail period, let each guest (or couple) wander over
and paint a square in any way he wishes. The first painter
may choose the beginning square, but each succeeding painter
must use a square adjacent to what has already been painted.
You may want to give the "happening" painting a name that
guests must use as inspiration. Follow with the buffet supper.
Arrange a still life of fruit, vegetables, flowers, or inanimate
objects. After the buffet, have a drawing and award the "happening" to the winner to take home.

❋ Follow the lead of one country club we know by giving a
Firewater Fling—a cocktail dance. Humorous golf rules are
provided for couples who want to play preceding the fling.
You could eliminate the golf and make it cocktails and dancing from 6 to 9, or a cocktail-buffet and dancing from 7 to 10
or 11. This calls for a rock 'n' roll combo and plenty of action!

❋ Europeans appear to enjoy their pre-dinner apéritif in a more
leisurely fashion than Americans do their cocktails. Try their
formula by making your next cocktail party an Apéritif Party.
Feature such drinks as Dubonnet, Lillet, Cinzano, Pernod.
They are less expensive than liquors and may be served plain
or on the rocks. Provide lemon and orange peel. (To prevent
having any unhappy guests, you may want to have handy a
choice of several cocktails.) Europeans also avoid rich hors

d'oeuvres, so make your accompanying fare simple, such as cheeses, crackers, and perhaps a pâté. For a Champs Elysées or Via Veneto influence, set up some small tables in one room or in corners where they won't obstruct traffic, so that guests may sit down to chat. One strolling musician would be pleasant at such a party.

Coffee Party

The Party. 10 A.M. to 12 noon. The only outstanding accomplishment required for giving a morning coffee is to be a superfast bedmaker. The rush to get things shipshape by 10 in the morning may leave you breathless, but anyone should be able to manage a simple morning party that requires little in the way of preparation or serving equipment. It's an inexpensive way to entertain, too. Of course, you can make it elegant if you wish. You'll find between 6 and 25 guests the best number to invite. A friendly way to get people together just to visit, to meet a new neighbor, to honor a friend, or to call a committee meeting. Although it's usually a ladies-only affair, we've found that the men love to be included on a weekend or holiday. If you wish to entertain a large number of couples with a non-alcoholic party, this is the way to do it. In fact, a morning coffee has such flexibility that it has contributed considerably to the social calendar of wives almost everywhere in this country. (A coffee party is also a good solution for a weekend or holiday brunch, or as an after-dinner party.)

The Menu. A coffee always means buffet service. Guests sit, stand, or circulate. Good hot coffee (or iced in summer) is the most important menu item. Always serve cream and granulated or lump sugar, and saccharin tablets for those who use them. There are also brown rock and pastel-tinted sugars. Serve some of the fancy blends of coffee found in coffeehouses. (See page 173 for other coffee suggestions.)

The menu can be as simple as a good coffee cake and bite-size

doughnuts from a bakery for the easy-does-it hostess. But for
the one who enjoys baking, there are many other goodies: homemade sweet muffins, nut bread, crumb cakes, biscuits, and un-
iced tea cakes. Just be sure the food isn't too rich. If butter is
served, use whipped or honey butter for easy spreading. Include
something non-sweet such as ham, bacon, or sausage in tiny rolls,
little cheese biscuits, or *tarte au fromage* (cheese pie). Fresh fruit
always makes a hit—strawberries with stems and a powdered-
sugar dip, melon balls, chunks of fresh pineapple served with
picks, and fresh cherries with stems.

The Ideas.

❋ There are so many new taste experiences emerging all the
   time that "tasting" parties are a sure hit. Since America's
   coffee tastes are becoming more sophisticated, try a Coffee
   Tasting Party. We suggest this for a mixed party between
   11 and 2 on a Saturday or Sunday, to take the place of brunch
   or lunch, or as an after-dinner party. Basics are quantities of
   regular American coffee and Italian espresso. Then provide
   all the embellishments you can think of: sugar cubes, un-
   refined sugar (which the British always use), multicolored
   sugar, hot milk, plain coffee cream, whipped cream, lemon
   and orange twists, brandy and liqueurs, hot chocolate, chocolate curls, cinnamon and nutmeg. This is the occasion to use
   a collection of cups and mugs, if you have one. You might
   provide mimeographed or handwritten sheets on how to make
   some of the foreign coffee drinks (see page 173). Or let guests
   compose and name their own recipes, writing them on cards
   or sheets of paper provided. Give a prize of a coffeepot, a
   basket of special blends of coffee, or a funny present of a can
   of coffee, for the most original. For a midday party, serve not-
   too-sweet coffee cakes, thinly sliced nut breads, and bacon
   sandwiches in tiny rolls. For after dinner, make it simple
   sweets, mints, and nuts. Avoid richness, as the coffees are likely
   to be rich themselves.

❋ Invite friends for coffee and ask them to bring a bundle for your local thrift shop. Park a station wagon in the driveway. Have the tailgate open and toward the street, so that as guests arrive they can deposit bundles in the wagon. This does away with clutter in the house and spares the hostess the unpleasant job of loading the car. Later, simply haul away the labeled (for tax-deduction purposes) rummage.

The Dance

The Party. The country has gone crazy over dancing, so the small, or not so small, dance in a home has come back as one of the most enjoyable ways of entertaining a group. It's easier than you may think, but there are certain requisites for a successful event:

❋ Forget about having the furniture in its proper place. Remove as much of it as possible to another room. Some enthusiasts have gone so far as to have a moving van cart it away for the evening. Others have whisked it into the garage.

❋ Have tables and chairs for "sitting out" and for supper.

❋ Have something liquid, such as punch, available throughout the whole evening to quench the thirst of the dancers.

❋ Good music is essential, even if only from records. If you have space and it is a sizable party, engage a combo to provide appropriate music. If you use records, organize them carefully beforehand, so that the different types are well spaced.

❋ Be sure your floor is in a condition conducive to dancing. It should look presentable, be clean, and be waxed but not slippery. If you prefer to keep the parquet flawless, there are portable dance floors made in panels to be placed over floors or rugs and taped together. They can then be untaped and stored until the next dance. You can also rent portable dance floors (see page 215).

❈ A buffet or supper should be served around midnight or a little after. If it's a young group that dances all night, scramble some eggs at dawn, as they'll be ravenous.

A dance at home would start between 10 and 11 o'clock in a large city, possibly between 9 and 10 in a smaller community. It would break up after supper around 1 or 2 in the morning, unless young people want to dance on and on. Naturally, for teen-agers, the hours would be earlier, as they should start home around midnight unless permitted to stay out later for a special occasion. However, this is usually for a prom not held in a home.

Decorations may be as simple or as elaborate as you like. A theme may be carried out such as An Evening at the Lido (Paris or Venice!). Your individual tables should look as pretty as possible, with tablecloths, candles, little lamps or other centerpieces, and your nicest table settings. The supper buffet table can have a centerpiece of flowers and candles, or something that harmonizes with the theme.

To keep the dancing lively, invite all the single men you know. A ratio of two men to a distaff guest isn't too much. The host should, of course, try to dance with as many feminine guests as possible—certainly with the guest of honor, if there is one—and at least once with his wife.

Unless all the guests know each other well, it's helpful and amusing to intersperse some mixers along with the regular dances. Try the Circle, with couples dancing in a circle formation or formations; when music stops, girls move clockwise to the next partner, and dancing continues until the music stops again. Or feature a Chain dance, with one couple starting the dancing, when music stops, each partner quickly chooses another and continues to dance until music stops again. Dancing continues until all are on the floor.

During the dancing and for the supper, let guests sit wherever they please at the tables. Of course, the host and hostess may direct the traffic and help guests find places.

If your dance is to be held in a hotel, club, or other outside place, it follows the same pattern (see Chapter 8 for information on making arrangements). In this event you would greet your guests at the door of the private room, be sure they are introduced to several others, that they know where the bar or punch table is, and that they know where to sit. Usually they sit wherever they like. Live music is almost always used at a dance outside the home. However, the discothèque has made records acceptable. The waiters can set the tables just before serving the supper, instead of having flatware and napkins on the buffet. Or guests may serve themselves at a buffet.

The Menu. You will want to have the buffet supper table set up and arranged in advance, so plan a punch bowl or bar elsewhere for serving beverages throughout the evening. A nice punch will suffice, and is easier and less expensive than a complete bar. You can rent the punch bowl and cups, if you don't own them. Be sure to provide several soft drinks, such as cola, for those who prefer. Have cigarettes and ashtrays on your small tables. At suppertime, all you have to do to convert the tables is to put on clean ashtrays and a new supply of cigarettes and add lovely wineglasses. Have the flatware and napkins on the buffet table to be picked up by the guests. Make the supper simple, but good and plentiful. A hot dish such as lobster Newburg, curry of shrimp or chicken, or creamed chicken, with rice and green peas is sufficient. Champagne is ideal, but a chilled white wine or rosé will do. Add an ice cream bombe, petits fours, and demitasses.

The Ideas.

❊ Nothing is more romantic than the thought of dancing your way to a foreign land on a luxury liner, or dancing on a fabulous private yacht. So invite guests to a dance on board the S. S. Smith (your own name, of course), leaving Pier 123 Riverway Road (your address). Buy nautical invitations or cards, if you can. Use nautical blue and white with accents of red in your decorations—blue tablecloth and white napkins with red-and-white centerpiece; or white tablecloth, red or blue napkins, with red-and-blue centerpiece. Rent a commodore's or captain's cap for your husband to wear while receiving. Use the obvious motifs of anchors, life preservers, and sailor's caps as decoration wherever they will fit in. But as always, don't overdo it. Bon voyage!

* "Intimate and elegant" might describe the little dances now being given, frequently at home. Having a ball in a small way—not more than 50 guests—makes a far more personal party and avoids the crush of the frequently over-extended guest lists of the big balls. Pick a color and ask feminine guests to dress in any tone they choose of the one color. A small club or several couples might combine efforts. Carry the featured color throughout.

* Today's dances demand uninhibited motion and are best done in pants for women as well as men. So theme your next rock 'n roll dance as a St. Tropez Party, named for the Mediterranean mecca for women in pants. Note on the invitations, "Everyone's for pants!" Provide the hottest music in town—best from a live combo—a good floor, a never-ending flow of good drink, "with-it" guests, and a light supper (or breakfast) to end the festivities. A night to remember!

* The Thirties are far enough away to make an interesting period piece. So plan a party themed to this decade of gorgeous blond movie queens like Carole Lombard and Jean Harlow. Make it a "tea" dansant on Saturday or Sunday afternoon. Emphasize top tunes of the period and the fox trot. To be really far out, ask feminine guests to wear blond wigs. Serve champagne punch.

* It adds to the gaiety to have a theme for a dance, and sometimes to make it a costume party. Try such ideas as:

   A Snow Ball with feminine guests wearing white dresses or white Snow Queen headdresses. Use white decorations.

~~ A Block Ball if you live on a congenial block. Dance in the street . . . have a teen end and an adult end, with punch and soft drink tables in between.

~~ On a summer evening when your lawn is at its best, have a Dancing-on-the-Green Party. Use lanterns and supplement your garden with blooming potted plants. Many of the modern dance steps are as easily done on the grass as on a polished floor. Specify sports clothes. Music may be recorded. Provide refreshment table and lawn chairs for sitting out. Similarly, a Poolside Hop could be given by a pool.

~~ A Night on the Moon Ball, see page 273.

~~ Beaux Arts Ball, see page 274.

The Debut

The Party.   The debut, which used to be limited to a few very large or very social cities, has spread across the country and is a civilized and charming custom to cultivate. If it has never been a part of the social life of your city, organize a group of your friends who have daughters around 18 years old for a group debut. The group debut can also be sponsored by an organization, or it can become a charity function for raising money. When the debut started, it actually was a symbolic launching of a daughter into society. Today, with young people starting their own kind of social life in the early teens, it is more a symbol of a girl's entrance into adult society, and is a reason for a season of parties and fun.

The debut may take the form of an at-home or reception with dancing, a dinner with dancing, or a dance. It is given by a girl's parents, grandparents, or other close sponsor such as a guardian, unless it is a group affair. The rules for these kinds of parties apply (pages 289, 296, 309). More formality is observed, and there are certain rules of dress. The debutante wears a white long formal dress for a dinner or dance. It may be trimmed with a pastel color; or the girls may elect to wear pastel dresses or white as they please. At a late afternoon reception, the guest of honor may wear a short white or pastel cocktail-type dress although in some cities it is customary to wear a long dress almost like an evening dress.

The debutante receives with her mother, while her father takes care of the pleasure of the guests. She has her first dance with her father. In the case of group debuts, the girls receive with their parents in a receiving line (at some large New York debutante cotillions, only the girls themselves are in the receiving line). There may be a formal presentation of the girls in a march or special dance that has been rehearsed beforehand. Engage the combo or orchestra that the young people love—not the one you prefer. The best possible music for dancing is essential. Following a girl's debut, there is a round of parties given for her and the other debutantes throughout the season—luncheons, dinners, dances. So the whole thing is one wonderful whirl for a girl.

The Menu.   Service would follow the pattern for whatever kind of party is chosen. Naturally it should be the finest available and with the prettiest decorations.

The Idea.   Just make it the prettiest and most memorable party possible. Use all the flowers you can afford in the decorations. The room for dancing or the ballroom may be draped in fabric to resemble a tent, or it may be literally lined with flowers and greenery. A color scheme of one or two colors should be carried throughout. A summer debut could of course take place outdoors in a tent erected for the purpose. Provide good company, music, food, and drink.

Dessert Party

The Party.   If you are looking for an easy, inexpensive, and versatile way to entertain, the Dessert Party is made to order. It's probably the easiest party to do, can be completely non-alcoholic, and thus is inexpensive. The food may be entirely purchased, if time and talent are a problem, or may be easily prepared by yourself ahead of time. For a busy mother, this party is certainly the answer. It's appropriate for a distaff group after lunch (about 2 o'clock), or for a mixed group after dinner (about 8 or 9 o'clock). You can follow the dessert service with bridge or some other game, with a shower for a guest of honor, a committee meeting—or just talk. Because of the ease of preparation and serving, the guest list can be stretched as far as you want to go. Follow any theme, or simply fill the house with flowers and leaves. Serve from a buffet table, but be sure it is as pretty as you can possibly make it. Or wheel around a dessert cart, and serve the coffee from a coffee table. Dessert is the climax to a meal—so make it look so. If bridge or games are to follow, you can use the game tables covered with pretty cloths for serving beforehand, or let guests sit informally wherever they please.

The Menu.   Since you will want to present a beautiful table, plan the menu around your nicest dishes, silver, and serving pieces. Of course, the dessert itself is the most important consideration. You might provide a lavish selection of desserts, such as a tray of fancy pastries, a special strawberry cheesecake, a compote of mixed fruits, and a variety of petits fours and cookies. Or set out a do-it-yourself table of several flavors of ice cream with fabulous fixings such as hot and cold fudge sauce, whipped cream, chopped nuts, crème de menthe, marrons, fruit, melba sauce. The best hot coffee you can make, caffein-free coffee, and tea are essentials. You might want to add a special beverage, such as caffè espresso. Complete the feast of sweets with compotes of plain and chocolate mints. If it is an evening party, you may want to offer liqueurs after the dessert, or highballs a little later.

The Idea.   To honor a new arrival in town or in the neighborhood, plan an afternoon dessert party to introduce the newcomer to your friends. Use as your table centerpiece something that suggests a characteristic of your city or something the city is famous for. In Boston it could be a handsome big bean pot filled with an informal bouquet of mixed flowers and leaves; in New Orleans, decorate the table with fluted paper balls, serpentine, and other paper carnival items; in Phoenix, use a cluster of pots of cactus plants. Every town or city has something distinctive. As a welcoming gift for the newcomer, purchase a pretty loose-leaf notebook with alphabetical index dividers. Ask each guest to write out on notebook pages her favorite addresses in town—the butcher, the baker, the shoemaker, the best restaurants, the hairdresser, where to get the poodle clipped and the cat boarded. So that the guest of honor will have a record of her new acquaintances, ask each guest to sign her recommendations: "Recommended by Mary Sanders, 123 River Drive, Plaza 4321."

Dinner

The Party.   A beautiful dinner party is the "Tiffany" of entertaining, and a compliment to your guests. On the other hand, it is probably the most difficult party to arrange, as it requires real cooking ability (or an able cook), much planning and work, and a great deal of time. Every hostess should learn to produce such a party creditably. A great deal of business entertaining revolves around dinners, as it is a harmonious way of meeting and negotiating—or getting acquainted before negotiations at another time. It is the best kind of party at which to get to know people. Eight is an ideal number for a dinner at home, as most houses will accommodate this number comfortably, almost everyone has table service for at least 8, and most recipes are scaled for 8. Although it requires a bit of practice and skill, a hostess can cook and serve a dinner for 8 without any help at all. Even 12 or 16 can be handled at home without help, but this is about the limit that most talented hostesses invite. Naturally, if you are the lucky owner of a staff of servants, you can go all out.

A theme appropriate for the occasion or season can be carried out in the décor, or it may be only flowers, greens, and fruit. If budget is a consideration, this is one time when it is better to spend it on excellent food than on fancy decorations. A beautifully set table is decoration enough. For suggestions on seating, place cards, and serving, see pages 138 and 187 to 192.

The Menu. Most hostesses serve cocktails or other drinks before dinner, with husband or bartender in charge. Dinner can be a simple three-course affair or a more elaborate five or six courses. Mrs. John F. Kennedy led the trend to fewer courses when she was First Lady by instituting the four-course, two-wine dinner. Basic courses are:

Three-Course Dinner	*Four-Course Dinner*	*Five-Course Dinner*
Soup, shellfish, melon, or fruit	Soup, shellfish, melon, or fruit	Shellfish, melon, or fruit
		Soup
Main course (meat, fish, or fowl) and salad	Main course (meat, fish, or fowl)	Main course (meat, fish, or fowl)
	Salad	Salad
Dessert and coffee	Dessert and coffee	Dessert and coffee

Serve at least one wine with dinner, or champagne throughout. If you wish, offer a liqueur with the coffee, and a highball later. See Chapter 5 for complete details on menu planning, the cocktail hour, and dinner wines.

The Ideas.

❊ Spain, a country of beauty, dignity, and romance, has captured the imagination of Americans. So plan an elegant Spanish dinner served late à la Madrid. Regular time for dinner there is between 10 and 11 P.M. Instead of American cocktails, serve Spanish sherry, salted almonds, and olives about 9 P.M. Start the dinner with the famous Spanish cold soup,

gazpacho. Follow with the main dish of Spain, paella. And
finish off with the Spanish custard, flan, as dessert. Check cookbooks in the local library for recipes, if you don't have them.
Use hot colors and Spanish flags in the decoration. A Spanish
dancer or guitarist would make wonderful entertainment, or
a pile of Spanish records.

❊ Travelers love to share their experiences with each other, so
if yours is a traveling set, plan a Globe-trotters Gabfest in the
fall after vacations. Ask an airline to cooperate by giving you
ticket envelopes for the invitations. Decorate with travel
posters and folders. Ask guests to bring any special objects
that they have brought back from foreign travel, and exhibit
the treasures on a felt-covered table. For dinner serve any foreign dishes, from Polynesian punch to Egyptian shish kebabs.
You or some of the guests may have interesting movies or
slides to show. But be sure they are interesting. Otherwise,
spend the evening exchanging experiences. This theme could
also be used for a lunch or after-dinner party.

❊ Chinese New Year's Day is an interesting holiday to celebrate.
It falls on a different day in January or February each year,
(check your laundryman!) and each year has its own sign or
insignia. The 12-year cycle, which keeps repeating, is:

1967	Year of the Ram
1968	Year of the Monkey
1969	Year of the Rooster
1970	Year of the Dog
1971	Year of the Boar
1972	Year of the Rat
1973	Year of the Bull
1974	Year of the Tiger
1975	Year of the Rabbit
1976	Year of the Dragon
1977	Year of the Snake
1978	Year of the Horse
1979	Cycle starts repeating with the Ram.

Decorate dinner table with Oriental objects such as Chinese dolls, fans, parasols. Seat guests at the traditional round table and serve one dish at a time from the center of the table. These courses are authentic, and any or all may be served in any order desired: cold cuts, hot soup, fowl (chicken), seafood (may have two, such as shrimp and lobster), beef, pork, vegetables, squab. You might be able to arrange with a Chinese restaurant to prepare all or part of the dishes. Also, there are some excellent frozen Chinese foods available. Oriental rice bowls can be found in many gift stores, and fortune cookies at the supermarket. Give chopsticks as favors, and have a prize for the one who best conquers the art of using them.

❋ Transport your guests on an imaginary trip to the French Riviera for a Friday night Bouillabaisse Supper. This is the famous fish stew or soup from the south of France. Find a recipe in a gourmet cookbook, and serve it from a handsome big earthenware tureen into earthenware bowls. Add a salad Niçoise and French bread or rolls and butter. Finish with fruit and cheese, a demitasse. Cover tables with fishnet and shells.

❋ Give a Sukiyaki Dinner with guests seated on cushions on the floor. Have them remove shoes before entering the house, and give them paper slippers or "tabbies." Serve on trays placed on mats. Use any Oriental items as decoration and provide chopsticks.

❋ Invite a group of weight-conscious dieting friends to a Calories-Do-Count Dinner. Plan the best menu possible with the fewest calories. Use diet foods (supermarkets usually have a whole section of these), but give them a special twist (a useful book to consult is *The Gourmet in The Low-Calorie Kitchen*, by Helen Belinkie, McKay, 1961). Print decorative menus, leaving space for calories to be filled in. Ask each guest to guess the number of calories in each dish and the calorie total for the dinner. Give a prize of a diet book or low-calorie cookbook for the one whose guess is nearest the correct number, a bottle of low-calorie cola drink as booby prize.

✤ Plan a Bavarian Biergarten party for a summer evening. Ask male guests to wear shorts and shirts (lederhosen are traditional in Bavaria), female guests to wear dirndl skirts and blouses. Instead of cocktails, serve seidels (steins) of beer with trays of sausages and cheese, and baskets of thinly sliced pumpernickel. Highlight the dinner menu with sauerbraten (pot roast), potato pancakes, and applesauce. Serve at tables covered with blue-and-white (colors of Bavaria) checked cloths and informal centerpieces of garden flowers. Pile some records of student drinking songs or folk music on the record player. Include a yodeling record and have a yodeling contest.

Engagement Party

The Party.   An engagement in the family is a clarion call for a party. While an announcement in the newspaper can suffice to break the news of a daughter's engagement, you will want to celebrate with a party. Or you can spring the announcement at the party as a grand surprise and follow with the newspaper announcement. Since parents (or guardians) announce the engagement of a daughter, they are the hosts for the party. You can make the announcement party strictly distaff at a lunch or tea, or you can choose a cocktail party, dinner, or reception for a mixed guest list. A party to celebrate the engagement after the announcement has been made is almost always a mixed affair in the late afternoon or evening. Follow our suggestions in this chapter for parties of this sort. Decorations should be pretty and can go a bit sentimental, but use restraint. Flowers and candlelight are the proper atmosphere. Leaves and fruit are pretty in the fall, and Christmas greens at the holiday season. You can add hearts and cupids if you do it with a light touch. Guests at an engagement party are, of course, family members and good friends of both the bride and the groom. This is not a time to invite casual acquaintances or pay off social debts.

The announcement of the engagement may be made in various ways but should never be too "gimmicky." At a party for all ladies, you might have the initials or first names of the couple lettered on a large cake or on small individual cakes— PB and RC, or Patricia and Ronald. Or the engaged girl may receive with her mother, wearing her new engagement ring. At a mixed party, the engaged couple may receive with the parents and tell each guest, or the girl's father may make the announcement in a toast, preferably champagne, at a reception or during the dessert course at a dinner. His toast might be something like, "I propose a toast filled with joy and happiness to my daughter Patricia and to Ronald, her fiancé."

The Menu. What you serve depends upon the kind of party. Whatever the menu, it should be especially chosen for the nicest possible service. At a luncheon, plan a pretty dessert, such as a molded mousse with petits fours. Fancy sandwiches and cakes should adorn the table at a tea. Though the atmosphere of a cocktail party is more sophisticated than pretty, do try to make the canapés especially attractive. Order ice cream molds for a dinner dessert. For a reception, concentrate on a beautiful punch bowl. Naturally, all dishes, silverware, and linens should be your finest.

The Idea. If the happy time has arrived for you to announce a daughter's engagement, plan a Mother-and-Daughter Tea to include guests of the two age groups from among your close friends. Use your daughter's favorite pastel color in the decorations. To break the news, have a basket piled full of fortune cookies with the names of the betrothed written on little slips of paper inside: Marian and John. (Order them made by a local bakery or by an Oriental restaurant that serves them.) Decorate the basket with a ribbon bow and a flower tied to the handle. Pour tea from a small table in the living room, if it is a small group. If not, use the dining room table and ask one of the mothers to pour.

Large Group Parties

The Party. Although most women prefer to give parties of moderate size, almost every woman is called upon to entertain a very large group at some time during her life. The occasions might be a party for a club, a neighborhood, an office, a high school class, sorority or fraternity alumni, an engagement party, a wedding reception, or you may be chairman of a church or organization event. Such a party appears to be an insurmountable task to some, but if handled efficiently, it *can* be fun—even for the hostess! This is the time when no detail can be slighted, and nothing can be left to chance.

If your guest list begins to take on the proportions of a mob scene and simply can't be cut down to size, consider renting a club or hotel room. You and your house—even the guests—might be better off without the stress and strain involved. On occasions when you prefer to use your home, yet find it difficult to limit the guest list, home facilities must be stretched to capacity. (See Chapters 7 and 8.)

If the party is a joint effort for an organization, either at home or elsewhere, appoint working committees for invitations, food, decorations, serving, entertainment, and especially cleanup. If it is a private party and the hosts are alone in the venture, be sure to start planning early. Issue invitations three or four weeks before the party so that you will know well in advance how many to plan for. Don't forget to consider parking problems involved and let guests know where to park, if special arrangements must be made.

When weather permits, it's a pleasant arrangement for a large group to overflow to the out-of-doors. But it's unrealistic to set your heart on this plan when you consider the uncertainty of the weather. After food has been prepared for 60 to 75 people, you have reached the point of no return and must carry on with the party, rain or shine. So plan within the realm of how many can be entertained inside and how you can best do it. Of course, you're safe with a covered porch, but if you must make use of an open terrace and yard, the only way to keep plans running smoothly is to rent in advance a large canopy or tent. Since this might have to be put up two or three days before the party, there is no canceling out at the last moment if the sun shines brightly. This adds a sizable expense to the party, but may be worth it to have peace of mind, and it does add a certain splendor, besides. One of our neighbors planned a wedding reception in her garden and, as fate would have it, the wedding day brought a drizzling rain. But the hostess could remain calm as she surveyed the beautiful big canopy that covered the terrace and half the yard, her party insurance.

When guests arrive, be sure there is someone at the door to greet them. If you have children old enough to take this responsibility, they can be very helpful. Or you could ask one or two friends to assist you. (See page 182 for details concerning arrival of guests.)

Make as much of your house available to guests as possible, so that they will spread out into smaller groups. Remove any possible hazards, such as a footstool that might trip an unsuspecting guest, or a coffee table that monopolizes the center of the floor. Our experience at large parties has been that guests persist in congregating around the buffet or bar, and it's next to impossible to pry them loose. Often two or three adjoining rooms are virtually empty. It's a wise hostess who anticipates this bottleneck and devises a few schemes to prevent it. Have something in each room you plan to use, that will attract the guests. The buffet could be in one room, bar in another (or two bars and two buffets), hi-fi in another, and perhaps games in a recreation room, either upstairs or down. If your guests still fail to circulate, ask a friend to entice some into another area. One couple hired a pair of folk singers for their big party and made sure that the musicians moved from room to room instead of remaining in one spot where guests might be tempted to crowd around. If the party is casual, and you plan to use several different levels or areas of your home, make decorative little signs with arrows indicating the different points of interest, or post signs over the doorways of the various rooms. Guests then feel free to wander and are not afraid of going off limits.

Open house, tea, and cocktail parties are not only stand-up, but also drop-in affairs, so that all guests are not present at the same time. Seating is then no problem. But when a lunch or supper is served, additional chairs must be provided. Certainly guests don't expect everyone to have his very own chair at a large party—they often perch on stairs to eat—but try to have enough small folding chairs tucked in corners to give at least adequate seating. If you plan to use your yard, set up tables and chairs outside.

Decorations can be flowers, greens, fruit, or anything indicative of the season or the occasion. Just be sure to place any large arrangements where they will be out of the way and won't be turned over accidentally. For suggestions on flowers, music, and entertainment see pages 130, 139, and 198 to 205.

The Menu. We recommend that you have some help in either preparing the food or serving, if you want to enjoy the party. The type of menu depends, of course, on type of party. If you prepare the food yourself, it's important to work out quantities in advance. There are recipe books that solve this problem for you, but if you use your own favorite recipes scaled for average amounts, carefully figure proportions and measurements as soon as you decide on the menu. Buying for large parties is economical because you can purchase the largest-size containers. One of the greatest problems when preparing food at home is insufficient refrigerator space. Be sure to take this into consideration when purchasing perishables.

Drinks can be served from one large punch bowl (see page 144). If you are serving a complete meal, don't undertake a great variety; prepare a few things skillfully. A large party in a home is almost always a buffet, so when planning the menu be sure everything can be eaten with the least equipment possible —finger food or food that can be eaten with a fork. The following dishes are practical for quantity serving: platters of assorted cold meats, or sliced ham or turkey; casseroles; salads such as chicken, potato, shrimp, or one all-inclusive green salad with raw vegetables and meats added. Easiest dessert is finger food that can be placed right on the saucer with the coffee cup. An assortment of cookies is adequate, if they are very special ones.

The following guide will help you when purchasing coffee for a very large party: a pound and a half of regular coffee or three 2-ounce jars of instant coffee will make 60 cups. So few people use sugar in their coffee now, a pound should be adequate for about 60 cups. Cream is also used less and less, so 1½ quarts should be more than enough for 60 cups.

Although we usually favor pretty linens, paper napkins of good quality are permissible at a large informal party. Dishes and linens can be rented in quantity (see page 215), and for casual outdoor parties some of the sturdy, plastic-coated paper plates could be used.

The Ideas.

❋ Next time you are chairman of a church or club dinner, make it a round-robin affair to get people acquainted. Long tables are generally used at these large dinners, and guests tend to converse only with persons next to them and sometimes never meet the ones at the other end of the table. Let the ladies keep their places, but ask the men to change places at the end of each course. If each man moves past two ladies, he will then be seated between two different ladies. If guests are seated at card tables, have the men progress to the next table between courses. If the dinner is a "ladies only" affair, let every third person do the moving.

❋ The urban life of apartment dwellers is often condemned for its unfriendly atmosphere, but there is a way to break the ice. If you are an outgoing, party-loving cave dweller, start the ball rolling and plan a get-acquainted weekend party for the tenants in your building. An enthusiastic response is inevitable. Line up a committee of organizers to help plan and prepare the food. Cook out, if your building is situated in a way that makes this possible. If not, what about a buffet picnic in the lobby, or on the roof? Easiest solution to equipment needed is to rent it and make up a kitty for expenses. Have games available for all, borrowed from tenants.

Lunch Party

The Party.   12:30 or 1 P.M. to 3 or 3:30 P.M. Although a lunch party requires good organization on the part of the hostess, it's considerably less demanding than a dinner party. The hour is convenient; the hostess has time to give the house a once-over-lightly dusting; schoolchildren are gone, and little ones should be napping. Lunching together is one of the most popular forms of entertaining among women (men can be included on holidays). This is a more personal invitation than a coffee or tea. The hostess who loves to cook can indulge her hobby and serve newly discovered specialties, since women are more receptive than men to new dishes. Eight to 18 guests make a pleasant group and can be handled without additional help.

A lunch might celebrate almost any occasion, and decorations can be carried out in keeping with the season or with a particular event. On Easter Sunday have a hat party and ask the ladies to wear their Easter bonnets. Let the husbands vote on the prettiest (secret ballot, of course) and give a prize. Honor a traveling friend by having a shower of small gifts for convenience in traveling. Honor a visitor or a friend who is moving away by carrying out a theme of her special interests, such as golf, bowling, or gardening. Use the theme of a current bestseller for a book club, or one from a theatrical hit for matinee buffs.

The Menu.   Lunch may begin with a light apéritif or sherry, which is preferable to anything as heady as a cocktail so early in the day. If you prefer a non-alcoholic drink, chilled cranberry juice in a big wine goblet or a snifter looks pretty. In this day of figure-conscious women, the menu should not be heavy. Plan to have something hot, even if it's just the rolls and coffee. Most lunches served in homes consist of only two courses, the main course and dessert with coffee. An appetizer is optional and could be a small serving of fish mousse, a cup of fruit, or bouillon. The main course can consist of a meat dish or meat substitute, with a vegetable or rice and/or salad. Any of the following dishes make an appetizing lunch menu:

* Ham loaf with raisin sauce

* Casseroles such as chicken Tetrazzini

* Chicken Stroganoff

* Hot fish dishes, such as shrimp or lobster Newburg

* Molded fish salad ring, such as tuna fish or salmon

* An all-inclusive salad bowl—greens, vegetables, ham, chicken, and cheese

A tomato aspic is good with any of the meat dishes and replaces salad, or can be served in addition to salad. Special breads —blueberry muffins, spoon bread, or Sally Lunn—are good with lunch. As a general rule, desserts should be light, but young people like the rich, gooey ones. It's more convenient, and prettier, to have something that can be brought to the table and served there with coffee or tea. This eliminates the confusion of many trips to the kitchen. Consider these or similar desserts when planning your menu:

* Charlotte russe

* Spanish cream

* Ice cream in a big meringue shell; pass sauces or crème de cacao, crème de menthe, or Tia Maria as a topping.

❋ Bowl of ice cream balls in assorted flavors; pass sauces.

❋ Fudge pie

❋ Hot chocolate soufflé with ice-cold cream or whipped cream

❋ Peach Melba or pears Hélène

❋ Hot stewed fruit with whipped cream

❋ Apricot or other fruit mousse

❋ Green grapes and sour cream sprinkled with sugar and nutmeg

❋ Cream puff shells filled with ice cream; pass hot fudge sauce.

The Ideas.

❋ Give a Welcome Spring! lunch party on the first day of spring. Decorate profusely with pots of blooming spring plants—geraniums, hyacinths, tulips, and daffodils. (You can set them out in your garden later.) Serve chilled rosé or May wine with a pansy floating in each wineglass. At each guest's place at the table, set a berry basket of blooming pansies with colored tissue paper masking the basket, or use blooming potted plants. These can be table decorations and favors combined. Ask your florist to give you a supply of little flat wooden identification sticks on which to print guests' names. On the other side, print horticultural name of the plant. Stick these in the flowers as place cards. Or favors could be packets of seeds tied to place cards with ribbon.

❋ A perfect way to enlarge your circle of friends is with a Half-and-Half Party. Give the affair to honor a friend. Invite half of the guests from your circle of friends, and the other half from friends of the person being honored. Or two hostesses may give the party together, each inviting her own friends as half of the guest list. Everyone will be enriched by meeting new people.

Open House

The Party. Being "at home" to a group of friends is an old-fashioned social custom that is coming back into vogue. It's such an easy and pleasant way to see people, repay social obligations, and bring friends together. The open house is a variable type of party that is good for a mixed gathering on Saturday or Sunday afternoon from 4 to 6 or 7, or after dinner from 9 on . . . for hostesses who do not want to give a cocktail party . . . for a young people's party without alcoholic beverages . . . for an all-female afternoon party . . . for high school or college girls . . . for women's clubs and sororities . . . for church groups . . . for a wedding anniversary or a special birthday anniversary. This is one party that requires a good-sized invitation list, as it would be dismal and ineffective for any number under 20. Like a tea, this should be a pretty party, with all of your best possessions used. You can cover the table completely with a sheer organdy or lace cloth, or can leave it bare (but polished!). Since this party is always in the late afternoon or evening, a candelabrum or candlesticks are called for. Flowers, figurines, birthday or anniversary cake, or seasonal arrangement is right for the centerpiece. Small napkins are laid out. If you have guests of honor, or if it's a club party, you may have a receiving line. For other occasions you may be as casual as at a cocktail party, where the host and hostess circulate most of the time.

The Menu. A beverage and pick-up food are the menu basics for an open house. For a mixed adult party, you can concentrate on one wonderful punch in the summer or one special hot beverage such as Swedish glogg or hot mulled cider in the winter; at holiday time, serve eggnog. If the party is after dinner, it may be a champagne punch and/or highballs. For young people or all ladies, a fruit punch is appropriate. The accompanying food is usually all cold, which may be prepared ahead. The menu may focus on small sandwiches, petits fours, slivers of fruitcake, nuts, and mints. Focal point of the table is the punch bowl. If you don't own one (they do take a lot of storage space), this is one time when it's acceptable to borrow from a close friend, or you can rent from a renting service, caterer, or possibly even from your local liquor store. If you have ingenuity, you could improvise prettily with a handsome big soup tureen or an antique washbowl. Attractive cups are essential, as are pretty trays and serving dishes of china, crystal, or silver. This is one party that requires no silver flatware.

The Idea.

❊ The next time you are drafted to head a fund drive of any sort in the neighborhood, give the neighbors something in return for their contributions by holding an open house reception on a Sunday afternoon. It's a chance for old neighbors to meet new ones, too. Make it clear on the invitations or in your telephone calls that contributions for the charity are welcome but not obligatory. Place a lovely silver bowl on a table near the entrance with a little card propped against it to name the charity. If donations are to be placed in envelopes, stack these on a small tray beside the bowl. Make refreshments very simple—a punch (or eggnog at holiday time), some little sandwiches, cookies, and salted nuts. Your neighborhood will be the better for your hospitality, and so will your cause.

Outdoor Party

The Party.   As long as the weather is clement, any hour of day, from sunrise to moonrise, is the right time for an outdoor party. Although other countries have caught the fever, the outdoor barbecue is America's own child. If anyone doubts that it is here to stay, take a look at statistics, which show that almost a billion dollars was spent in one year on alfresco dining. Some barbecue grills are in a Rolls-Royce class and cost as much as $1000, but you don't need status equipment for a good meal. Simple grills will do the trick, and more easily, too. Some who start out with custom-made equipment find it much too complicated and often resort to an unencumbered, inexpensive setup that they can sit back and enjoy, without having to decipher a manual of operation.

If you have a spacious porch and yard, plan your entertaining for when it's warm enough to take advantage of nature's help. There are so many ways to entertain outside, there's bound to be one to suit you: a cookout breakfast, after-church brunch, picnic lunch, luau, strawberry festival, evening barbecue, and boat or barge party if you're near water. Have a neighborhood or block party, a barbecue honoring houseguests, or a club or class party for your children. Celebrate Independence Day after the local parade, or before fireworks begin, with a picnic.

Since both young and old enjoy eating alfresco, there is no better way to combine all ages. It makes for carefree parties to have the children burn up their excess energy outdoors, instead of inside. Invite 4 to 40, however many you can handle, but most hostesses will hit their stride with 15 to 30. Stress informality in dress as well as in décor. When entertaining a large party of city dwellers at a country home, consider chartering a bus to transport them safely and to keep guests from getting lost.

An outdoor party can be as simple as you wish to make it. But if expending yourself to do things in a very special way is your style, give an elegant outdoor party and decorate porch, patio, and yard profusely with baskets of flowers, bowls of fruit and vegetables, and hanging baskets. Fill a child's wheelbarrow or wagon with flowers. When your garden is thriving, decoration is built right in; when it isn't, fill painted wooden tubs with greens and wild flowers, and set out potted ferns. For an evening party, use strings of electrified lanterns in the yard, or make a border around the party area with the perforated paper bags of sand containing burning candles. Wherever candles and lanterns are used, don't forget safety precautions. If the party is around a swimming pool, turn the pool into a floating garden. Make rings of floating flowers by tying fresh garden flowers and leaves to inflated round life preservers. Also float small lighted oil wicks in the pool. Cover tables with bright-colored cloths in checks, stripes, or floral patterns.

The Menu. Simple fare is usually best, but the important thing is to have plenty, since appetites are piqued in fresh air. You can serve hearty foods such as baked beans and corn on the cob, some of the things that you wouldn't serve at a less informal dinner. Of course, children are happiest with hamburgers and frankfurters, so why waste expensive cuts of steak on them? Desserts should be good and ample, but nothing difficult to serve. Drinks can be hot coffee or cold lemonade, but if everything else is cold, a hot drink is usually preferred. Soft drinks can be kept in a tub of ice for convenience.

If you have paper plates, choose well-designed ones. There are complete paper ensembles in a variety of designs and colors. Be sure they are sturdy enough to last out the meal and that you have the kind of food that can be eaten on paper. Soggy paper plates and collapsing paper cups can spoil a party. If you entertain often in summer, you might want to purchase a set of casual dishes for this purpose. After all, nothing would happen outside that couldn't happen indoors as well. Don't forget to provide an effective spray for winged invaders. Bug-repellent candles and torches are good, too.

The Ideas.

❋ If your property is adequate and you'd like to have one big, memorable party during the season, plan a miniature country fair for the close of summer. To alert guests, send invitations several months ahead in the form of free passes with an explanation of various competitions—and a rain date. Then send one or two amusing reminders during the summer. Give hobby-happy friends a chance to compete with each other and show off their accomplishments. Guests may enter whatever category they choose: crafts, painting, sewing, cooking, raising flowers and vegetables. Give blue ribbons or prizes to the

best entries. Set up games such as pitching horseshoes, shuf-
fleboard, a wheel of chance, and fishing for prizes (these could
be "white elephants"). Decorate with balloons, and have a
lemonade and cold-drink bar. After awards are made, serve
a picnic supper. This could be strictly a fun affair on a small
scale among good friends and neighbors, or an elaborate venture with the combined efforts of several couples, a club, or a
whole neighborhood. The more the merrier! If children are
included, let them enter their hobbies, too, and compete with
each other. You could become famous for planning such a
party every year with your circle, making plans the year round.
This type of party could also be converted easily to a benefit
for charity by selling tickets to include supper and charging
extra for cold drinks, balloons, and fudge, to swell the kitty.

❋ Carry out a theme of the French sidewalk café on a summer
evening. Send invitations written in French. Set up gaily covered card tables on the lawn or terrace. Set each table with a
different color by making tablecloths and napkins of inexpensive cotton in whatever colors you like. Dishes and flowers
should carry out the color scheme on each table, too. Decorate
with French travel posters set on easels or tacked on tree
trunks. Serve from a cart of assorted French pastries and
petits fours, and try your hand at flaming café brûlot. Hire an
accordionist to stroll among the tables, or set up a record
player outside with a stack of French records. The girls would
love tiny bottles of French perfume as favors. Furnish sketch
pads and pencils for guests to play quick-sketch artists and
sketch each other.

❋ If you long for June in January, rush the season and give a
Winter Picnic Lunch. Find a nice mountain or a pretty
stream, or drive to a summer home. Take along wood for a
fire (don't trust to luck) and blankets. Have one Thermos
full of hot mulled wine to start things off, and another of hot
coffee laced with brandy to wind things up after lunch.

❦ Folk costumes and customs make a colorful party. For inspiration you can choose any country you like, possibly one from which your family might have sprung. One of the most charming folk areas in America is the Pennsylvania Dutch. A Pennsylvania Dutch market theme can convert your yard into a Pennsylvania Dutch marketplace on a summer evening. Write invitations in the vernacular. Informal arrangements of garden vegetables in baskets, garden flowers in painted buckets, and painted hex signs are persuasive props. Use hex signs on front of house and over doors (bone up at your local library). As a centerpiece for the table, make a pretty still life using a cutting or cheese board laden with fruit, nuts, cheese. Serve a Pennsylvania Dutch dinner, including sweets and sours, and shoofly pie or apple pandowdy.

❦ Who doesn't occasionally feel compelled to have a Spaghetti Supper, whether you're of Irish, Indian, or Italian descent! Do it with zest, and plan an Italian Carnovale outdoors. A perfect kickoff for travelers, especially those headed for sunny Italy. Decorate with plenty of reed-covered Chianti wine bottles (to open as needed), Italian flags, and use flag colors of red, white, and green in flowers and linens. Fill the air with Neapolitan music, live or recorded, and encourage guests to join in the arias. To protect guests from sauce while they twirl their spaghetti, use little colored fingertip towels for napkins, or provide little bibs.

❦ For those who summer at the seashore or by their own pools, a Beachcomber Party will liven up things on a weekend. For entertainment, hide numerous little gifts in the sand or in obscure spots around the pool. These could be individual shell dishes for serving, or just unusually pretty shells, a can of shrimp or tuna fish, a jar of shrimp sauce, toy fish, or miniature boats. Give guests sand pails for their loot. If you prefer pirates to beachcombers, make it a treasure hunt, with little notes to guide guests to the treasure. Bury in the sand a box or chest that holds favors for all. After the hunt, serve a seafood dinner or have a clambake.

❋ For a children's, teen-agers', or adults' picnic or cookout, look around your town for a clean, attractive hot-dog vendor with a wagon. Buy the best-quality frankfurters, rolls, and mustard, and have him do the honors at his wagon.

❋ The luau is a favorite party, especially of the teen-age and college crowd. Name it a South Sea Island Party to be different. Since the custom is to sit on the floor or ground, a luau is a natural for midsummer entertainment when a lavish feast can be spread on a carpet of grass or on a sandy beach. Give guests cushions for comfort. Ask the boys to come in bright shirts and white duck trousers, and the girls in muumuus. Let them go barefoot if they wish. Flower leis, symbolizing friendship, are a part of the party. Purchase paper ones from a party or 10-cent store. Engage a local dance teacher to instruct in the hula to the tune of Hawaiian records. Prepare the luau setting on a low, *low* table, or make a flat base on the ground with a layer of boards or a blanket or even newspapers. Lay over this a paper or cotton tablecloth and literally cover with leaves, flowers, fresh pineapples, and bananas for a lush tropical effect. Though roast pig is traditional, there are other typical dishes that you can find in your cookbook library.

Sherry Party

The Party. 3:30 or 4 to 5:30 or 6 P.M. A sherry party can celebrate any occasion, but has a festiveness that makes it especially appropriate for holidays. Homes look their prettiest at Christmastime, yet the busy season makes it difficult to have as many friends in as we'd like. An easy way to do it, once the house is decorated, is to have a late afternoon sherry party. Ask as many as you can accommodate, or only a few close friends. Follow the British custom of including men, or invite only women. It makes a pleasant hour of relaxation, and since the hostess has very little to do after the guests arrive, she is able to enjoy the party as much as they do.

The Menu. Serve a good medium sherry, which appeals to almost anyone. Or give guests a choice between dry or medium and cream sherry. Pour from good-looking decanters set on a tray or on wine coasters. If you haven't enough matching wineglasses, you can rent them from liquor stores or from a rental service. It's thoughtful to provide coffee, if there are guests who don't imbibe wines. There are two schools of thought on what to serve with sherry. Some say sweets only, such as fruitcake, shortbread, and pound cake. But we like to follow the more liberal point of view and include cheese straws, salted nuts, tiny sandwiches, or assorted crackers with a pâté. However, the menu should be kept simple, and very rich food is taboo. Offer buffet service from the dining room table, or from a table of adequate size in the living room, if your group is small.

The Idea.

❋ During the Christmas holiday season, give a late afternoon candlelight sherry party. Tie a tiny Christmas bell with red velvet ribbon to the stem of each glass. Serve bell-shaped cookies, and carry out a Christmas bell theme in decorations.

Shower

The Party. A shower is a happy party planned to celebrate a special event—it's usually bridal or baby, but may also be going-away, housewarming, birthday. Almost any kind of party can be the background for a shower, from a morning coffee to an evening event. It's the kind of party women and girls adore, probably because it's a sentimental expression of love for someone, as well as a material expression. It's quite acceptable, though, to have men present at an evening shower, provided it's not a baby shower and the gifts are not of an intimate nature. Invited guests should be close friends of the guest of honor, since they must bring gifts. And since it costs the guests money to come to the party, be sure to give them a good one.

The shower has its own special protocol, which good taste demands that you follow:

❦ A shower is never given by a member of the family, but is usually given by close friends.

❦ The type of shower you give should not force guests to buy expensive presents—unless your guests can afford it and lavish gifts are the rule in your group.

❦ Guests should not be asked to give money toward one big item that you intend to buy unless it is an intimate group, a club, a neighborhood group, an office, or a Dutch-treat party.

❦ Be careful about surprise showers—it might be a shock!

❦ If you accept an invitation to a shower, you must bring a gift.

❦ If you regret, follow the local custom about whether to send a gift.

The theme of the shower stems from the type of shower, or a theme can be taken from the life of the guest of honor. For example, if a bridal shower is given for a girl who is an avid sailor, the theme could be bridal or nautical. Use imagination rather than accepting the trite. Since the presentation of the gifts is the focal point of the party and provides the chief entertainment, use imagination here, too. Avoid the ubiquitous umbrella. Instead improvise something that can be a useful gift for the guest of honor:

❦ Pick a pretty basket for the catch.

❦ For a baby shower, pile gifts in and around a baby basket, bassinet, crib, or cradle.

❧ Any re-usable article is welcomed by the bride—a clothes basket, wastebasket, fireside wood basket, a small antique trunk.

❧ A going-away shower calls for small, easy-to-carry gifts that can be presented in a traveling or tote bag.

❧ For a completely inexpensive container, cover or paint corrugated cartons or crates.

❧ Piñata animals or birds are always gay and attractive.

The Menu. Pretty food is the order for an all-ladies party. If it's a mixed evening party, it can go casual or not, but shouldn't be too pretty-pretty. Depending on the type of party you give, the service can be seated, buffet, or tea-table. Since the present-opening is a ceremony, seating should be provided for all guests.

The Ideas.

❋ Give a Shower-by-Mail for an engaged friend or a mother-to-be who has moved to another city, but has left behind a circle of close friends in her former home town. Ask guests to bring shower gifts unwrapped. Arrange them on a table for all to see. Provide an assortment of gift-wrapping papers, ribbons, and cards. For entertainment set up card tables and have guests gift-wrap the packages. Give a prize for the prettiest. Then pack all in a big carton provided for the purpose. Next day post the package. Take photos during the whole procedure and send later to the absent guest of honor.

❋ It's fun to see how ingenious guests can be in their gifts when you give an Around-the-Clock Shower for a bride or a house-warming. Assign each guest a specific hour of the day or night for the present, which must be something that can be used at that time. For example, 9 A.M. might be dish towels, or 5 P.M. might be cocktail glasses.

❋ Photographic equipment to record all of Baby's milestones makes a wonderful shower for a mother-to-be. Call it a Baby

Album Shower, and suggest that guests bring any items for picture-taking and filling an album—such as exposure meter, film, album, flashbulbs, camera. You as hostess can give the camera and let guests know film and flashbulb sizes.

❊ Any husband or wife with a green thumb regrets leaving behind cherished plants when a move is made. So for them plan a Green Thumb Shower of all kinds of plants, shrubs, seeds, and gardening implements. Present them in and around a shiny new wheelbarrow. Use pots of flowers for the table décor. Plan ahead for a guest with a station wagon to help the honorees home with the haul.

Soup Party

The Party.   11 A.M. to 1 P.M. Have a hot-soup party for a winter get-together in the snowbelt or a cold-soup party in the sunny South. An inexpensive party to give, and comparatively easy for a large group. Guest list might include neighbors or just friends you want to see, or the soup could precede a committee meeting. The party can take the place of a luncheon before a meeting or matinee, or it can be the first course of a progressive luncheon. A Sunday soup party after church could include husbands. From 6 to 25 can make a lively group, but don't have so many that guests jostle cups. Any party theme can be carried out, and decorations can be simple or very festive.

The Menu.   A large variety of food isn't necessary. One kind of soup is adequate, but it's nicer to give guests a choice of clear or cream soup. Serve any of these you like:

> Hot or cold vichyssoise
> Onion soup
> Split pea soup
> Chicken soup
> Minestrone

Continued on page 320.

Bean soup
Tomato soup
Clam chowder
Hot or jellied bouillon
Hot or jellied madrilene
Vegetable soup
Asparagus soup
Hot or cold borsch

Let guests choose their own seasonings from a tray that might include any of the following: Parmesan cheese, chopped parsley, croutons, herbs, curry powder, nutmeg, paprika, pepper, chives, and toppings of sour cream or whipped cream. Crackers of all kinds and special toasts are good with soup. Also hot cheese biscuits, toasted English muffins, slender crisp breadsticks, hot French bread with herb butter, and a tray of assorted cheeses. If the party is to replace lunch, you might add fruit and cookies, or simply a plate of mints.

For serving, use tureen, copper container (if properly lined; insert a glass liner if not), large silver punch bowl, giant earthenware saucepan, or one of the porcelainized iron pots. Be sure that whatever you use is heatproof. Serve buffet and use soup cups and round-bowled soup spoons. Regular teacups can be substituted for soup cups. Guests may stand or sit.

The Idea.

❧ Give a soup party on a Saturday morning before Christmas. Invite couples to stop by and fortify themselves with hot soup before last-minute shopping. Invite children, too, and have a game room set up separately for them with milk-and-cookie bar. Give them balloons and other favors. Or have fixings for them to make Christmas tree ornaments. Hire a sitter to keep them in tow. Let parents return for them after their shopping.

Stag Party

The Party. Though *les girls* get together almost daily for socializing of various degrees, even if only for a cup of coffee, we tend to forget that *les boys* enjoy their own company, too. In many cases the pre-wedding stag party was their last. Most husbands wouldn't dare suggest that their wives plan and produce a stag party for their benefit. We propose a new deal for the men in our lives and suggest that they host a stag party at least once a year. It's certainly an easy project for a wife to undertake, since men like simplicity and directness. Just be aware of a few cautions:

❊ Forget the fancy decorations, and concentrate on comfort.

❊ Provide plenty of big, functional ashtrays that they aren't afraid to use.

❊ Plain, hearty, plentiful food is what most males prefer. Keep the carrot curls for the girls.

❊ Whatever the beverage, be sure there's a more-than-adequate supply.

❊ Use man-sized napkins, preferably of linen or other fabric.

❊ Make the seating as comfortable as possible.

❊ Conserve the candles and provide good lighting.

❊ After the stage is set, make yourself scarce!

There are many occasions when the man in your life would enjoy a stag party—an evening of bridge or poker . . . before or after golf, riding, sailing, bowling with the boys . . . to view a sporting event on TV . . . while the wives are attending a female party.

The Menu. Any straightforward food served in man-sized portions is welcome. Forget the casseroles and fancy foods the girls adore. Be sure dishes and serving pieces are in kind. Coffee and beverages should "flow like water." The do-it-yourself buffet described on page 285 is an excellent way to serve, since you can prepare everything ahead, post a list in the kitchen, and disappear.

The Ideas.

❋ Your husband will bless you if you plan a World Series Stag Party for him during this annual sports event. Naturally it would have to be a game that falls on a weekend. Make it a really great party by renting a color TV set with big screen. Or for a larger party, rent several sets and place them in different rooms for groups of viewers. Be sure there's an ample supply of cold beer during the game, and plenty of ashtrays. Serve a buffet lunch before, or a buffet supper afterwards, and be sure it's hearty. Make score sheets for each guest—and have a score-guessing contest, with an appropriate bottle as prize.

❋ On your husband's or son's birthday, plan a Father-Son Rally. The theme or the entertainment has to be compatible with the ages of the boys. Small boys are interested in active games. Medium-sized boys can be more content with quieter games. Teen-age boys love cars and sports. A good icebreaker for all is the always-interesting game of guessing who is who from baby pictures obtained beforehand. A do-it-yourself meal or refreshments will keep both dads and sons busy. Have everything prepared, and post the menu. Let them organize themselves for putting it together. Be sure to include some boy favorites such as French fries.

❋ For an early breakfast before a morning of golf, hunting, sailing, or other sport, see page 260.

❋ Have a Commuters Special stag bridge party for your husband's bridge companions on the 8:02 and the 5:05. Let him invite his own foursome and neighboring foursomes from the train for an evening of more leisurely bridge. Filch a few extra timetables from the station, covering his usual morning run, to use as invitations. Write across the schedule with a red or orange felt marker:

"Seats are reserved for members of the 8:02 bridge players for a relaxed evening in the Club Car at 821 Parkway Road on Friday, March 27th, at 8:02 P.M. Join us for bridge, beer, and buffet. R.S.V.P., Pete Van Dyke, Central 4-1234."

Follow the general rules for a stag party given above. As bridge prizes, give a commutation ticket, "bottles," or any of the zany items now available for the man-who-has-everything.

Supper Party

The Party. A supper party can be played up or down. It can be quiet and simple, or gay and festive. A Sunday night supper implies great informality and coziness. This is a favorite time for intimate friends and families to get together for an early supper between six and seven, either pre-planned or impromptu. A time for relaxed conversation, instead of great activity. An early evening party gives commuters a chance to get plenty of sleep and be bright-eyed on Monday morning. For the same reason, it is also a suitable party for groups that include children or the high school or college set. Best to keep the group small, with 6 to 12 guests, 18 at the most.

A very late supper party usually follows some other event, such as the theater, opera, concert, movies, dance, or sports. Then there is a more frivolous atmosphere, since guests are already in a party mood from whatever event preceded the supper. It's the kind of party young people love, since their endurance is boundless.

The Menu. At a Sunday night supper, cocktails or wine may be served first. Plan the menu around one main dish, preferably a hot chafing dish or casserole with a vegetable or salad. Add dessert and coffee. If you want to start with an appetizer, it could be cups of madrilene, or seashells filled with shrimp and

topped with a piquant sauce. Serve this in the living room
before supper, to eliminate fussing with hors d'oeuvres. Seat
guests at the dining table, or serve buffet and provide snack
tables. Small groups are always cozy by fireside.

A late, late supper may call for a slightly different menu and
a lot of efficiency on the part of the hostess. Everything must
be prepared in advance, to be quickly and easily served with a
minimum of last-minute kitchen work. Because of the late hour,
a basically simple menu is best, perhaps a good salad or Welsh
rabbit on toast triangles, with rolls, dessert, and coffee. Some
night people consistently prefer scrambled eggs or an omelette
with plain or Canadian bacon. Let the host make highballs for
thirsty guests while the hostess is taking care of supper preparations. Or serve a wine with supper instead.

The Ideas.

❋ Give a Critics Supper after a concert, the theater, or a movie
   by inviting the group to come to your house to discuss the
   performance. Arrange the table early in the day for a simple
   buffet. If a dinner party has preceded the performance, keep
   the menu very light. Plan a dish that can be made in advance
   and reheated, or a cold salad or mousse that can simply be
   taken out of the refrigerator. Serve champagne "nightcaps"
   with the buffet. Coffee to climax all.

❋ The French custom of Le Réveillon after midnight mass on
   Christmas Eve is a friendly and warm tradition. This is a
   light supper such as baked ham, omelette, salad, cheese, fruit,
   French bread, and wine. Set it out on an informal table lit
   with a cluster of chunky candles—and begin Christmas Day
   happily. It's fortification for trimming the tree or for playing Santa to children. Try it next Christmas and see.

❋ For a Mexican Chili Party decorate your table with a big
   upturned sombrero filled brimful of fruit spilling out onto
   the table—or with a bunch of the big, floppy Mexican paper
   flowers. If you have a Mexican shop near you, other items

that add to the decoration are pottery figurines, baskets, tin figures, and candelabra. Serve a tequila drink at cocktail time, along with guacamole dip and crackers. Ladle chili from a big kettle into earthenware bowls. Complete the menu with tortillas, relishes, oyster crackers, Spanish cream, and coffee.

Tea

The Party. 3 or 3:30 P.M. to 5 or 5:30 P.M. A tea party is probably the most feminine party of all, and the hour suits busy mothers who have too many demands on them earlier in the day to entertain. Whether the party is large or small, it's the time to make everything lovely-to-see with flowers, pretty linens, tea napkins, dainty food, prettiest cups and saucers and tea plates. This is a fitting way to entertain friends of varied ages and interests: your own contemporaries, mothers and grandmothers; a minister's wife, or other church representatives; a neighbor moving in, or a neighbor departing. It's especially nice for older ladies who don't like to dress early and rush off to a morning coffee. A mother might honor her new daughter-in-law (or future daughter-in-law) by introducing her to friends at at teatime. College sororities and women's clubs have always been devotees of this gracious tradition, but younger girls of junior high and high school age should be encouraged to give teas, as well. It's wonderful training for them in the social graces. We probably honored the youngest guest ever when we invited friends for tea to meet our three-year-old godchild. She went along charmingly with the idea, and her behavior was beyond our fondest hopes. Even at that tender age, she took it in feminine fashion, enjoying party clothes, cake, and especially the attention.

The Menu. The most important thing on the menu is good tea. There are special mixtures and spiced teas, but don't serve anything too far out, because a real tea drinker prefers traditional blends. Be sure it's hot, not lukewarm, and have lemon, sugar, cream (the English insist on milk), and hot water on the tray. Coffee is becoming more and more a part of the tea service, but it is not a must. Also optional is a decanter of sherry.

You must have some sort of tea service, although it need not be silver (see page 121). If the party is large, serve from the dining room table; guests can stand or sit. Ask a friend in advance to pour. With a very large number of guests, it's desirable to have a tea service at each end of the table. In this case, the two sets should be similar, and you will need two friends to pour. In order to let the pourers enjoy the party, too, ask additional friends to assist, and change during the second hour. At a small tea, when everyone is seated, it's cozy in winter to set a table near the fireside and serve there yourself. Bring out your prettiest cake plates and serving dishes of silver, china, or glass, and fill them with an assortment of sweets, such as cookies, petits fours, bite-size cream puffs, tea cakes, tiny individual tarts, little sandwiches of sweet bread and butter, fruitcake, and pastel mints. Most guests like a few non-sweets, such as nuts and small sandwiches of watercress, cheese, shrimp, or crabmeat.

The Ideas.

❀ Invite a few friends with young daughters to tea. Girls could be from 10 to 16—mothers, any age! It may surprise you how the girls respond by putting best foot forward when treated like young ladies. They will feel important being included as special guests at a grown-ups' party. It would be appropriate to plan a party the week before Mother's Day. Tie pairs of tiny velvet bows in different colors and pin matching pairs on mothers and daughters to identify which two belong together.

❀ On May Day invite friends to an afternoon tea. Instead of using tea plates, give each guest a little basket to hang on her arm and fill with goodies. Line each basket with a paper lace doily and put a flower-printed paper napkin inside. Tie a spring flower, real or artificial, on each handle with pastel ribbon. Use pastel tablecloth and a centerpiece of May flowers.

❊ At an afternoon tea in summer, add variety and dash by including a punch bowl of iced coffee topped all over with mountains of whipped cream dusted very lightly with cocoa. Ladle into punch cups. You can sweeten the whipped cream slightly or have very fine granulated sugar for those who like their coffee sweet.

Teen-age Party

• **The Party.** Of course a party for teen-agers may take almost any form, and almost anything in their life can be an excuse or an occasion for a party. It can take place any time but early morning (they like to sleep). Teen-age festivities should come to an end by midnight or 12:30, depending on local customs. Record parties, after-game parties, slumber parties, Sweet Sixteen Parties are all popular and obvious ideas. Each can be given a new twist—and there are many other ideas that would be right. When your teen-agers want to entertain, help them do it right and do it differently. However, don't try to dictate to them. They know what they will enjoy, and it may not be exactly your idea of a good time! Here we just want to point up a few essentials of entertaining this age group. Teen-agers are of two minds. They like their parties informal and out of doors whenever possible. But when holiday and prom times come, they like them proper and formal. There's practically no in-between. They adore thematic ideas and special decorations, and they have the energy to put them up. A teen-age party in a home can be for anywhere from 6 to 30, but from 10 to 16 is the best sized group to be under control. And so that all teen-age parties will always be under control, do be *un*-obviously present at all times. Never leave home when a party is going on. Post the house rules conspicuously on a blackboard or bulletin board and place signs around the house to remind

guests of the rules, such as: CURFEW AT MIDNIGHT ... NO
SMOKING ... LIGHTS ON AT ALL TIMES ... LADIES
FIRST.

Popular informal parties are luaus, Sadie Hawkins parties,
Western, hillbilly, hobo, come-as-you-are or -were. A little more
dignified are progressive dinners and parties themed to various
countries or parts of the world, such as Spanish, Italian, Mexican, Oriental. The Sweet Sixteen Party, whether an all-girl
luncheon or a mixed evening party, should have the beauty and
dignity befitting this milestone.

Junior and senior proms are in most cities among the biggest
and most important teen-age parties. Here the school usually
has charge of arrangements and working committees: decoration, food, music (book early), ticket, publicity, invitation, program. School colors are always appropriate for decoration, but
why not be more original—like the class in a Birmingham, Mich-
igan, high school which turned the whole gym into a medieval
castle. Through use of crepe paper streamers, a gym may be
turned into a festive tent. This is one time to let your imagination soar.

The Menu.   Since the food likes of teen-agers are simple and
unsophisticated, the menu for a party never presents a problem.
Perennial favorites are hamburgers, hot dogs, sandwiches, pizza,
pancakes, French fries, and cola drinks. If budget is no problem, they love steaks at a cookout. For dessert, the gooier the
better—sundaes and other ice cream dishes, layer cake, fancy
pies. Let them help plan the menu, and don't be horrified at
their ideas. Their stomachs seem to have built-in protective
chemistry. You don't have to have a lengthy menu, but do have
vast quantities of everything. Informal buffet service suits their
casualness to a T, and they even love to cook the food themselves. Because they aren't enthusiastic about cleaning up afterwards, this is one time when paper table accessories are not only
appropriate, but desirable. There are many attractive and well-
designed paper items available that will give the party a fillip.

The Ideas.

❋ In the winter when young people are shut in, they tend to get explosive and restless for something to do. To help them let off steam, plan a Blizzard Blast at your house during the first winter snow or blizzard. Tell guests not to dress up, but to wear ski clothes or other cold-weather sportswear. Put a big box at the door with a sign on it, "PARK BOOTS HERE." As guests arrive, serve antifreeze "cocktails" of hot mulled cider or hot chocolate. For entertainment, let guests take off their shoes and have a sock hop to records. Or if yours is a musically inclined group, have a hootenanny sing-along. By 10 o'clock they will have worked up an appetite, so end the party with bowls of hot chili, crackers, plenty of relishes, cole slaw. Send them packing home early.

❋ It's a safe bet that among teen-age and college crowds, nine out of ten times it's the girls who give the parties. For a turn-the-tables party, a group of boys could plan a We-Can-Do-It-Too Party as a thank-you to all the girls who provide the fun and food all year. Let each participating host invite four girls, so that pulchritude will prevail four to one. Boys share the expense and responsibilities. Girls arrive unescorted and "rush" the boys all evening, asking for dances and tagging.

❋ If you don't have room for your teen-agers to give a dance at home, make it a Carport Hop, using your garage or carport for dancing. If you are near a party rental agency, you can have a good dance floor laid—or let the teen-agers scrub the floor clean. Cover the walls with colored crepe paper streamers—ceiling, too, if possible—to give a tent effect. For a crowd, extend the dancing to the driveway, too. Put some garden furniture around and set up a buffet table in the yard. Ask guests to bring their favorite records (labeled with their names). Serve soft drinks from colored tubs filled with ice (buy plastic ones or spray regular tubs). Between 11 and midnight, serve sandwiches, fruit salad, potato chips, more soft drinks, ice cream and cake.

❊ Invite guests to come to a Spy Party looking the way they imagine spies look. Boys may want to wear trench coats or just look dashing à la James Bond. Girls may wear Mata Hari costume, or look formidable with dagger pushed through garter, or pack a toy pocket pistol. Invitations could assign secret operator number to each guest, such as 779. Use the numbers on place cards, and let each guest detect his place. As an icebreaker for the party, have guests write down the names of all of the spies they can think of, either real or fictional. Give the newest spy novel as a prize to the one who can name the most.

❊ For Sweet Sixteen Parties, see "Birthday Party," page 257.

❊ Though girls much prefer parties with boys, they do love to have slumber parties, when most of the night is spent doing anything but slumbering. They love to eat, drink quantities of soft drinks, talk, listen to records, "do" their hair and nails. Help your teen-ager give a Japanese Slumber Party at which the girls sit and sleep on cushions on the floor (they bring their own). Though sukiyaki is the Japanese dish, chop suey or chow mein is easier to serve for an Oriental flavor, since it may be made beforehand and reheated. Chopsticks are guaranteed to keep the party lively—and fortune cookies will, too.

❊ Give girls a big treat at a morning or afternoon party by hiring a hairdresser to "do" everyone's hair. Ask each girl to bring her own hair dryer and set up shop in a big bedroom with bathroom adjacent.

❊ Teen-agers love outdoor parties and have plenty of time for these during summer vacation. So keep your teen-agers busy with pool or beach parties, cookouts, treasure or scavenger hunts, backyard parties, luaus, Western and hillbilly outdoor parties, outdoor dances, bicycle meets, car rallies.

Weekend

The Party. Entertaining weekend guests is for the hostess the equivalent of a 48-hour party. Not that it's one continuous round of activity wthout sleep, but it does require being on the job morning, noon, and night without letting down. Weekend guests are usually close friends or family, except when it's business entertaining, but whoever the guests, the one running the show must be on her toes—and feet—most of the time. Houseguests may be invited for from Friday night or Saturday morning until Sunday night or Monday morning. Send maps with easy-to-read directions for those coming by car, and tell them how long it takes to get there. Make the invitation clear as to when guests are expected and how long you wish them to stay. Knowing prevents embarrassment on the part of both guests and hosts. Also give them some indication of what is planned, so that they will know which clothes to bring. A hostess will be happier if she invites only 2 to 4 guests at one time, unless she has an estate with a staff of servants. Don't bite off more than you can chew, or Monday morning will seem an eternity away. For guests' comfort, it's important to have adequate sleeping and bath facilities. Don't feel that guests must be entertained every second. They will appreciate time to relax with a book or magazine. If golf, swimming, or tennis is on the schedule, let guests in on your plans, so that they can be ready at the right time—and be sure they like to play! But don't regiment them into perpetual athletic activity like Boy Scouts on a camping trip. Give them a taste of easy living, too.

Devise a subtle way of letting everyone know the house rules. It's easier to have model guests if you do. One painless way of informing them is to keep a little slate or decorative news board in guest room or wherever they are sure to see it. Note the breakfast hour and what time the station wagon leaves for the golf course. Also include any warning, such as "Our cat loves mink. Keep your furs out of reach," or "Beware of feeding candy to the dog." Remember to provide drawer space and closet space with plenty of hangers. This will encourage neatness! A luggage rack is a must in the guest room, and a small clock helps guests to arise on time. It's thoughtful to equip one drawer with personal items that may be forgotten—hand lotion, tissues, pins, needle and thread, shaving cream, comb, hair spray, clothes brush, toothpaste, and a new toothbrush. Provide a small tray with clean glasses. Extra little attentions, beyond the call of duty, please guests and make them feel pampered—a bowl of flowers or fruit in the room, a cookie or candy jar, a chocolate bar, or a small decanter of sherry.

It's difficult for the weekend hostess to give sufficient time to both her guests and her children. So arrange for a sitter (could be a high school student) to come in at least part of the time to look after young children. Older ones usually have their own activities that keep them busy. If children of houseguests have been invited, activities should be planned for them so that they won't be at loose ends. Children usually enjoy games—croquet, Ping-Pong, tennis, bowling, badminton—and swimming, movies, and picnics. When activities for adults and children are combined, appoint one person (a teen-ager in the family or a hired sitter) to be responsible for the very small children at all times. They will then have constant supervision, will be less likely to have mishaps or accidents, and the hostess will have peace of mind.

The Menu. Since there will be a number of meals to plan, don't have anything too complicated unless you can do it before guests arrive. Write out menus for all meals in advance. Breakfasts should be the simplest of all. Serve only things that don't have to be eaten immediately, since rising habits vary. A buffet or do-it-yourself breakfast is easiest. Let each one pour his own fruit juice and serve himself as he makes an appearance. Sweet rolls and plenty of hot coffee will keep most people happy. They don't expect you to flip pancakes or cater to individual whims. If you feel that the day must begin with an egg, make a chafing dish of creamed hard-boiled eggs to be served on toast triangles. (Eggs can be boiled the day before.) This can be kept hot and served as guests are ready. And bacon can be kept warm on an electric tray.

Lunches should also be simple, but if men are present and have had a morning of sports, serve something hot, such as a hearty soup with sandwiches, a casserole made in advance and reheated, or grilled hamburgers with an assortment of relishes. If it's a summer weekend, serve lunch outside in individual baskets. Saves dishwashing and leaves kitchen free for dinner activity.

The cocktail hour and dinner will be the highlight of the day, when everyone gets together for a time of sociability. The dinner can be simple, but it should be as nice as possible and served attractively. Try to make it festive and partylike. Have the kind of food that doesn't require lots of attention. A ham or roast takes care of itself, once it is in the oven. Outdoor cooking has been a boon to the weekend hostess and gets men into the act; gives the wife more freedom.

The Ideas.

❋ Invite guests for a "play-as-you-please" weekend. Anyone who leads a busy, pressing life during the week will snap up this chance to unwind. Tell guests to bring whatever hobbies or amusements they enjoy—sewing, knitting, rug hooking, archery, crossword puzzles, or just plain whittling. Let them play golf or tennis, or swim. Give sun worshippers comfortable chairs and plenty of sunburn lotion. Don't *plan* activity; guests plan their own. Have on hand a few games such as darts, badminton, croquet, jigsaw puzzles, or cards for those who come unprepared.

❋ Get together a group of affluent friends or a club for a High-Flying Weekend party in Bermuda, Puerto Rico, Jamaica, Honolulu, or any interesting resort. Check with your local travel agent on the possibility of chartering a plane, if it's a large group. There are special rates for as few as 25 persons on regular passenger planes, if it is a specific organization. Then there are very reasonable excursion rates to some resorts for as long as two-week stays. This is really the easiest arrangement, because you don't have to guarantee any certain number of people and it doesn't have to be a club or organization. Your travel agent can arrange everything for you, both plane and hotel reservations. Try to book on a plane with a movie. If anyone in the group has a portable musical instrument—an accordion, a non-electric guitar, or a banjo—ask him to bring it along for entertainment. Plan ahead carefully to make the most of your time. Research the sights to see and the featured foods, and compile a guidebook for the group. Mimeograph schedules for everyone.

❧ ❧ ❧ ❧ ❧

Although most women enjoy giving a variety of parties, there is usually one type that becomes a favorite and brings the most satisfaction to the hostess. Within the framework of your own favorite, plan one very special party a year as your social signature. Establish an idea that is interpreted differently each year, such as a movie theme, which would mean that a new movie becomes the idea for each party. Or it could be an opera or a play. Or a significant date on which you entertain, always with a different sort of party. In New York, the fashion industry annually joins in one great Party of the Year the week before Thanksgiving. Each year there is a new theme. Since Christmas is a time for tradition, your party could be built around the reading of a Christmas poem or story that you love—one of the New Testament versions, Van Dyke's "The Story of the Other Wise Man," or Dickens's "Christmas Carol." If you choose the last, follow it by a typical English holiday dinner. Make yourself notable among your friends for a Party of the Year and they will look forward to sharing the tradition that becomes the signature of you the hostess.

❋ Your favorite holiday could be the key to your signature party: a post-Thanksgiving buffet on Friday, Saturday, or Sunday; an Easter brunch following church; French Réveillon after midnight services on Christmas Eve (see page 324); a July Fourth all-day spree.

❋ Select a day or an event that has not been commercially exploited, yet has significance. This will inspire a more original party. Why not choose an event indicative of your own state —the Boston Tea Party in Massachusetts, the Gold Rush in Western states, the Run of 1889 when the Oklahoma Territory was opened, election day in Maine ("As Maine goes, so goes the nation"), the Louisiana Purchase, the statehood of Hawaii or Alaska.

❋ Some of us are more inspired by seasons than by events. If you find yourself in this strange category, give an "all in good season" party, whether your inspiration comes from a crackling fireside during winter snow, the first spring flowers, a full moon in a summer sky, or frost on the pumpkin in autumn. Yours might be the very first Christmas party each year, during the first weekend in December. The party that opens the holiday season is usually the one most enjoyed, before the social rush becomes frenzied. If you have a country home, give city friends a treat each fall by inviting them to enjoy the beauties of nature.

❋ If you belong to a women's bridge, golf, bowling, or book club, consider giving an annual party for your group and include the husbands. Make this the highlight of the club year.

❋ If you take pride in your ancestry, start there to build your signature party. Carry out a French theme in menu and decorations on Bastille Day (unless your ancestors were Royalists!). Someone of Italian descent would prefer to glorify Columbus Day.

❀ If you are interested in a particular hobby, get a group together annually who have the same interest, whether it's
painting, photography, or woodworking. Or mix the hobbies.
During cocktails or after dinner, have an attractive display
of the guests' accomplishments during the previous year.

❀ An annual event that holds special interest for you might be
celebrated as your Party of the Year:

∿ A cocktail-buffet after the first football game of the season.

∿ A champagne supper to open or close the concert season.

∿ A cocktail-buffet following a golf or tennis annual tournament.

∿ An open house following a sports car exhibition.

∿ A brunch before a favorite antiques show.

∿ A bouillabaisse supper on the first day of the fishing season.

∿ A midnight supper for the cast in an amateur theater
presentation on opening night.

 Part Three

Backing *Up Your Family*
by *Business Entertaining*

When a man meets his fitting mate, society begins.
—Emerson

The American male needs a wife who is "the right *kind* of girl, not the right girl," once wrote anthropologist Margaret Mead. This can be stated even more emphatically about the needs of the American male executive. For in our country, entertaining has gone beyond the simple purpose of getting good friends together. It has become an integral part of the corporate life—and of the life of the corporate wife, as well. The right *kind* of wife is sometimes so important that she is scrutinized by her husband's company before he is given an advancement, if entertaining is part of this post or subsequent ones up the ladder of success. For behind every successful man, there's a wife. A few unusually brilliant bachelors have made it to the top, but we're sure this is in spite of, rather than because of.

Some sedate Wall Street firms are so picky about wives of executives that a man about to be married is more likely to take the girl of his choice "home" to his boss for approval than to take her home to his mother. Men have even been known to switch wives in order to come up with one more acceptable to the establishment, an act we can't say we condone.

One accomplished young female friend of ours was actually wooed by a rich industrialist as a likely wife for one of his five sons and heirs because he believed her social attributes would make her the perfect executive's wife. This father was reviving the old *mariage de convenance* and systematically searching for young women of talent as prospective wives for his sons, who would eventually inherit the business. Being of more romantic bent, our friend withstood the parental siege and married a poor artist, instead.

The challenging new social career of executive's wife has come about as a result of this American business trend. We group professional, business, and political wives together as executives' wives for the purpose of this chapter. The work pays well in prestige, and frequently in luxuries, but usually not directly in dollars to the woman herself. And it requires more personal talent than almost any other career for women.

Prime function of the executive's wife is directing the business-connected entertaining and social life for her husband. It's a key public relations job that helps advance her husband's career and wins friends for her husband's company. Of course, to have such a career, you must first have a husband who's an executive, or who has the potential or desire to be one. If you aspire to be a champion instead of chattel, this is for you.

Wanted: Wonderful Wife

If the executive's wife has the asset of an outgoing personality and likes being with people, she is a natural as hostess and helpmate to her husband on his way up the ladder. And she can enjoy the trip, as well. Entertaining for strictly business purposes might be described as two or more sets of people trying to make the best possible impression on each other. Since these are often very interesting people, and since everybody is out to be agreeable, it's quite possible to have a good time, too. Business entertaining brings together people of varied levels, backgrounds, nationalities, and interests to exchange ideas. This can result in experiences almost as broadening as travel.

As with any other kind of life, there is bitter with the sweet, and demands put on an entertaining wife may sometimes seem far beyond the call of duty. The young bride of the junior executive is usually just learning to run a home, and if she must also learn the art of business diplomacy and protocol at the same time, the climb may seem uphill in more ways than one. But ten years later, when she has earned her campaign ribbons with a Purple Heart thrown in, she will be the enviable one whom the other young wives are copying as they begin the climb.

The wife of one executive, who is now firmly entrenched at the top, recounts with amusement the first innocent experience of her indoctrination. She and her husband, who had just been tapped by the top echelon, were invited to what they believed to be a large formal dinner and theater party. The wife's wardrobe was limited, and worse yet, she was wearing maternity clothes. Since she had no maternity dinner dress, she decided to wear with a smile the best she had in a cocktail dress, and let it go at that. She was sure that she and her husband would be lost in the crowd, anyway, and if she felt conspicuous she could always hide behind a potted palm. Much to their surprise, the "large dinner" turned out to be a very formal, select affair for 14—with no potted palms! To add to her embarrassment, she drew as her theater partner one of the wealthiest and most famous tycoons in the country. An appearance with him would never permit obscurity!

This same wife has now become so adept at handling any situation that she is able to carry on with the greatest aplomb, come what may. She was put to the acid test recently when an entire day of best-laid plans went awry. Called upon to entertain two Texas tycoons and their wives at lunch, she took them to the country club, but they arrived too late to be served. Unruffled, she headed her Lincoln Continental straight down the road to the town diner, an unimposing structure where the only "atmosphere" was that of frying hamburgers. The very same day, her husband sprained his ankle just before he was to take over as host at golf. Though a rank amateur, the wife had to replace him among a pack of avid golfers. She didn't even know her way around the course, but confided in the caddy so that he could point her in the right direction from green to green. Such a day would have broken the spirit of the uninitiated, but it went off with gaiety and grace in her now skillful hands.

It is not unusual for a wife to be called upon to take over at a moment's notice. If her tired husband begins to get sleepy in a nightclub when entertaining an oil man whose money he's eager to invest, she must look interested and intelligent and carry the conversation alone. This happened to a wife we know, and her comment was that it's easy enough to *love* an oil well, but not to talk about one!

Above all, it is the wife's place to make guests and visitors feel welcome and comfortable. She never actually participates in any business transactions among the men, so her part is to create an atmosphere of hospitality and ease among the guests, whether it's in her own home, a country club, or a hotel. And her attitude must be that of the proverbial shopkeeper, "The customer is always right." This sometimes calls for a cool head under fire. One wife was faced with weekend guests who arrived a whole day early without warning. Up to that point she was relaxed in her knowledge that she was right on schedule. But she did not fall apart at this turn of events. She simply raced for the freezer and started rescheduling the rest of the day in her mind while preparing brunch.

Smile When You Can't Say That. The language barrier has always been one of the greatest hurdles in human relationships, and when a man represents his company internationally, language difficulties can create troubling situations. In a Latin American city, a group of the most important and influential bankers in the Western Hemisphere were invited with their wives to a highly exclusive dinner party. After dinner the men went off to another room to discuss money, leaving the wives to get acquainted. But the Spanish wives spoke no English, and the American wives spoke no Spanish, so they sat out the evening beaming at each other, occasionally exchanging an understanding and sympathetic pat. Not everyone is linguistically inclined, but it is helpful in carrying out the good-neighbor policy to learn at least a few sentences of the language before you go to another country. Merely making the effort delights the nationals. And they love teaching key words to you, so ask their help.

While we are on the subject of language, we believe strongly that every cultivated woman should have a nodding acquaintance with the French language. Though English may be spoken 'round the world, French in our estimation is the social language. You should be able to read simple French phrases and pronounce correctly the most universally used French words. Remember how helpful Jacqueline Kennedy was to her husband on their first state visit to France, when she was able to give a little speech in her charming French. While you may never be able to make a speech in French, you can learn enough to get along.

Pampered Guests Are Happy Guests. There are many little courtesies a wife can take over that pave the way to pleasant relations with other businessmen and their wives. Make out-of-town guests feel welcome by sending flowers to their hotel rooms upon arrival. This is a Continental custom, so it's good to reciprocate when foreign visitors arrive, but Americans enjoy such attentions, too. It is also thoughtful to offer to take a foreign woman shopping, if she is unsophisticated in the ways of our country. An American wife would probably prefer to shop alone (she might not want you to know that she pays for her clothes), but if she implies that she would like a guide, then make the gesture.

When visitors are expected to travel from a hotel in a city to a home in the suburbs, one of the kindest things you can do for them is to provide door-to-door limousine service. Everyone enjoys comfort, and this puts them in a pampered mood from the start. This is especially important when the guests are not familiar with transportation in the area.

When entertaining foreign visitors, remember to respect their customs. If you don't know what the customs are, find out, so your party won't trigger an international incident. When foreigners are in your home, try to serve at least one dish that is familiar to them, so that they will not be subjected to complete upheaval in eating habits. It also helps to see a little bit of home in a strange land, so whenever possible, make use of anything you have that is reminiscent of their country, no matter how small. As table decoration you could use a piece of Lalique glass from France, china from England, or a brass fruit bowl from India. One wife who is often called upon to entertain business visitors from all over the world keeps a supply of the miniature flags we've talked about, and uses appropriate ones in her centerpiece or to decorate hors d'oeuvre platters. This would surely warm the cockles of the coldest heart.

It is a safe guess that more business entertaining is done outside the home than in it, although it is more personal and less businesslike to invite guests to your home. People enjoy going to homes in other cities or other lands, but on the other hand, when coming to a metropolitan area they usually want to carry the last word back home on the latest hit in the theater or on that famous restaurant they've been reading about. Trips to the suburbs can focus on golf or swimming, followed by dinner at the country club or at the host's home. Latin Americans enjoy being entertained in a private home where children in the family are also present, because of their appreciation for strong family relationships.

What Is She Really Like?

We know of no matrimonial agency that turns out the ideal wife and helpmate for an ambitious executive. There is many a mother who would like to turn out such a daughter, but she usually "pushes" her offspring right out of the running. In Washington a wife can go to school to learn diplomacy, social graces, and protocol, but that's a very limited group. Other wives must be born with the abilities, or figure it out for themselves. The former group is again very limited, so most wives must enroll in the School of Trial and Error to learn by practice and experience.

Any woman of intelligence can train herself in the ideal attributes of the wife who is a social asset to her husband as he climbs upward in his career, whether it is business, professional, or political. Check yourself against these required requisites:

A Friend Indeed. Friendliness and a sympathetic feeling toward other people are basic. The woman who puts on a front of false friendliness is quickly discovered. She fools no one but herself. If you sincerely care about people, they will care about you. And an important man needs friends.

The Ability of Flexibility. To progress, a man must move around, and this may literally mean *move*. You have to be ready and willing to change your whole way and place of life at a moment's notice. Or the change may only be from one level of living up to the next as your husband advances, calling for new friends and new social responsibilities, with possibly a move to a better house and neighborhood. You must be able to roll with the chances as they come along.

Conversation Piece. Knowing how to be a *good* talker—not just a talker—is a blessing. Many women are born talkers, but never learn *how* to talk. Others are born tongue-tied, and become great conversationalists. We actually believe it is easier for the second group, because they must plot and plan how to develop an ability to talk well, while the long-distance talker finds it hard to pause long enough to evaluate what she's saying. Whichever group you belong to, you can and must learn to be a disciplined talker on different levels (from the office boy to the boss), and on different subjects (from how many eggs make an omelet to how many innings make a ball game).

❊ Don't talk too much—know when to stop.

❊ Never be tempted to gossip.

❊ Don't talk in a loud-booming voice.

❊ Off-color words and stories are taboo from the lips of ladies.

❊ Avoid discussing your husband's business affairs.

❊ Think ahead about some of the topics you can touch on before you go out with a business group.

In the Best Manner. You must learn all the rules of the etiquette of entertaining, and must have impeccable manners. This book will give you the former—we are sure you already have the latter! This includes exemplary conduct at all times and restraint in all things, especially in the intoxicating-beverage department and in the department of the other wife's husband!

Leave a Good Taste. The quality of taste is defined as critical judgment or discernment. This you must exercise in everything that represents you and your husband—your own appearance, your home, your manners, and certainly your entertaining. It's knowing when to stop and not go overboard. It's being understated, rather than obvious. It's being thoughtful and understanding. If we had to summarize taste in one word, we would say it's *appropriateness* in everything that surrounds your life. Or even more simply, "Taste is nothing but a delicate good sense," as de Chénier put it. The world's most elegant women have this sensitivity, but it can be cultivated by anyone.

My Brother's Keeper. Every man of substance in the business world is expected by his company to be a good citizen and a doer of good deeds. He must father the Cub Scouts in his younger executive years. He must chairman the charity fund drive in his maturity. Like husband, like wife. So the executive's wife must do her share in the civic, charity, and church life of her city. She must mother the Brownies and graduate to the charity ball. This is a natural instinct of the elegant woman and her husband—caring about others.

The Winning Way. In the keen competition of today, the wife who's successful socially must be pleasingly aggressive, but never annoyingly so. She must have the ability to take the initiative, but the tact to do it with a gloved hand. Some wives are misguided in their attempts to help their husbands, and don't know when to stop. A wife who performs like a backstage mother fired with ambition for her protégé is distasteful not only to the husband's business associates, but also to the husband himself. It is up to the husband to decide if and when he should aim at the next plateau. And it is up to him to complain to the boss about salary, never up to her. Neither should a wife push her husband socially beyond sensible bounds. Any activity is to be pursued within reason and within the limits of his health. There are times when he may want to relax with a tennis racquet or a book. Don't insist on a never-ending round of parties. Plan your entertaining so that it still leaves time for his hobbies or sports. A well-balanced diet is usually best.

Keeping Up with the Husbands. There's just no more pitiful plight than that of the wife who was a darling at 20 and becomes a drudge at 40. You must move hand in hand with your husband as he takes each step upward. You cannot sit still while he progresses. If your education was light on languages and you are thrown with a traveling set, enroll in a French or Spanish class. If you want to beat them all, take Russian or Japanese! If your husband's off-hours revolve around a country club and golf, learn to play, too. If you find yourself integrated with intellectuals, and you spent your college days as queen of the campus, take up the study of philosophy or literature or ancient history. If there's no university near you, take a correspondence course.

The Executive's Executive Wife

The executive's wife who is herself an executive is a latter-day phenomenon with her own set of problems that must be correlated with her husband's. The wives of most executives concentrate on a home life because of their many responsibilities and their fortunate economic status. In some of the large cities, however, many wives choose challenging careers themselves, and the family ends up with two executives at the helm. In these two-wheeling executive families, there are a number of benefits, but there are problems as well.

While two top incomes may not exactly double the family's standard of living, they certainly do expand it appreciably—and obviously. The home can be a little grander, the clothes and cars a little more posh, the children's schools a little finer. The circle of executive associates and acquaintances is certainly wider, and possibly even double. The business and social scope of both executive husband and executive wife is thus considerably more expansive, which can pay off in still more advancement and more income for both partners in the marriage.

The successful executive's executive wife has more than her share of responsibility. Her days, and many nights, are filled with her own business demands. Her family and social duties must be telescoped into evenings and weekends. Most women in this group can afford regular help in the home, but managing help adds to their problems. On the other hand, this wife has certain one-upmanship over the non-career wife. To achieve her personal business status she has had to cultivate the ability to juggle home and mix people with skill, and to look and dress well from early morning to late evening.

As capable as they may be, there are executives' executive wives who because of business responsibilities have not found the formula for handling the addition of a pleasant and rewarding social life for themselves and their husbands. They are cheating themselves out of one of life's happiest and most meaningful aspects. If you are one of these women who haven't quite been able to face up to entertaining, whether business or personal, don't wait another minute to start.

※ Just as you are forced to schedule everything else in your life, schedule regular entertaining—perhaps a small group once every week or two, a real party once a month, and an all-out bash once or twice a year. In this way you won't be tempted to let business duties deter you.

※ Plan specifically to do part of your entertaining outside the home, so that responsibility will be shifted to someone else's shoulders.

※ Many times, you and your husband can discharge your respective business obligations together, *if* the two groups of people are wholly compatible. But if each of you has a big deal cooking, don't try this, because you won't be able to divide your attention evenly enough. You will probably both come out with a failure.

※ Face up to it that sometimes you or your husband must go it alone as host if the other is detained or even called out of town by business. Make the necessary apologies, but don't dwell on it. One of our friends found herself the sole owner of a sizable patio party when an emergency in London demanded her husband's presence. It was too late to postpone, so she enlisted another couple as co-hosts. The guest husband filled in for the missing one at the bar and barbecue.

One of our executive female friends is frequently forced by her job to arrive home after the guests. Her executive husband and young son take over in the interim. She slips upstairs, changes into a stunning hostess gown, and makes an advantage of her late appearance by dramatically descending her beautiful stairway with a warm welcome to everyone. How much better than rushing in distraught and apologetic.

Problems! Problems! Problems!

We've chatted and corresponded with executives' wives around the world, and if it's any consolation to you, all have four common problems stemming from the entertaining lives they must lead. These problems are not insurmountable if you develop know-how.

1. *Insuring Security.* Not all—but many—wives of executives feel insecure about taking the plunge into the business social swim. They are afraid they can't organize a smooth party, or can't provide a delectable dinner, or can't master the guest mix with finesse. Sometimes the heart of the most courageous trooper is struck with fear when the husband moves up to a higher level and she must entertain "upwards." We assure you that anyone who wants to become a successful hostess at any level can do it if she learns the basics and plans her parties carefully. That's what this book is about.

2. *Clothes on the Go.* Almost every wife we queried immediately cited clothes as her biggest problem. A wardrobe expandable and exciting, versatile and variable, must always be ready to go. In Washington, clothes are considered so important to a wife that there are very discreet clothing consultants who may be called in to doctor a wardrobe. For women elsewhere, we have a complete plan in Chapter 12 for the benefit of your clothes closet.

3. *Minding the Moppets.* The next biggest problem among executives' wives involves their children. Even if you can afford competent help to care for them when you are out, it isn't always available. We wish we could reel off a built-in solution, but the answer, like the problem, is a local one. Mother,

mother-in-law, and the local high school baby-sitters are obvious. After that, check the ministers of local churches for the names of women who need extra income and are looking for small jobs. Sometimes a young mother needs extra money and can mind your children in the evening while her husband minds theirs. Another source might be student nurses or regular nurses who are interested in a part-time secondary job.

A penalty to pay for entertaining and party-going is lack of time to enjoy being with your children. We have two suggestions to make about this. When you entertain at home, make it a practice to let the children participate in the opening festivities. They can be taught to assist in receiving the guests when they are as young as five or six, and even to pass a tray of appetizers (but never drinks). Then off to bed. Secondly, when you are going out for the evening, plan to be present at the children's dinner or to tuck them in at bedtime, depending on your departure time. They will feel more secure, and you will, too.

4. *The Guest Guess.* Wives who entertain for their husbands are often stumped by the problem of planning a successful guest list—whether to make it all business, whether to invite associates of lower rank, whether to mix personal friends along with business obligations, whether to invite the boss. Here we will say that mixing a few flexible social friends with the business guests makes the whole affair less pointedly commercial and is flattering to the business guests. It also lessens the chances of your being accused of any ulterior motives. We help you answer the other troubling questions about guests in the following section and in Chapter 2 (page 19).

Practical Protocol

Though *protocol* is a word Washingtonians live by, it has considerable meaning for the executive and his wife, too. In Washington it prescribes with precision almost every move an official and his wife make socially, many times the exact opposite of what is done elsewhere. That's a whole story unto itself and one you must learn in that city, if that is your life.

Outside the capital circle, social procedures are more casual and less demanding. There are a few rules that you must know and respect, however, in your combined business-social life.

The Social Pattern. The pattern your husband's company has set is the one you must follow. Some companies have developed a strict protocol on entertaining—or even on non-entertaining. On the other hand, today's informality has led others to an informal approach. Tread softly until you sense what is expected of you.

The Expense Account. These three little words have become the basis for a great deal of entertaining today. It has been estimated that a great number of the better restaurants in New York and other large cities could not remain open if it weren't for the patrons who enjoy their fine food and service at the expense of someone's company. It has become a tribal custom in our affluent society for companies to encourage their executives to do business in an elegant atmosphere while consuming gourmet food. Even the Government recognizes this as a part of business, allowing entertaining in certain cases as a legitimate tax deduction.

If your husband is an expense-account executive and you are called upon to assist in his entertaining from time to time, let him plan the extent and kind of entertaining. Don't urge him to do something or go somewhere that he believes is not right. Maybe you have been pining to dine at that fabulous new restaurant that is too rich for your pocketbook. But let your husband be the judge of whether it is also too rich for his company to patronize. In other words, never try to talk your husband into taking unfair advantage of the trust and tender his company has given him. If his company *wants* him to lead the high, wide, and handsome life, lucky you!

Entertaining on Your Own Level. As the old proverb goes, "Like attracts like." It applies to the executive and his wife in entertaining. You may always feel perfectly comfortable and correct in making a social gesture toward someone on your husband's executive level, either inside or outside his company. In fact, a great deal of executive entertaining falls outside the company—between an executive and his client or customer in another company. Too much familiarity, however, can breed danger. If you are on too intimate terms with a man and his wife, it can become embarrassing if your husband must reject a business proposition from the other man, or if he passes him on the way to the top executive suite. So be cordial, warm, and sincere—but don't invite the business acquaintance to be godfather to your child!

Entertaining Higher Rank. This requires uncommon finesse and tact. You cannot skip over your immediate boss, but must work your way up gradually. Beware of climbing so hard that you take a hard fall. We know of one crass couple who resolved when they joined forces to entertain only persons of higher social and business position who could do something for them. The ambitious husband made it up the ladder in record time, but fell down it even faster!

Entertaining the Boss—and His Wife. What to do about invitations to your husband's boss and his wife is not so simple. As a general rule, you should *not* invite the boss and his wife first. Even after they have invited you, it is a delicate matter. Be sure that they *want* to continue a social relationship before you extend a return invitation. Unless your husband is near the boss in rank and works closely with him all of the time, it is probably better that you not try to become intimate with him and his mate unless they indicate this is their choice. Of course, all rules are made to have exceptions, so there are some. You may be located in a small town or an isolated spot where there is no social life except within the company. In this situation, there may tend to be more informality and less emphasis on rank. The Cabots may talk only to God, but perhaps the boss prefers a wider scope. Also, there are bosses who are extremely gregarious and democratic and who want to fraternize with executives up and down the line. So our advice is to develop a sensitivity toward how far the boss wants *you* to go toward a social relationship. Restraint, but not rebuff, is a wise approach toward him.

In any social contacts with the boss and his wife, your actions and words must be exemplary. Take pains to be dressed properly for the occasion, not overdressed or underdressed. Be warm and natural, not aggressive. Eat and drink moderately. Let the boss and his wife take the lead in everything, from what you do to what you say. If you feel called on to change the subject or fill a conversational lull, keep it impersonal. Best not to talk about your husband. (See page 197 for conversational suggestions.)

Entertaining Lower Rank. In becoming socially involved with business associates of your husband, you naturally do not make a practice of going too far down in rank. If your husband came up the hard way from the mailroom, he certainly doesn't continue to fraternize with the mail clerks! He may want to entertain his subordinate executives and their wives at a party or picnic once a year; or if he heads a department or division of the company, he may want to entertain all at an annual family-type party. But this is not at all necessary. (If you are on the receiving end of this kind of strictly *group* invitation, it *never* calls for a return invitation to the boss.) So the general rule here is that it is best to maintain your rank with those of lesser rank, except as a group, and not become too familiar. It can become embarrassing on both sides if you don't.

Entertaining an Out-of-Town Executive. You may entertain *any* executive (and his wife, if she's along) from out of town if his business with your husband's company is directly with your husband, even though the visitor's rank in his company may be higher than your husband's rank in his own company. This is a matter of simple courtesy to a guest for whom you are responsible. No one is more dismal than a man alone in a hotel room staring at a TV set. Most visiting executives appreciate your thoughtfulness in planning at least one evening for them. And we believe they appreciate it even more if the wife is co-host with her husband. This becomes a personal compliment to him, rather than strictly business. After talking business all day, he would probably prefer to talk about his children or his garden in the evening. If two men dine together, it's still business. In inviting him, your husband issues a verbal invitation such as, "My wife and I hope you can join us for dinner tomorrow night about seven. We'll pick you up at your hotel and drive out to our club." (Remind your husband to refer to you as "my wife," not as "Mrs. Jamison.")

Rank Skipping. This is a dangerous game sometimes played by couples who are overly aggressive. In your eagerness to get ahead and associate with the "right people," you must never skip over the boss and aim at the next level above him socially. This is sure death the minute the boss discovers your plot. This also goes for any associate of your husband's boss outside your company. If the outside person regularly deals with the boss, and encounters your husband only as an assistant to the boss, it is *verboten* to attempt to cultivate this contact socially. It sometimes happens that your personal social contacts may be a cut or two above those of the boss. If so, the least said to him about it, the better. Never be tempted to name-drop.

Entertaining Customers. To fete someone to whom you want to sell something—whether it's an idea, a service, or merchandise—is the basis of all business entertaining. You are complimenting the person by your invitation and by the entertainment itself. You are hopeful that the friendly gesture and the quasi-personal relationship thus established will lead to a receptive attitude on the part of the other person. The way is laid for the consummation of a transaction later.

Unless your husband has specifically asked you to take some part in the business discussion, better leave it all to him. Could be that the little pressure you decide to exert is the thing that kills, instead of clinches, the deal. Your part is to be a charming foil for your husband, to be a gracious hostess for him, and to make his business guests feel important. The entertainment you offer, whether it is in or out of your home, should be of excellent quality and taste. Naturally you would not offer a customer or prospective customer careless or thoughtless hospitality—but neither should it be ostentatious. It should be appropriate to your husband's position and that of the customer. Sincerity is as important here as in any other social situation.

Entertaining Competitors.   Sometimes the situation arises when your husband must entertain a competitor in business. This is not unusual, since he and the competitor may belong to the same clubs or the same church, or their type of business may be one in which all competitors are banded together in an association. On the other hand, the competitor may simply be a personal friend or a next-door neighbor. If the competitive guests are not personal friends, you can keep the situation from becoming personal or awkward by making it a group party, such as a cocktail or sherry party. Then the conversation is unlikely to become embarrassing in any way. If your husband's competitor is also his best friend, you and the other wife are likely to be intimates. A natural social life together would follow. There may be some business areas that the two husbands would discuss together for their common good, but there will undoubtedly be many that would be taboo. The best policy for you is to stay out of any business discussions with the other wife. There are plenty of other subjects to discuss. Leave the shoptalk to the men. Most of all, never boast to the other wife about your husband's successes and triumphs.

Entertaining Not. "When in doubt, don't" is a good rule to follow. If you seriously question whether or not it is proper to entertain someone, or for someone, it is better not to risk a social fiasco. If there is some way to check, or someone to ask whether your idea is acceptable, do so. If not, forget it. In this instance, a sin of omission is more excusable than one of commission. Never do you want to embarrass your husband or yourself. If a man shows poor social judgment, you can bet that his boss will doubt his business judgment and be afraid to entrust the company's reputation to him.

The Office Party

We can't close this chapter without discussing that subject sometimes considered a sore one—the office party. In this friendly, casual country, it is a development that probably could never have been avoided. People who spend the majority of their days shut up in an office together have something in common, even if they are not otherwise homogeneous. (That's why the secretary sometimes understands a husband better than his wife!) So from time to time office form, routine, and caste are set aside while the office party takes place. It's usually a Christmas holiday party or a summer outing. We don't condemn this evidence of good will, but there are pitfalls to avoid and precautions to take. As a wife you may never be involved except as counsel to your husband. On the other hand, you may become involved in being co-host with him, or in attending such a party when families are invited, or you may be an executive yourself, or an executive secretary who has to arrange such an event.

1. The one big danger in the office party confined to employees is the convivial drinking with which they start. Soon the business barriers are down, and familiarity may set in. While familiarity does not always mean trouble, in this situation it may. The boss suddenly feels called upon to demonstrate what a good fellow he is, while some of the lesser lights (who

might be pretty girls) suddenly lose their inhibitions. The next day when all is back to business as usual, there can be some very red faces. A few precautions can avoid the problems:

~ The boss himself is the keynoter. He *must* maintain his dignity while at the same time being friendly and cordial to everyone.

~ Be sure there is plenty of food to accompany the libation, so that empty stomachs don't lead to giddiness or illness.

~ Have an array of soft drinks so that those not used to stronger beverages aren't embarrassed or led to drink something that they otherwise wouldn't.

~ Establish definite hours for the party, and close the bar at the end of the time.

2. An office party with wives and husbands present has more dignity, but it, too, has its problems. This kind of party is difficult for girls who have no one with whom to come. The employees will have a great deal in common, but the husbands and wives who don't know anyone but their mates may feel out in the cold. So the affair can be awkward and dull. To avoid this:

~ Appoint a host committee of employees whose responsibility it is to see that everyone has a way to come and someone to come with. Make it plain that single employees may come alone, if they prefer not to bring a date.

~ Though name badges are not elegant, this is one time when they have a place. They serve as a sort of mass introduction and imply that anyone may talk to anyone else.

~ Have planned entertainment of a light nature, such as a roaming accordionist, a combo, or a popular singer, to break the ice and relax the atmosphere.

∼❧ Consider a seated dinner with an executive and his wife as hosts at each table. But let employees specify with whom they want to sit, and try to arrange seating as close to their wishes as possible.

∼❧ If it is an outdoor family party, start off with some games that will help everyone get acquainted.

3. If your husband feels that he should entertain his subordinate executives or the employees of his department in your home, your role is to be the most gracious and dignified hostess possible. You must put everyone at ease, and at the same time maintain dignity and reserve. Your husband is still the boss, even if he is the host.

4. If you are a female executive and want to entertain the girls who work under you, a luncheon in a private room of a club or hotel is a treat for them and keeps the party on an impersonal plane. If you prefer a dinner or buffet supper in your home, the party will take on more intimacy and informality. Try to avoid office talk and office gossip by some planned activity or by steering the conversation yourself in other directions.

Making Friends in a New Community

Home is where the heart is.
—Pliny

CHAPTER

11

Before the current American trend of periodic long-distance moving, a person could be born and bred, married and buried in the same town, forever snug and secure within the same social cocoon. In many areas there was not even the desire to broaden the base of friendships. On the contrary, there was a tendency to block the entry of any newcomers to "the group." Our mother has told us of suggesting to a close friend that she meet her former college roommate, as she thought the two would be compatible. The friend's answer was, "I'm not interested in meeting any new people." Today this attitude is likely to be the exception, instead of the rule. Americans are on the move as never before, which has created a whole new social problem: how to become a part of the social scene in a new neighborhood, city, or country. This is a problem that faces all brides, too, as they establish homes of their own. Before you can entertain and give parties, you have to be accepted.

Here Today, Gone Tomorrow

In any kind of move, a wife is more affected than her husband. A promotion eagerly hoped for by him often brings with it a transfer not so eagerly hoped for by her. She is sometimes faced with the problem of being abruptly uprooted every time she begins to feel established in a new community. In many instances she has barely discovered the best supermarket, and acquired a few friends, when off she goes with her husband to a new post to start all over again. Most companies are willing to pick up the tab for transporting a complete household, including everything from the children's playhouse to the rosebushes Grandmother gave them. But other than telling a man what time to show up at the office, a corporation rarely does anything further to help with adjusting, and it's sink or swim for the rest of the family.

This life of the camp follower is more difficult for some wives than for others, and little does the husband really know what the settling-in process entails. He goes off to his new office to be cordially greeted by business associates. They are eager to see that he meets everyone and that he has everything he needs to make him happy, including a personable secretary to wait on him. But all the while, what is the wife doing? She is at home unpacking crates and attempting to make old curtains fit new windows. At the same time, in case any of the neighbors catch a glimpse of her, she is trying to look the part of a desirable addition to the neighborhood who won't lower real estate values on the block. She can't help wondering: what will this town be like, will we make friends easily, and will we fit into the new locale?

In some communities there is an atmosphere of friendliness from the start, while in others, where the old guard sets the pattern, the going can be rough. When one land-loving couple moved into a strictly nautical neighborhood, they wondered whether they would ever be accepted into the inner circle, since they didn't know *fore* from *aft*. During the first year, they were careful to show proper respect for this obsession of the neighbors. They knew they had it made when the unofficial spokesman of the block enthusiastically exclaimed one day, "Glad to have you aboard!"

Occasionally, if an entire office of several hundred employees is being moved to another town, the company will maintain a relocation center temporarily to provide information about real estate and schools. They are willing to give the man and his wife a trip—on the house—to size up the new town and find a home. But after that, it's up to the couple to solve their own problems and integrate socially. When this type of transfer involves many employees, those being moved tend to gravitate toward one another. They locate in the same section of town and may find themselves caught up in a tight little group, seeing only each other socially because it's the easiest way—instant social status! Such an ingrown circle insulates a person from new contacts, because others hesitate to break through. It's all right to have company friendships, but not to the exclusion of others. It calls for special effort on the part of the wife to widen horizons.

When in foreign countries, Americans are notorious for clinging to each other. A friend whose husband is assigned to North Africa for a lengthy stint wrote us about her experiences abroad. There are intracompany parties whenever new transfers arrive, to introduce them to other Americans, and there are morning coffees about once a month among all the wives. Our friend includes acquaintances from without the company whenever possible, so that she and her family will have a broader experience.

The length of time for becoming acclimated and forming a nucleus of new friends is just about the same in any move, whether at home or abroad. It takes a good six months for roots to take hold. Unquestionably, it is the wife who makes the inroads for the whole family that lead to recognition, good or bad, in a community. Success or failure of the move depends on her acceptance of it and the way she handles it. A husband may be busy integrating into civic affairs, but the whole responsibility for their social life ultimately falls on his wife. Reference to suburban towns as "bedrooms" has become a common expression, because of the many men who work in one town and go home to sleep in another. Wherever this system prevails, the wife almost always becomes acquainted in town first, and it is sometimes months before husbands meet.

Think Happy. When your husband comes home and announces another move, start thinking positively and have an open mind. If you arrive in a new area with a preconceived notion of disliking your new home, it's a cinch you won't like it. To complain and to think that the grass is greener elsewhere can easily become habit-forming. It's understandable that elderly people find it hard when uprooted, and even young people when it happens every year, but ordinarily most of us should be able to adjust to new surroundings. We once heard of a woman who refused to accept her husband's transfer gracefully. She continually told her new neighbors how much she disliked her house and how much better the one she left suited her. After a miserable year, her husband moved the family back to their former home, which they still owned. A few years later, the neighbors who had bent a sympathetic ear to her complaints were surprised and amused when they learned that she had completely remodeled the house "back home," which she constantly praised, to become an identical copy of the one she had criticized and abandoned.

Another mobile wife complained that everyone in the neighborhood where she moved was much too old—even the postman! This came as a rude shock to those who considered themselves in the prime of life and in reality were only about 10 years her senior. That family also returned to their home town where, we assume, everybody is young, or else they have cornered the Fountain of Youth.

Don't be a displaced person, never taking interest in the new community and constantly talking about the way it was where you lived before. The utmost tact and diplomacy are needed by the wife who is with her husband on a foreign assignment. She shouldn't irritate and antagonize the nationals of a country by telling them how many more washing machines we have in the States. If you are still residing in your former home mentally, unwilling to transfer your loyalty to the new one, you are neither here nor there. You are living in a state of suspension that is emotionally unsettling to you and your entire family.

There are nice people everywhere, and if you are enthusiastic about your new community, it's likely that you will be received enthusiastically. If you say enough good things about a place, you will begin to believe them yourself! The newcomer who appears interested in others and in the town itself is generally the one who makes the adjustment quickly. In fact, some find constant moving to be a stimulating challenge. The wife who knows that she and her husband are between moves and subject to transfer at any time will be happier if she settles down and "thinks permanent." She will always feel like a gypsy, if she does nothing but sit and wait to pack.

No Pushing, Please

Although we advocate participation as a means of making friends, it's not wise to plunge in blindly without any discrimination regarding the direction your new life is taking. If you allow yourself to be propelled into an all-consuming social circle that doesn't meet your standards, you will shut out other avenues that may lead to more congenial and appropriate friendships. Also avoid seeming to be like an over-friendly puppy that attaches itself to someone and keeps jumping in where it isn't wanted. Pushiness will get you nowhere. The trick is to go 90 percent of the way, but look as though you are going only 50 percent. In other words, conquer the delicate art of trying hard without really showing it.

Workers Welcome!   There are all sorts of little ways for the wife to *let* herself be "discovered," but the one sure game that anybody can play is a four-letter word called WORK. Every-

body loves a worker, but never a drone. Joiners are many, but
workers are few. When asked to help on civic affairs, such as
Red Cross and United Fund drives, never decline in a new
neighborhood. Americans are compulsive do-gooders, always
raising money for a cause, so it's not hard to find a bandwagon
to jump on. Older residents are usually looking for someone
new to pass the torch to, because they're tired of doing it themselves. It's a great way to meet everybody on the block—and
legitimate, too! In our moves, we have walked miles on door-to-
door fund-raising, have struggled with literally gallons of coffee
and mountains of fudge at benefits, and have blown enough air
from our own lungs into balloons for hospital carnivals to create a medium-sized tornado. And as though that weren't enough,
the cast-offs we have sorted at thrift shops and rummage sales
would clothe a good-sized town.

So Glad You Came

Immediately following any move, most wives are consumed
by the tasks of decorating the house, arranging furniture, and
helping the children to adjust. One wife told us that the only
persons she knew well for the first year were the pediatrician
and the milkman. It isn't easy to carry out the role of a gracious
hostess just waiting for someone to call. Casual dropping in is
all but extinct in busy communities. At times we long for the
good old days when entertaining was more impromptu and
guests were always welcome. Now the stock question when a
friend telephones or stops by is, "Are you on your way out?"
We assume that the other person's schedule is crammed full
every day and it usually is! The British have managed to cling
to their afternoon tea hour, which helps to retain graciousness
in living, because it can bring friends together and create a
pause in the day. We read of one incident when this custom was
carried to such an extreme that it brought alarm to passengers
on a London subway as it glided 600 yards without motorman

or conductor; the two had jumped out to fill their teapot with hot water!

A friend of ours speaks nostalgically of her childhood, when birthdays were the most special event of the year in their Swedish household. Not a single invitation was sent, yet when the day arrived, many friends and relatives, both young and old, appeared spontaneously bearing gifts and good wishes. The celebration sometimes lasted several days, but her mother was always prepared for these "surprise" visitors with a magnificent smorgasbord, including a big birthday cake. They never knew how many would come, but they had such faith in their Scandinavian heritage that no one ever considered the possibility of being forgotten. As charming as this sounds, we know deep inside that today a party without special invitation just wouldn't come off. Our lives are usually busy and too organized to permit the luxury of spontaneity.

Going back further into the past, we have a news clipping that gives an account of our grandmother's wedding at a time when guests came from far and wide to celebrate. The minister arrived by mistake a day early, but this didn't upset either the bride or her family. He was invited in to spend the night, and then he stayed several days more, as friends and relatives continued the festivities. We admire their ability to manage unexpected arrivals plus days of entertaining, but we must remember that it was a day of more spacious houses and adequate domestic help.

Today, neighbors hesitate to call for fear of intruding at the wrong time, so it's up to you to make them feel welcome when they do come. One new arrival intimidated a well-meaning neighbor who asked to call when she said, "Do come, but be sure to bring some handwork, because I can't waste time!" No offense was intended; she simply wanted to do her own mending while visiting. But because of her abrupt manner, it was a long time before her neighbor worked up enough courage to make the call. In direct contrast to this, we know the wife of a young doctor who was just establishing his practice in town. She had four little children to cope with, besides the offbeat schedule of the doctor, yet whenever we dropped in unexpectedly she had the gift of making us feel she was actually hoping we'd come.

You Can't Win Them All.   No matter how hard the newcomer tries to make a good impression, occasionally efforts are thwarted. One woman we know waited patiently for her next-door neighbor, a very reserved and dignified person, to make the first gesture. When the neighbor finally came to call, it was disastrous. The newcomer, preparing for dinner guests, was taking stock of the liquor cabinet. She never drank herself, but became curious to know the difference between Scotch and Bourbon, so decided that the only way to find out was to taste. After taking a generous swig from each bottle, she looked out the window and to her horror saw her dignified neighbor coming up the walk on her first call. Since there was no escape, she greeted the visitor, reeking with alcohol and nervously trying to explain what she was doing. She became more ill at ease, and explanations went from bad to worse when the woman informed her that she never kept alcohol in her home. The call she had long anticipated turned into sheer torment. She knew that her behavior from then on had to be exemplary at all times, and if she so much as stumbled, she'd be suspected as a problem drinker. It was two years before this same neighbor relaxed and extended an invitation to join her bridge club.

An equally traumatic experience happened to another friend who moved into a neighborhood of ardent gardeners. He heard of a bargain in fertilizer, to be purchased by the carload, so decided to win friends by letting them in on the kill. He became self-elected chairman in charge of ordering and parceling out the fertilizer but, husbandlike, he neglected to inform his wife of the plans. She was caught unprepared the day of delivery for either the carload of fertilizer or the whopping bill presented with it. After a hasty call to the bank to find out whether their checking account could stand the strain, she had the truck unload in the garage. The following weekend brought a rush of excited neighbors to stake their claims, and our friend did more than his share of work in the distribution. But when the excitement subsided, he was mortified to discover that one of the neighbors he most wanted to please had come out of the melee with nothing. He felt obliged to sacrifice the meager supply for his own yard in order to avoid hurt feelings. So after a frenzied week, he ended up with only the pungent aroma of his neighbors' well-fertilized lawns—and a strained back!

Follow Suit

Willingness to go along with the established trend is essential to being accepted in any neighborhood. If doghouses are frowned on, bring Rover inside. If clotheslines are not in vogue, buy a dryer or purchase one of the circular, collapsible lines. And if you secretly long for a fence, postpone it until you can convince the neighbors that you're really fencing the kids in, not the neighbors out. One woman made herself unpopular when she moved into a neighborhood of cat fanciers and immediately wrote a letter to the town newspaper maligning all the cats. She has since moved away, but the wounds inflicted on the cat-lovers have not yet healed. Wait until relations are well cemented before deviating noticeably from the set pattern. Then if you can't lick them, join them happily. Most building restrictions in an area are for the sole purpose of preserving its beauty and are probably responsible for the location's appeal to you in the first place. So don't try to circumvent set rules. You *can* beat city hall, but not neighbors!

If formality in names is customary, wait until Mrs. Brown asks you to call her "Ann" before taking liberties. But if everybody else starts right out on a first-name basis, don't be shy about doing the same. In our neighborhood there is such informality that neighbors would think it odd if you didn't use first names —even for great-grandmothers. Yet in the city where we grew up, our mother's friends were still calling each other "Mrs." after twenty years.

A new arrival is not expected to know the customs in a particular neighborhood the day she moves in, but if she is alert she won't make the same mistake twice. A young wife we know found that her weightiest decisions were whether to dress up or dress down when going to a party. If you do guess wrong, she told us, it helps to have an understanding husband who always thinks you're the prettiest girl at the party, whatever you wear. But if you zig when you should have zagged, take two aspirin tablets and make the best of it.

Welcome, Stranger!

We have always been lucky enough to move into neighborhoods where people make a concerted effort to welcome newcomers, yet respect privacy (the perfect combination). When a new family arrives, it's not long before someone is at the door with an apple pie or an invitation to dinner. One neighbor took in a family of five overnight, because the moving van hadn't finished unloading. In another town where we lived, one dear little old lady scooted across the back way with a cake to get there ahead of the neighbor heading for the front way with a pie. She explained sweetly that she wanted to be the first to invite the new arrivals to church. This sounds competitive, but her heart was in the right place.

The more people you meet, the more you will find who have interests compatible with yours. It's easiest to become acquainted when there are a number of new families moving into a neighborhood within the same year. This often happens, with so many transfers taking place. Since all newcomers have the same objective, that of making friends, the give and take involved in relationships is on a very casual basis. There is not the waiting game that is essential if you are the only new arrival. During this period when you are meeting people and being evaluated, it is important to write little bread-and-butter notes for courtesies extended you. Others like to know that what they do is appreciated, even though they do it willingly.

There is often one good organizer in a neighborhood who sees that people with similar interests meet. Among our friends is one person who went to great lengths in giving categorized parties. Individual groups might be invited because they were mothers of preschool children, mothers of second-graders, wives in her husband's business, new couples who lived on the same street, or fathers who liked to play with electric trains. She was teased unmercifully, though affectionately, because we all felt like catalogued numbers in a little slot in her file. But she did get others together and was responsible for launching many new friendships.

It's Up to You

Always encourage any entree. If you have a friend who knows someone in the town where you are moving and suggests your getting in touch with her, don't hesitate to do so. Ask the friend if she would mind writing to say that you are coming.

Parents often become acquainted through their children. An invitation to join a car pool for taxiing the kids may be a nuisance to carry out, but in some neighborhoods it's your bid to join the clan. If your neighbors don't put out the welcome mat, there are many activities to enter into without waiting to be invited. Only a person devoid of interests could miss.

The church or temple is one of the first places that many people think of on moving to a new area, but it's unlikely that you could get to know anyone intimately just by attending a service. As with any organization, it's necessary to participate in the projects within. If you are musical, join the choir. You might meet someone who will invite you to a music club. Every town has a hospital within reach, and all hospitals need volunteer help. Women's hospital auxiliaries are generally eager for workers, and even though these organizations often have nominal dues, it's merely a matter of mentioning to a member that you are interested.

One person we know always continued her interest in mental-health projects when moving to a new state. Another continued working with UNICEF and became known throughout the entire state after she moved. Someone else entered enthusiastically into supporting the symphony orchestra in any city she moved to. The League of Women Voters is another possibility. There are Red Cross chapters in most communities that welcome workers, as do Boy and Girl Scout groups. Anyone who is willing to become a den mother will gain the admiration of other mothers! Although some friends say it is every bit as hectic as they imagined, others say that the camaraderie among the co-working mothers is equal to that of the Scouts themselves. At least give it a go for the sake of your children. P.T.A. brings you into contact with parents of children the same ages as yours.

The YWCA is open to all, and their newcomers' clubs have become famous as a means of meeting other new people and also getting acquainted with the town itself. One of our most cherished friendships of long standing blossomed within a newcomers' club. In some areas the YWCA sponsors a "ladies' day out" program, which provides classes at a nominal fee on a variety of subjects such as bridge, art, hat making, and gourmet cooking. Many towns have adult education classes at night, when husbands can baby-sit, on anything from paleontology to picture framing. In a group of this nature you will find congenial people who are interested in the same things you are.

Crafts make for binding friendships. Women become obsessed with painting, ceramics, knitting, or rug making, and they love to pursue these hobbies in groups, to compare results. And people interested in doing things are generally interesting people. A friend of ours who sews beautifully moved to a part of the country where she knew no one. But when the young wives on her block discovered her talents, they were eager to share it. First thing she knew, she had a weekly kaffeeklatsch with sewing lessons on the side. This same friend also became one of the mainstays in little theater work in the new town—she is their authority on costumes.

By Invitation Only

Many organizations take in new members only by special invitation and often require a year's residence before a name can be proposed. By this time, most newcomers have made friends who take pleasure in sponsoring them for clubs. Among such possibilities are women's clubs, college clubs, country clubs, swimming clubs, tennis clubs, service leagues, and Junior League. If you have belonged to such an organization in another town, ask them to write ahead to the club in the town where you are going. This facilitates joining, and in some clubs brings about an automatic transfer, eliminating the waiting period. It's a simple matter to join sorority and college alumni groups. It's up to you to make yourself known to them.

Setting a Social Trap

Some wives are simply not joiners, and they shrink from organized activity. Or some find themselves tied down without reliable baby-sitters. If this is your predicament, and neighbors fail to make gestures your way, take matters into your own hands—but subtly! If you have a little one, get out there and stroll. Everybody loves to coo over babies. They're irresistible. Look out the window and find out the popular hour of day for neighbors to be out gardening or wheeling their children. Put on something attractive but casual, no hair curlers or blue jeans, and look your prettiest—baby, too. A smile always helps. Only a person with a heart of stone could resist this trap.

If you're not lucky enough to have a baby on hand, buy a dog—a cute dog—and walk it often. We can guarantee that you'll meet someone who will at least talk to the dog. Although we are fervent ailurophiles, we recommend dogs instead of cats for this purpose because walking a cat on a leash is destined to end in defeat. This animal trick was carried to what we consider rather extreme lengths when one family bought a horse to attract the neighbors!

The Children's Hour

Any wife who is also a mother has a double adjustment in moving. She must see that her children adapt as well as she does. The younger the child, the easier it is. Any child young enough to play outside is found by other children. No formal introductions are needed here. First thing you know, they're merrily tricycling down the street together. If you provide plenty of play equipment, such as swings, sandbox, and playhouse, it attracts children as honey attracts bears. A rustic log "fort" in our neighborhood draws them from blocks away.

Of course, children of school age become acquainted in class, but for those who move in summer this is delayed. One family arrived in town immediately after school closed, so the mother made a special effort to take her children to a supervised playground each day, where they soon made friends quickly. Children can also become acquainted through Boy and Girl Scout troops or in classes of various kinds, such as dancing or music.

As the age group advances to the teen-age set, the children are more restrained in getting acquainted and are too old to want parents to start friendships for them. In some suburban towns the YW and YMCA do an excellent service for teen-agers in providing after-school activities such as Ping-Pong, dancing, music, gymnastics, and swimming. Some high schools sponsor clubs that are open to all and promote different interests, such as skiing, science, or French.

Your Turn

As soon as the family is settled, the house is in order, and you have made a few acquaintances, don't wait too long to repay the courtesies shown you. It's unthinkable to be like "unsinkable" Molly Brown, who invited her neighbors to a bash as soon as she moved in. Of course, nobody came to the party, and she was shunned by one and all. But once you have been entertained by several people, your invitation will be an anticlimax if it comes too late and the relationship has begun to crumble in the interim. When you do entertain, don't overlook the person who launched you. It would be rude and ungrateful. One newcomer we know was entertained several times by a neighbor who graciously introduced her to a large circle of friends. These invitations were never repaid, and the final insult occurred when the newcomer requested her hostess's favorite recipe for a luncheon to which she failed to invite her neighbor.

You have to develop a little extrasensory perception to know how far you can go in issuing first invitations. If you have been entertained by a number of other wives, yet haven't met every husband, you can repay them as couples. Just say that you are looking forward to having them in your home to meet your husband.

When you finally reach the stage of that first real party you've looked forward to giving, make it a *smashing* success. It will never lose its glow if it's a hit—nor cease to haunt you if it flops! We're not urging extravagance, but we do mean to make everything as attractive as possible—yourself, your home, your food— even your husband. Splurge a little this time on flowers, and have silver and brass sparkling. Serve only the never-fail recipes in your file, and above all make guests feel welcome in your home so that they will *want* to come back. We know of one incident when the spectacular success of the hostess was almost her undoing. A male guest was so complimentary that his wife became jealous. We trust this won't happen to you, but if it does, smooth it over with something extravagantly flattering to the wife. Ask for her fondue recipe, which you simply *adored,* or persuade her to tell you how she raises such beautiful roses!

Past Imperfect, Future Perfect

If your debut doesn't live up to your high hopes, don't go into seclusion. Better luck next time! We believe in looking forward with optimism instead of backward with regret. Mrs. Herbert Hoover was such a perfectionist that when giving parties in the White House she always reviewed them later with her staff so that she could make the next parties even better. If you are "the staff" in your house, confer with yourself to improve your next try.

After a few moves, a wife becomes sensitive to the plight of others, and she is the one to welcome the next new neighbor. It means so much to find someone at the door on moving day with a plate of sandwiches and cookies. That first person who breaks the ice and makes you feel at home usually occupies a special place in your heart forever. And the only way you can really even the score is to do the same thing for someone else.

The Clothes You Need for Your Social Life

A fair exterior is a silent recommendation.
—Publilius Syrus

The age-old debate is whether women dress to please men, other women, or themselves. We couldn't possibly take sides because we believe every woman who seeks self-confidence and social success should dress well to please all three.

A well-turned-out woman never fails to be noticed and admired by a man—whether husband, male guest, or just the friendly truck driver who can't resist an appreciative whistle! Another woman may experience a tinge of envy upon seeing you perfectly dressed, but you go *up* in her estimation. At the same time, your own personality is enhanced when you are beautifully packaged with tasteful and fashion-right clothes, harmonizing accessories, and appropriate coiffure and makeup.

Some lucky women seem to be born with a talent for looking wonderful and could probably survive a shipwreck with chic. Jacqueline Kennedy and the Duchess of Windsor are prime examples of our time. Others, not so lucky, go through life looking as if their clothes were only an afterthought. If you feel you belong to this latter group, read this chapter carefully and take heart. You, too, can learn to qualify for the "Ten Best Dressed" in your own social circle, whether your clothes budget is little or lavish. Actually, being well dressed has nothing to do with money. We can think of at least two rich celebrities in New York who are the objects of incredulous stares at theater and opera openings because they are so gaudily and lavishly overdressed. They mistakenly take the stares and flashbulbs as a token of admiration. In notable contrast is Mrs. Rudolf Bing, wife of the managing director of the Metropolitan Opera, who always attends opening night in a distinguished gown of utter simplicity, but exquisite in color and fabric. Her hair, makeup, and accessories are in the same key.

On-Stage Dressing

Clothes are important to every woman, and especially to those who entertain to any extent. All hostesses should heed these checkpoints in their clothes closets:

1. A *knowledgeable* wardrobe that fits into the pattern of the community—not obviously above it, and certainly never below it.

A couple we know almost ruined their chances of being accepted by a social set of comparable economic status by not being dressed compatibly. Moving to an ultraconservative city, they found the most "in" neighborhood and bought a beautiful house. Their first invitation arrived for a cocktail party on a spring afternoon at a palatial home nearby. With every intention of making the right impression, the wife outfitted herself in a new understated, but very good, little black cocktail dress. Her husband wore his best Brooks Brothers. Shock is the only word for their reaction when they arrived and discovered that the cocktail uniform of this snobbish set was the ultimate in reverse snobbism—immaculately tailored Bermudas and shirts for both the women and the men!

We have much more to say on this subject of clothes to fit the community later in this chapter. We just want to register the point here as a major wardrobe consideration.

2. An *interchangeable and versatile* wardrobe that multiplies as fast as an electronic computer, yielding up a maximum of costumes that can attend any kind of occasion from a picnic to a ball.

Indiscriminate buying will get you nowhere in building this kind of wardrobe that you need to take you everywhere. You must *plan,* and the best way is on paper (see page 381).

We'd like to interject here that a friend of any wardrobe is the feast of fabulous sportswear we have today. Much of it isn't really sporting any more. There are dressy skirts, blouses, sweaters, and jackets that switch and combine into many marvelous looks. One wife we know must be ready to fly or sail off at a moment's notice with her travel-executive husband. Concentrating on separates, she prides herself on being able to go around the world with one suitcase and be among the best-dressed anywhere, whether she's at the captain's party or dining at Maxim's.

Separates may net you a great bargain. Frequently you can pick up one wonderful skirt here or one heavenly blouse there that might be left in stock at the end of the season. Otherwise, we're not for bargains, as we believe very few real ones exist. If it's marked down, there's often a reason.

3. An *instant* wardrobe, always clean, pressed, mended, and ready to go at a moment's notice—whether to a party next door or halfway around the globe.

Putting clothes back into your closet when there's a rip or a tear, a spot or a hanging hem, may seem expedient at the moment, but in the long run it's more than annoying. Woo the habit of keeping your wardrobe "go." A little mending kit nearby makes it easy to take that stitch in time. Sending off your soiled clothes weekly to the dry cleaner assures you an instantly ready wardrobe. Then when your husband telephones to relay a last-minute invitation to help entertain a visitor or to accompany him on a sudden trip, you'll never have to plead, "But I haven't a thing to wear."

4. A complement of *accessories* to achieve a total look for each outfit.

Accessories are the accents to any costume and can make or break it. Never underestimate the power these small pieces pack. Choose the finest you can afford and be sure that they complement more than one outfit.

A Matter of Taste

The first consideration of the well-dressed woman is the almost indefinable matter of taste. Webster calls taste "The power of discerning and appreciating fitness, beauty, order, or whatever constitutes excellence . . ." Emerson said simply, "Love of beauty is taste." Schiller believed taste is "The finer impulse of our nature." Various others have said that good taste is synonymous with good sense.

Actually, taste changes with the changes in time and place. It may have been tasteful in another age to sit in a Roman arena and cheer the pitting of lions against human beings, or today in another country to sit in a Spanish *plaza de toros* and watch a handsome bullfighter present a dusty, bloody bull's tail to a beautiful señorita. Or it may be in good taste to parade in a bikini at St. Tropez, but a scandalous shock to wear one in your home town if you're over twenty-five. Near nudity was taste in post-Revolution France, but a disgrace in Victorian England. Taste today may be a wristful of gold bracelets, but never a single one on the ankle.

To zero in on taste in dress, it means being able to discern what is acceptable at the particular time and place . . . with the addition of a large dash of good sense! This doesn't mean you have to be dull. Be daring enough to try the new, if it's appropriate. Have the courage to be individual, but not queer. Have the grace never to shock.

In another vein, taste is simplicity. It's quality stripped of the obvious non-essential. To return to our paragons of looks and manners, Jacqueline Kennedy and the Duchess of Windsor are never overdone or conspicuous, although both are always exquisitely dressed in the best of fashion and are trend-setters.

If you feel insecure about your own taste, you *can* develop it to the point of security. Choose the friend (or enemy!) whom you consider to have the best taste and whom you envy most. Try to analyze why you admire her appearance. Every time you see her, figure out what she has done to make herself appear the ultimate in good taste. Later, when you're alone, analyze it on paper! Is her hairdo subtly a bit smoother than the others? Is her makeup designed to make the most of her good features? Are her clothes well-fitting, of good quality, fashion-right, clean, pressed, the right length, a foil for her type? Are her accessories and jewelry really accessories to the whole, and not overpowering or too conspicuous? Is her voice pleasant and well modulated? Is her manner considerate and thoughtful? Do *you* get the idea?

A Thing to Wear

To prescribe a specific wardrobe that would answer the social needs of women everywhere would be impossible. This country is much too big and varied; fashion is much too fleeting. There are general rules, though, that will insure a well-dressed appearance anywhere.

1. Keep posted on the new and right in fashion by watching the windows and displays of the better department stores and

shops and by reading their ads. Study the fashion magazines. Take clues and cues from the top designers by looking at their clothes in the stores, even if you can't afford to buy them. But don't be misguided by television, where fashion is a stranger.

2. List the activities that make up your social life, such as country club luncheons, dinners in homes, committee meetings, P.T.A. gatherings. Then note the kinds of clothes that are essential for your attendance at these functions, such as little wool dresses for winter luncheons, and linens for summer; tweed suits for committee meetings; and so on, according to the customs of your group.

3. Start your new wardrobe each season by using your holdovers from the preceding season as the springboard. List what is still presentable, along with the blouses, sweaters, and accessories you still have. Then plan what major new purchases you have to make to be dressed for every kind of occasion that will turn up on your social calendar. Since coats are the most expensive items in a wardrobe, buy these first. Then coordinate all else, including accessories. Try to have accessories as interchangeable as possible for multiple effects. Every ensemble should be planned to have a *total look* from head to toe. Personally, we sometimes catalog our wardrobe for an entire season on little cards. Each costume, with its accessories and jewelry, is listed on a separate card. This makes dressing easier, our look more complete, and packing for a trip a breeze.

4. Color sense makes fashion sense. As wonderful as color is, it can be a tender trap if you don't discipline yourself when buying. Don't let yourself fall in love with the most divine little orange dress if green is your basic color. It could be horrendous! Luckily, we have arrived at a sophistication in fashion that says that everything doesn't have to match. In fact, better if it doesn't. Now we can wear unusual colors together that formerly were taboo. This gives more leeway in combining clothes for multiple effects.

At the beginning of each season, decide which color you want to make the basis of your wardrobe. This doesn't have to be a basic color in the narrow sense of the word (such as black or navy blue)—it can be a new fashion color. Build all other clothes around this in colors that are compatible, so that clothes, coats, and accessories are not only harmonious together, but also interesting in contrast.

5. Accessories make a major contribution to the total appearance and should be carefully selected to *enhance* the ensemble. They are not inconsequential bits and pieces to be bought with little thought and money. Nothing stands out more conspicuously than a cheap hat, or a plastic handbag, or poorly made shoes. In fact, good accessories can make a little nothing of a dress look like a couture model.

In planning accessories, try to achieve individual effects—not just the same safe basic black. It's no longer the fashion to match everything—such as shoes, bag, and gloves; or earrings, pin, and necklace. If you must match, at least try for contrast of texture, such as black patent or calf shoes with black lizard or alligator handbag. The knowing way is to choose each piece on its own merits, but naturally with the thought of compatibility in mind. For example, a pink, yellow, pale green, or beige suit might be accessorized with mushroom-colored calf shoes, olive-y green lizard bag, and beige leather gloves. Gold shell earrings would look pretty with a pearl necklace. A colored enamel or gold pin, and an armful of gold bangles combine well with almost any ensemble in the daytime. We must note here that we believe the well-dressed woman should not be hung with costume jewelry. It should be real, no matter how simple. The sole exceptions are fake pearls, although we lean to cultured versions, and hand-set costume jewelry for evening. Most of us are *not* the possessors of a set of diamonds or emeralds!

6. If you lack confidence in selecting and putting your clothes together, put yourself in the hands of one of the shopping

consultants. Most of the leading stores have these personal shoppers who will suggest and select for you.

7. Ask the help of the fashion coordinator in your favorite department store, when you have a fashion question. These knowledgeable women know not only what is fashion-right, but also what is right to wear where. This is particularly helpful if you have just moved to a new community.

The Hostess Receives.   Time was when etiquette demanded that the hostess appear at her own parties in understated dress, so she wouldn't upstage her guests. Today's hostess happily plays quite the opposite role and can be as colorful as a peacock. She can dress in a completely different fashion from her guests if she wishes, and at an evening party can be much more elaborate. Not only does she direct the show, but she stars in it, too—and can look the part.

At a morning party or meeting, the hostess is likely to wear the same type of dress as her guests, but she doesn't have to. She can choose a pants suit appropriate for the season and time of day.

Both hostess and guests should choose a dress, ensemble, or suit for lunch, except at a resort where silk pants and shirt, or a simple shift, might be the order. An afternoon dessert or card party calls for the same kind of dressing.

At the tea or cocktail hour, the hostess can really begin to shine. For tea an afternoon dress is pretty and right—a lace suit, a soft chiffon, a pretty silk print. For cocktails she may be a bit more dressy and sophisticated in a typical cocktail dress, or she may decide on a long hostess dress or skirt and dressy top.

For a dinner at home the hostess may elect to wear a long at-home skirt or dress, or at-home pajamas with full legs. The guests may be wearing only simple street-length dresses, but it's fun for the hostess to have a different look. Even if her party is black-tie, she can wear a hostess gown or pajamas. For entertaining at dinner outside the home, hostess and guests would be dressed similarly in whatever fashion prevails at the time and place.

"Black Tie" or "White Tie."   These words added to an invitation mean a formal evening party and demand the prettiest clothes hostess and guests can corral. For most cities and towns in this country, "black tie" is the most formal kind of party given. It denotes a dinner jacket or tuxedo (never say "tux") worn with a black bow tie for the men. The degree of formality of the women's dresses depends on the occasion and the customs of the community. For a dinner it could be anywhere from a short, simple dinner dress to a long, lavish dress. It should never be "bare," but could have a low neckline. For a dance or a ball, black tie signifies that the ladies are expected to wear an evening dress (or "formal," as it is called in some cities). The elaborateness of this dress follows the local pattern, and it might be anything from a short décolleté dress to the most elaborate long dress.

Men's dinner jackets may change with fashion or with the season. Traditional is the midnight navy blue or black fine worsted, but now some men who enjoy wearing nonconformist clothes may decide to wear dark plaid or deep-maroon jackets or even brocades. Personally, we think the traditional more distinguished. In summer the white dinner jacket is popular and acceptable almost everywhere, although absolute traditionalists still accept only black, summer or winter. Men's evening shirts and accessories also vary, so a local tailor or fine men's store should be consulted on what is being worn locally at the time.

When an invitation reads "white tie," the men must wear the most formal evening attire, meaning tailcoat and white piqué bow tie. Ladies follow suit with the most formal kind of dress in fashion at the moment. Today this is a long dress. It doesn't necessarily have to be low-cut, but does have to be dressy in fabric and detail.

An invitation that gives the choice of black tie or white tie leaves it up to the guests to decide how dressy they want to be. The majority of men would probably choose black tie because they are more likely to have that attire and to feel more comfortable. The women, though, don't necessarily have to be influenced by this male inclination. They may go all out in light of such an invitation.

We have known couples who turn down invitations that call for formal clothes because they simply don't own them. There's no need for this denial of pleasure today, as it is perfectly acceptable, and quite usual, for men to rent the evening attire they need. In fact, many men of means who do not have regular occasion to attend formal functions find it more convenient and more economical to rent clothing when they need it. Some of the best tailors have this service available, and we do suggest renting from the best supplier. Women can always improvise easily and economically with a long skirt and evening blouse or sweater.

A near-necessity in a woman's wardrobe today is an evening coat. Never wear a daytime coat over an evening dress, even if the coat is mink! A long cloth coat is smartest. The ultimate is a long fur coat, if your budget is limitless! A street length is acceptable if it is an evening coat in a dressy fabric or fur with dressy styling and made to be worn only with evening or dinner clothes. A waist-length coat or jacket may even be styled to ensemble with the evening dress. And finally there's the mink stole, but it is so ubiquitous today that it lacks distinction.

Happily Hatted—or Unhatted. Where and when to wear a hat is no longer the problem it used to be, because you can appear almost anywhere today unhatted. Beautifully groomed hair has stolen the show. It is completely proper to attend any kind of social function bareheaded. In fact, the only time a hat is required is for the formal ceremonies of life: church, funerals, weddings. You can even dispense with a hat or little headpiece after a wedding ceremony and enjoy the reception with your crowning glory in full view. Naturally, you can keep your hat on through the whole thing if you prefer.

Although we have seen some hostesses wear hats when giving luncheons or other daytime parties in their own homes, to us this seems a bit silly and unnatural, especially in this day when many women never wear a hat. With some few rugged individualists a hat is a trademark. The Comtesse de Toulouse-Lautrec is reported to put on a hat the minute she gets up in the morning. And we rather imagine Hedda Hopper might do the same. But we can bet that you don't—so why put on a hat when you're hostessing? If your party is outside the home at a club or hotel, do as you wish.

A guest who wears a hat to a morning party, a luncheon, or an afternoon bridge may keep her hat on—or she may take it off when she takes off her coat, if she would feel more comfortable bareheaded. A hat worn to a tea, cocktail party, or reception (except wedding reception) should be kept on, since these are drop-in affairs.

A hat is usually not worn to dinner or the theater in the evening unless it is especially designed for that purpose and is almost an integral part of your total look. Then it is not taken off, but remains a part of the ensemble you are wearing. The exception is a hat worn to the theater that will cause everybody in the next 15 rows back to have to lean sideways. Then, by all means, take it off before someone has to ask you.

For really formal occasions, the rule is no hat. If you want to wear a hair ornament such as a bow or jewel or flower that relates to your dress, this can be very pretty. Need we say that for such an occasion your coiffure should be fresh and special? An added hairpiece can be quite dramatic.

The Gloved Hand.   We hope you share our love for beautiful gloves. They can elevate a costume to elegance. Except for active sports, when you may or may not wear special gloves, we can think of no social occasion when gloves are not only correct but called for. Gloves have always been a symbol of importance since they were adopted by the church and court as a part of ceremonial dress centuries ago.

The mobile automobile life we lead today is conducive to running out barehanded—but don't. Naturally, don't drive in good gloves, but take them along to put on before you get out of the car, whether it's a shopping spree downtown or an elegant party you're going to. And as for whether you can wear gloves when you don't wear a hat, you most certainly can—and should.

The fashion length of gloves changes periodically, so no set rules can be given. Also, in selecting gloves, the current sleeve lengths must be considered. With no sleeves or short sleeves, longer gloves are called for. With long sleeves, shorter ones are natural. The only gloves we like for teen-age girls are little wristbone-length shorties. But these are so young that they don't belong on anyone over 32, except perhaps with a casual sleeveless summer dress. Mid-arm gloves (8-button length) are smartest with any daytime sleeve except a really long sleeve. With a bracelet-length sleeve, just crush them a bit.

With a cocktail or dinner dress that is sleeveless, or has only short cap sleeves, select the 8-button mid-arm glove or the 10- or 12-button, which comes below the elbow. If you are young, a shortie is appropriate.

With formal evening clothes, the elbow-length glove (10- or 12-button) or the long 16-button model is correct. Teen-age girls and young women may choose between these and white kid shorties. In deciding, consider how you think your own arms look, and what length harmonizes best with the lines of the dress you will wear. If it has a bare top with string straps, or is strapless, do wear the 16-button white kid.

Leather gloves are the criterion of quality, but there are many beautiful fabric ones, too. Leather should always be chosen, though, for dressy and formal occasions. Fabrics are fine for daytime events. As for the styling, the simpler the better. Actually, just beautiful leather in a beautiful color is enough. No little embroidered flowers or beads, please. The colors of

leather gloves should be subtle, rather than obvious—basic colors
are always appropriate. For daytime wear, an off-white or beige
is now smarter than pure white. If you choose a real color for a
glove, be sure it is a pastel or muted tone, because brightly colored hands have a way of looking garish. For informal daytime
summer wear, some of the embroidered polka dots or printed
stripes are amusing on cottons.

When to take gloves off and when to leave them on is a puzzlement to many. In Grandmother's day, stringent rules applied
about a lady's gloves. Today common sense prevails.

❋ Always wear gloves outside going to and from a social event.

❋ If your gloves are beautiful and complete your costume, you
don't have to take them off at *any* social function, except when
eating, drinking, or smoking. However, it would look odd to
keep them on at an informal or casual affair.

❋ Though it is customary in Europe for a woman to whip off
her right glove when shaking hands, it is done in this country
only when meeting a high official of church or state.

❋ When you are hostess in your own home, you don't don gloves
to greet your guests except for a very formal affair, such as
receiving at a reception, a black-tie dinner, or for a formal
ball in your own ballroom. In today's casual world, this isn't
necessary, and you can appear naturally in your own home
barehanded as you would bareheaded. Mrs. Lyndon B. Johnson has received at the White House without gloves. On the
other hand, if you believe it adds to your total look, it is perfectly correct.

❋ When you are part of a receiving line *not* in your own home,
and when you are a guest going through a receiving line, keep
your gloves on.

❋ No matter where you are, *always* take your gloves off entirely
when eating, drinking, smoking, or serving. If you are wearing long gloves buttoned at the wrist, don't wad the hands

into little balls and stuff them into the arms of the gloves. That was Grandmother's way.

❋ When you wear gloves to a formal ball, you may keep them on while dancing, if you desire. It looks very pretty on the dance floor.

❋ As for wearing any jewelry over gloves, *don't*. It is considered bad taste to wear rings over gloves. Through the years, bracelets have on occasion been worn on top of gloves. Currently this is not done, but could change with fashion. In any event, a beautiful glove doesn't need to be "gilded," and wearing bracelets on top tends to soil them.

The Inconstant Corsage.   When we attend a big party in New York, there's scarcely a woman who wears a flower. When we are guests out of town, we are frequently the recipient of a corsage of tearoses surrounded by silver ribbons and dotted with little bees. We say a plague on both the customs and on the florists of America who have let this happen.

There's nothing in the world more beautiful than flowers, and they *can* have a place in fashion. Unfortunately, smart women have rejected the old corsage and haven't established a new fashion for a chic way to say it with flowers. They just leave them off. The teen-age group is an exception, as girls still expect a corsage from a beau for a big party.

If you live in an area where corsages are worn for social or ceremonial occasions, *force* your florist to arrange something chic for you:

❋ No net bows and frills, please. If you want a little ribbon bow, have it made of soft mossy-green velvet or the color of your dress.

❋ Leave off the birds and bees.

❋ One or two larger flowers are smarter than a cluster of itty-bitty buds.

❦ Carnations and lilies of many kinds are charming flowers to wear.

❦ The orchid is still the queen of the flowers—but don't wear orchid-colored orchids unless you are 80 or over—and even then, we don't plan to. Choose a more unusual one, such as green, brown, white, or pink.

❦ The matter of whether to wear a corsage right side up or upside down will probably be debated forever. We are fanatics over wearing the flowers as God made them—with heads up!

❦ For teen-agers, the arm corsage tied on with a ribbon is young and charming, but only for teen-agers.

❦ If you don't want to wear a flower, you can pin it on your bag or carry it in your hand. That's what we usually do with those tearoses!

A Thing of Beauty

One of the exciting developments of the past few years is the emergence of one's own person as a thing of beauty and fashion. We're talking about hair, makeup, hands, and feet. Formerly, a clean body and a neat hairdo were the only additions needed to your clothes. The new beauty movement not only makes every woman totally attractive, but also adds zest to life. Today being well-dressed means tip to toe, inside-outside.

We used to go to the beauty parlor to have our hair washed and set—usually not very well. Now we go to the *hairdresser* for a fashion look and a fillip to our spirits. This man has become the second most important male in our lives after our husbands. (We say "man" advisedly because we believe that all the great hairdressers are men.) In fact, several of the New York hairdressers have become social lions, sought after as guests at important parties. So seek until you find—a hairdresser who understands you, your personality, and your activities. And don't tell him—let him tell you how you should be done. Remember, he sees you as others do. If he's really an artist, he can also make helpful suggestions about makeup, because hair and makeup are part and parcel. Granted, this service is expensive today, but well worth every cent. Economize on caviar or some other such little luxury—never on your hairdresser!

A specialist in makeup, or *maquillage,* as the French call it, has become almost as essential as a hairdresser to many women in larger cities where such specialists congregate. For an important party, a hostess or guest may go for a face makeup as she goes to have her hair set or combed just before the party. This certainly isn't yet for everyone, but the idea is. You can learn to be your own creator of beauty.

First study the editorial pages of the fashion magazines for the current look. Then read the ads of the leading cosmetic manufacturers, to keep posted on what's new. Visit the cosmetic department of your favorite store to see and sample the products. Many of the saleswomen are actually representatives of the cosmetic manufacturers and are carefully trained to advise. Watch the papers for the appearance of a special representative from New York or Europe who may be in town and available for consultation. Take advantage of all this help that the stores and cosmeticians provide for you.

Design a daytime look, an evening look, and a Big Date look for yourself and splurge on the makings. You'll never make a better investment that will pay higher dividends. But easy on—don't get so carried away that you end up grotesque enough to qualify for a monster show on TV. We go back to our theme line—appropriateness and understatement.

If you are basically beautiful, don't try to hide it with a hard-chic makeup. Everyone loves a pretty woman, and most of all, men. So make up to bring out your beauty. The Gabor family of beautiful women is an example. They are always turned out to look just plain pretty. They never strive for obvious chic. And look at their fame and fortune!

If real beauty passed you by at birth, you still have the possibility of being attractive and interesting. Frequently, ugly women are more attractive than pretty ones because they must try harder. The first step is to look for your best features—hair, eyes, mouth, even legs. Always emphasize this feature with careful makeup, while "making down" your unattractive features. For example, if your eyes are too close together, don't load on the eye makeup. Rather, use it sparingly but skillfully to draw the eyes apart more, while perhaps emphasizing your hair and mouth. A large nose or an overly square face can be partially camouflaged by the use of two tones of powder or with one of the brush-on colorings. Put yourself in the hands of a local cosmetician in a store, or a specialist, to learn these tricks. There are several companies that have makeup shops across the country whose managers and personnel are trained to help you achieve the most attractive you.

Hands and feet are expressive extremities you should not forget. Second only to your face, your hands reveal what you are like. They are always on stage. You eat with them, shake hands with them, gesticulate with them, serve with them. Their grooming shows whether you are careless or careful. Nails should always be beautifully manicured and wearing polish that doesn't scream. Chipped or peeling polish is absolutely *verboten*. Use a good hand lotion regularly to keep the skin soft and smooth.

We've always rued the fact that American women pay very little attention to the grooming of their feet and toenails. Feet should have the same tender, loving care as hands—pedicures and softening lotions. Though American women may have the most beautiful legs in the world—long, smooth and de-fuzzed—their feet too often leave much to be desired. In the Eternal City, every chic Roman woman has a pedicurist who's as important to her as her hairdresser and manicurist. Although you may never see Rome, we say "Do as the Romans!"

Fragrance is the intangible ingredient that completes the woman of elegance. You can choose one as your signature, using cologne or toilet water for casual wear and perfume for other occasions. Or you can be adventuresome with a whole collection. Be sure the fragrances you choose wear well on your skin and are in keeping with your personality and appearance.

Know Your Public

No matter how generous your husband may be with your clothing allowance, you must still spend it on the kind of clothes that are the pattern of the community, and especially of your own social group. You can't look like Mrs. Diamond Jim Brady (nor would you ever want to!) if everyone else in your circle is wearing Indian silver and turquoise.

If you've lived in a place for a number of years, you are tuned in to the accepted manner of dress. In fact, you've probably added your bit to the establishment of what's acceptable and what's "in" at the moment. Dress varies from one part of this giant country to another and develops idiosyncrasies from community to community.

Although we are fortunately in a period where individuality is appreciated, it must still flourish within established custom. Your own pattern of dress must fit into the broad pattern of your city and social group like a jigsawed bit that must fit into the whole picture of the puzzle. It must *fit;* it mustn't stand out like a misfit. If you stray too far off the beam, you become a friendly freak or an ostracized outcast. Neither one will get you anywhere socially.

If you can afford it, certainly it's pleasant to have the very best clothes that are appropriate for your life. There's no stigma attached to being known as the best-dressed. But your clothes should never be ostentatious. They should be fashion-right without being extreme. They should be of fine quality—always a comfort, as well as an investment. Better one good dress to last five years than five bargains that won't look good even one year!

To *know* the right thing to wear in the community and for any occasion in the social life of the community is social security. The mother of one of our friends tells the story of how she married and moved to a new and conservative city with the fond hope of making a permanent place in the social and civic life for her husband and herself. She quickly made a good and

lifelong friend of another young wife who seemed attracted to
her. Years later she discovered why, when her friend confided,
"I knew immediately I'd like you because you always wore those
nice little Peck & Peck suits!"

A move to a new community may mean a whole new orien-
tation of dress. In your old home the ladies may wear madras
and loafers for lunch on the country club terrace, but in your
new home they may prefer linens and heels.

There are two simple ways to learn the secrets of the social
set you hope to join: observe and ask. Watch what other women
wear for shopping, for lunching or dining in a restaurant or
club, even to the A. & P. Try parking your car near social meccas
and look at the guests as they enter a hotel or a club dressed for
a party or evening out. Or simply look out your window.

For a lunch party on the terrace of a neighbor, we donned
an appropriate pale-blue linen dress and white kid pumps. Just
as we were about to depart for the party, we saw a new wife in
the neighborhood, who had also been invited, drive up to her
home with a baby-sitter. She was obviously dressed for the party,
too—but much too dressed in a flowered silk and sandals. We
couldn't believe our eyes when she arrived only five minutes
later looking like one of us in a pink linen dress and matching
linen pumps. She confessed to us that when she looked out of
her window and saw us crossing the street, she knew she was all
wrong and made a quick change that saved the day—and reputation—for her!

You aren't even safe in a new community with a prescribed
kind of dress for a particular activity. A tennis aficionado we
know moved from one Connecticut town to another. The first
day on the courts at her newly joined club she confidently appeared in her prettiest white tennis dress that she thought could
play any court in the world. But she was the only player who
thought so. All others at that club were knowingly slashing away
in trim Bermudas and attractive shirts. This same friend attended her first Junior League morning committee meeting in
her new home as understated as she possibly could be in a good

black suit, but when the uniform turned out to be simple sweaters and skirts, she felt overdressed.

Our saddest story is that of the wife who moved with her husband into a rather proper New Jersey neighborhood from the breezy Southwest. An afternoon-into-evening Fourth of July celebration at a neighbor's included the new couple. He arrived and immediately blended with the other men in an attractive sports shirt and slacks. She stood out so painfully as to be an embarrassment to all. The other women guests were prettily dressed in summer cottons or linens, while she had on short shorts and an old shirt. After about an hour of obvious misery and squirming over her predicament, she mysteriously vanished, to return half an hour later looking very attractive and right in an appropriate dress and shoes. If only she had looked out the window!

If you can't catch the local act from the window or other vantage points, simply ask about what's being worn, when an occasion arises that puzzles you. Everyone is flattered to be asked her opinion and usually will go out of the way to help. When you receive an invitation and aren't sure what the proper local attire is for the occasion and place, ask "What do you usually wear for lunch at your club?" Or, "Are you wearing a short or long dress to dinner?" Or "Will Bermudas and sweater be all right for the cookout?" The answer will probably be a complete report on what all the other guests are likely to turn up in. And you'll not be marked as unknowing at the beginning of your social life with a new group.

$\mathcal{H}$ow to $\mathcal{B}$e a $\mathcal{P}$opular $\mathcal{G}$uest

> Good guests are too valuable to good hosts to be dropped
> lightly and without reason. The fault in such a case is
> necessarily with the guest.—Elsa Maxwell, *How to Do It*

CHAPTER

13

Most of this book has been devoted to the good host or hostess,
but it's time to view the other side of the coin and devote some
space to the good guest. Nobody wants to be a wallflower. We
all like to be a part of the group. As one of our teen-age friends
said, when her parents wouldn't allow her to go out on a date,
"I don't really care if I can't go, just as long as I'm invited."

Most people go to more parties than they give. Every time
you invite seven friends to lunch, you will probably reap at
least four or five invitations from that one group. But if the
social "swim" is passing you by without so much as a splash,
it's time to do a little soul-searching to find out why. We're not
suggesting that you keep a scorecard or make a career of "guest-
ing," but it's good for all of us to evaluate our behavior once in
a while. A blend of simple courtesy, basic rules of etiquette, and
a good dash of common sense will earn a passing grade for al-

most anyone. And this chapter is merely to provide a refresher course.

Certainly most of us try to be good guests, but in some instances our intentions are sadly misguided. Any party is a cooperative affair, and no matter how much effort the host puts forth, a successful party isn't possible without the guests who participate. It may not be a 50-50 proposition, but it's at least 60-40. There's surely more to being a guest than just providing a body to fill up a chair. A good guest *contributes* to the party and, most importantly, gives of himself. We recall a friend who often said of her neighbor, "She's such a pleasant person—but oh, how I wish she'd *give* a little."

It shouldn't be too difficult for anyone to be an agreeable guest, assuming that you really like your host. And you wouldn't accept the invitation in the first place if you didn't. You should never accept an invitation unless you sincerely wish to pursue that particular relationship, which means inviting that person to your home in turn. It's unwise to accept any invitation merely because it's an "in" group and you'd like to be seen at the Joneses'. Sincerity is a must in becoming either a good host or a good guest.

R.S.V.P. Tout de Suite

When you receive any kind of invitation, either written or by telephone, reply in some way immediately (see page 31).

It's customary in many communities, when giving a large tea or cocktail party, to send written invitations without a request for reply. In this case, it is usually expected that you will respond only if you cannot come, thus sparing the hostess many telephone calls.

Always use discretion when a hostess suggests that you bring your houseguest to a party. Be sure the houseguest will fit in. For instance, if your 80-year-old aunt is visiting, it's unlikely that she would be an addition to a Watusi party. Better to take Auntie to a tea party instead—unless her name is Auntie Mame.

Your Entrance

If cleanliness is next to godliness, punctuality must be third in line. We recently heard someone say that she has a "punctuality neurosis," and we tend to suffer from that same affliction. We feel that if the hostess invites you for 7 P.M., she expects you near that hour—not more than 15 minutes afterward. If she wanted you at 8, she would have said so in the first place.

We consider each invitation as a form of compliment. The very fact that the hostess wants *you* at *her* party is in itself complimentary. Return that compliment by making your arrival show that you have anticipated the event. Don't worry about arriving first. Somebody has to.

If you know in advance that you cannot possibly arrive at the scheduled time, tell your hostess and ask if this will inconvenience her. She will then know when to expect you and won't be wondering whether or not to call the missing persons bureau. If your emergency is at the very last moment, and you find that you will be considerably late, our advice is that your story had better be good. Never, never keep your hostess on the telephone with lengthy explanations at the very time that guests are due to arrive. Nothing is more upsetting and inconvenient. Make your excuse as brief as possible at that time and give the unpleasant details later if you must.

Exit Here

Assuming that your arrival has been punctual, your departure should follow the same pattern. You may not turn into a Cinderella at midnight, in fairy-tale fashion, but you may become the least popular guest if you wear your welcome thin. Since nearly every hostess must carry on her usual household or family routine the following day, besides performing as cleanup squad, guests should show some consideration for her and not stay on until the wee hours of the morning.

Of course, if your hostess is the hyperthyroid type who still has boundless energy at the end of the evening, she may urge you to stay longer. In this case, it's up to you. However, if you feel that you must leave, you can always do so by telling her gently but firmly that you've had a wonderful evening, but you must now say good-by.

We have often been amused by one decisive friend who is always the first guest to arrive and the first to leave. At the end of the evening, she quickly arises on the stroke of 11, expresses her appreciation to the hostess, gets her coat, and leaves within a very few minutes. Her direct and uncomplicated explanation is, "I have said all I have to say by that time and have heard all I want to hear." It's as simple as that. Although not all of us fit the role of the rugged individualist, it's certainly a boon to the hostess, at times, to have one person begin the general exodus. Another friend deliberately plans to end her parties early by "planting" a very close friend to set the pace and make the first move to leave. At least this gives others the idea.

It's much easier to make a set rule to cover arrivals than to cover departures, because the latter depends on the customs of your crowd and the circumstances involved. If the party is a drop-in and drop-out affair, you may leave after one cup of tea or one cocktail, or you can stay longer if you wish. When it's lunch, we find that many guests must leave immediately afterward to be home when children return from school. A general rule is to stay about 30 to 45 minutes following lunch. If bridge or canasta has been planned, guests should arrange in advance to stay longer. Guests are generally expected to stay after dinner for a considerable period of relaxation, which might be games or simply conversation. The hostess would be disappointed if guests rushed away following dinner, for this is her time to enjoy them without other party details on her mind. As a guide, stay about two hours following dinner. But it does depend on local customs and the hour when dinner is served. Generally, midnight is the witching hour, beyond which you should not stay.

Who Should Leave First?   Where the decorum of royalty must be observed, no one leaves a social function until after the person of royal status. We have neither kings nor queens to worry about, but persons of high rank, such as the President, receive this same consideration. Also, guests at any strictly formal affair are expected to wait until the guest of honor leaves. But to get down to everyday life on a strictly informal plane, where we're all commoners together, the trend in most communities is the reverse of this rule. It is generally customary for the guest of honor to arrive a few minutes before the other guests and to leave a few minutes after they have departed. In other words, the guest of honor is there to help greet the arrivals, and remains so that they may all bid their farewells to the one for whom the party was given. If it is a surprise party or shower, naturally, the hostess arranges for the person being honored to arrive after all others.

The Heart of the Matter

Between the time of arrival and the time of departure, guests have an obligation to the hostess to be pleasant and agreeable. As we have said before, it's a give-and-take affair, so the key word is "participation." Surely no one would attend a party with the attitude, "Here I am. Now entertain me." And when we say *participate,* we don't mean take over. We have all been subjected to the guest who outdoes everyone else and is an authority on all subjects, whether it's rearing children or headshrinking. But do enter into whatever is planned. Be a good sport at games—and especially a good loser.

The most important ingredient of the good guest is probably genuineness. Be yourself—but your best self. This point was vividly illustrated at a very glamorous and cosmopolitan gathering in New York. A prominent decorator was entertaining for an internationally known artist. The guest list included an art collector, a wealthy socialite, an attractive Italian count, and a famous voice coach, among other celebrities. In the midst of this group were two attractive but unsophisticated young ladies visiting from another state. After everyone had left, the host and guest of honor were discussing the various interesting people who had been present. The artist said to her host, "Who do you think were the most charming ones here?" He immediately answered, "The two young visitors." When she pointed out that there were so many elegant and accomplished guests that she was puzzled by his choice, he observed, "They were the only completely natural people in this room, and the only ones who would be the same in their own homes as they were here." Coco Chanel expressed a similar thought when she said, "In the difficult and wonderful battle of life, the simple woman emerges victorious, the sophisticated one, defeated."

Be Not a Problem Guest. This may sound unbending, but we believe that you should eat whatever the hostess serves, whether you like it or not, or at least go through the motions. This is just one of the little courtesies of life. The hostess has spent considerable time and energy attempting to please you, so why not reciprocate and try to please her?

In your attempt to be the polite guest, you may occasionally find yourself wishing that you had not been invited. This happened in Paris when a friend was eager for us to enjoy some of the dishes that are served as daily fare throughout France. The meal became memorable for us, but not in the way she intended. We got off to a bad start when the first course turned out to be our first encounter with snails. By mustering all our courage, we managed to consume a respectable number, thinking all the while that the menu could only improve. The next course was a tasty stew, but our hearts sank when we discovered that it was rabbit stew. The dinner climaxed with goat cheese. We're all for trying new dishes, but found ourselves in the position of the proverbial tourist longing for the good old American hamburger. Our hostess got "A" for effort in attempting to educate us in French cuisine, but we deserved "A+" for being model guests even though our stomachs rebelled every step of the way.

If you are on a strict medical diet of some sort, explain briefly to the hostess when you accept the invitation, but make it clear that you expect no special attention. Even though there are certain things you are not permitted to eat, there is enough variety at most meals to keep you from going hungry. Of course, if you're fasting, stay at home! Or ask whether you may drop in after the meal.

In the case of serious food allergies, any hostess is sympathetic and understanding, so quietly explain to her if you consider an explanation necessary. In many cases you could get by without mentioning it. Don't be like the lady invited for tea who, the minute she set foot inside the door, announced that she never drank tea, but preferred coffee. Incidentally, if you can't drink wine or coffee, don't turn the glass or cup upside down. Accept it and pretend to sip.

If you have an allergy to animals, or just dislike them, don't shriek and carry on if a cat walks through the room. Contain yourself. We recall one dinner party when the host's cat was merely mentioned. Kitty wasn't even in the house, but one man suddenly made a hasty exit without stopping to collect his wife and was not seen again that evening. Maybe he had good reason, but we couldn't help wondering, "Was it allergy or antipathy?"

The Helping Hand.   Where there are servants, of course you omit any offer to help. However, in a household devoid of servants, the hostess does have her hands full when entertaining. Therefore, it's thoughtful to offer your help, but take her at her word if she declines. If she asks to be alone, she works better that way. And since we are of this bent ourselves, we have a particular understanding of the "loner" in the kitchen. It's distracting to have to watch the guest as well as the pot, but occasionally it is helpful to have someone pour water, light candles, or do a little last-minute chore—preferably outside the kitchen.

Never force the hostess to clean up the minute dinner is over by forcing your assistance. This is the time when she can relax and stay with her guests.

Frankly, when we're guests, dressed in our best, we don't wish to do K.P. duty in anybody's kitchen, and we don't expect others to do it in ours. Once in a while, when there is an exceptionally high mound of dishes, a very close friend stays to help after the rest have gone home. This is a generous gesture and greatly appreciated, but it is not expected of any guest.

The Sweetest Sound. William James once said, "The deepest principle in human nature is the craving to be appreciated." Any hostess enjoys hearing her praises sung—or at least hummed —but continual and ecstatic raves are in questionable taste and serve only to embarrass her. Without overdoing it, let her know that you are aware of the thought that she has put into her hospitality. Complete silence on the part of a guest baffled our cousin Charlotte when she was living on the coast of Italy. She planned a full day for the pleasure of a visiting Oriental friend and eagerly looked forward to showing him the beauties of the Mediterranean coast. As they drove along the Amalfi Drive, she pointed out particular spots of beauty, but as time went by she became more and more concerned, because Mr. Wu spoke not a word of appreciation. In fact, Mr. Wu spoke not a word! They lunched at a magnificent hotel overlooking the sea, but still there was no comment from the mysterious Oriental, and the end of the day brought forth no explanation. The next morning, Charlotte could endure the suspense no longer, so she called Mr. Wu at his hotel to express her concern that perhaps she had offended him in some way, which would account for his reluctance to converse the previous day. He quickly reassured her, "Oh, you gave me a wonderful day, and I thank you. Why, the reason I didn't speak was that I took a vow of silence for the day."

You've Come to Stay

There are two cardinal rules for the overnight guest. Don't come unless invited, and don't overstay your time. In this age of no servants, we might as well face the bald truth, that entertaining company from out of town is exhausting, no matter how much you love and cherish your houseguests, and regardless of how fervently you desire to make their stay pleasant.

We practice a system that virtually guarantees that the glow will still be on your hosts when it comes time to leave. No matter how much we're tempted to prolong a visit, we usually limit our stay to four days, even with each other: the day we arrive, two full days for chatting, and the day we leave. Few people wear out their welcome in that short time. As one friend remarked, "You can do a lot of visiting if you visit fast!" (We are not referring to situations when family members are separated by many miles and see one another infrequently. A parent might visit a daughter or son once a year for several weeks.) A brief stay will usually endear you to your hostess, unless you are a prima donna who demands constant attention. In that case, the only thing that could possibly endear you to her is your absence.

Probably the least welcome guest is the one who arrives without warning. The lame excuse is generally, "I didn't write because I didn't want you to go to any trouble." Everyone knows, of course, that it's far *more* trouble to have unexpected guests. Most people prefer not to have this kind of surprise—or shock! It could involve extra shopping, extra cooking, changing beds, doubling up the children for sleeping, getting a substitute driver for the car pool, canceling a dental appointment, and many other extras, all of which could have been taken care of in advance, if the hostess had only known.

Try to make sure that your visit is convenient to your hosts. No one ever knows what particular complications exist in a family, and the announcement of your visit could be that last straw. Our sympathies went out to a young mother who had a succession of visitors during the New York World's Fair. They came not alone, but in packs—four to six in a family. This occurred half a dozen times during one summer. The poor hostess, who had no domestic help, acted as cook, maid, baby-sitter, and, in addition, had to look after her own three young children and keep her husband happy. Needless to say, by the end of the summer, she was ready for a sanitarium.

Disorder in a household is upsetting to the family, yet order is one of the most difficult things to maintain while entertaining overnight guests. So do your part in keeping your room and bath neat. Have things looking as attractive as when you arrived. Hide your clutter wherever you can, either in closet or drawers provided for your use, or inside your traveling bag—even under the bed if necessary, unless someone else has beaten you to it. If you're a splatter-bug in the bath, wipe up water spots with tissues. Remember that the nice lady of the house is your hostess, not your personal maid. And go prepared with your own personal cosmetic and toilet articles, in case your hostess is like the frugal New England woman who said to a houseguest who kept borrowing small necessaries, "Let me know what you need for your room, and I'll tell you how to get along without it."

When you've come to stay with friends for the purpose of sightseeing, be willing to go it alone at least part of the time. The guest can return to the nest, take a nap and rest before dinner, but who cooks that dinner? The hostess! And she may have to cope with a den of Cub Scouts along the way. There's no escape from her daily routine, which in itself may be a full-time job.

The Golden Rule is a good one for any houseguest to follow. "Do unto others as you would have others do unto you." Sometimes a careless remark tossed out thoughtlessly can shatter the hostess completely. One woman we know entertained her houseguest, supposedly a dear friend, by inviting a large number of people to dinner, in spite of the fact that a record-breaking heat wave was in full sway. After the party was over, when the hostess was drooping with fatigue, her guest tactlessly remarked, "Wasn't it too bad that Helen was unable to come—and she's my favorite friend!" Such a remark would make any hostess feel let down, and that particular friendship has been a wee bit tarnished ever since.

Refrain from deprecating the community you are visiting, no matter how backward or unattractive it might appear to you. Better to say nothing than to criticize unkindly. Be open-minded and look for points of interest. There surely must be some.

Try to abide by rules of the household when you are visiting. It's up to you to adapt yourself to them. Don't expect a whole family to readjust to you. Assume that the hostess is always right, and follow suit. Inquire what time you are expected for breakfast, and appear at that time. If you're a heavy sleeper and don't have a travel alarm clock, ask the hostess to call you when it's time to get up. In some homes the wife prefers to give the husband breakfast first, if he has to leave early for business. The morning rush can get frantic enough without added complications, so if this is the rule, be a good guest and stay out of sight until your presence is appreciated.

Respect the privacy of the home and try not to be omnipresent. Don't poke around in closets, desk, medicine cabinet, or drawers, unless they have been assigned to your use.

When it's time to retire, the habits of the host and hostess should again prevail. If you have insomnia, stay up later if you wish, but pursue only quiet activities such as yoga, crossword puzzles, solitaire—or thinking!

When entertainment is planned for you, be ready on time, whether it's a party or a shopping spree. Try not to keep your hosts standing around waiting while you relax in a shower or fuss with your hair.

To sum up the perfect houseguest, we could describe one of our cherished friends. When she comes for a few days, she informs us exactly when she will arrive and whether or not she will be here for lunch or dinner. If traffic delays her, she telephones. Instead of inviting all her other friends in town to drop by, she pays them brief visits. If we've planned a party for her, she offers to help in any way possible, but when we decline, she finds errands to do that take her out of the house. She always asks exactly what time to be back and, without fail, returns at that time. Since she likes to retire early, she never exhausts us by staying up till the morning hours to visit, yet she is enthusiastic over anything we plan. (There is nothing like enthusiasm to cheer a hostess on.) Consequently, we look forward to her visits with pleasure, not panic. What greater compliment could we pay than to say she's always welcome?

Gifting the Hostess

Any gift should come straight from the heart, whether to a hostess or anyone else; therefore, the offering of a hostess gift is optional. A guest of honor usually *wants* to make this gesture of appreciation to the hostess. In some places it is customary for him or her to send flowers the day of the party. However, there is no set rule, and if you know of another gift that would please your hostess, it's perfectly proper and sometimes more interesting to deviate from custom. If you are not the guest of honor at a party, it is certainly not required that you take a gift, but it is a thoughtful gesture and sometimes depends on particular circumstances involved. In this case, the gift should be only a token gift and of less value than that given by an honored guest. The same rule applies if you are invited to lunch or dinner when it's not a party.

When You Say It with Flowers. It is preferable to send or take flowers in advance of party time, or send them the day after with a thank-you note. A hostess can become completely unstrung if faced with an enormous bouquet as guests arrive. Flowers take a great deal of time to arrange, and besides, few people have an assortment of containers ready. If you *must* bring them with you, arrange them in a container at home, or offer to arrange them for the hostess, or bring a potted plant that requires no immediate attention. The hostess is bound to appreciate something small and prearranged more than a big bouquet that she must take care of at her busiest moment. If you send a king-size floral tribute, be sure to have it delivered in plenty of time for the hostess to rearrange her furniture!

What Shall It Be? If you are not familiar with the taste of the hostess, don't give anything that may clash with her house and put her in the embarrassing position of having to bring it out of the closet every time you pay a visit. A friend of ours had the misfortune to receive a monstrous purple vase. She spent several years tolerating it, afraid of alienating the donor if she disposed of it. Every month or so she moved it to a new spot, hoping that somewhere, somehow, it would blend into obscurity. But a purple vase could hardly go unnoticed. Finally, in a fit of despair, she said to herself, "This horror *must* go," and off it went to the nearest thrift shop. But she still feels uncomfortable when the one who gave it comes to visit and always sees the flowers in other containers.

It's usually safe to give something that can be used up or consumed. Nice soap is a very acceptable gift, or gourmet goodies such as special jellies or preserves, glazed nuts, almond-stuffed olives, pickled fruits, special candies, petits fours, an assortment of interesting cocktail tidbits, or a bottle of wine. A very useful and original gift we once received was an attractive assortment of gift wrappings, with gift cards to match, for various occasions. Choice fruit is always appreciated and can be a very special gift if arranged with originality.

A Little Bit of You. We have always felt that any gift you make is like giving a little of yourself. Your own specialties, such as shortbread, cookies, nut bread, jellies, or relish, are acceptable and appropriate gifts—that is, *if* you're a good cook. A nice touch is to enclose the recipe, if your hostess enjoys cooking herself. If sewing is your talent, make a pert apron for someone who enjoys the kitchen. Near Christmastime a particularly beautiful tree ornament is an attractive gift. This too could be one you have made. Flowers from your own garden are a treat to most people.

There is no end to the choice of patio accessories for the summer hostess who entertains outdoors—colorful candles in glass containers for safety, gay paper napkins, a plant, or useful gadgets for the barbecue grill. Berries in season are always a delight and can be dressed up by covering the box inside and out with wallpaper or gift paper. Or present them in an inexpensive basket that can be used later for rolls or snacks.

Look Ahead. We find the most satisfactory system is to buy small, unusual gifts throughout the year, whenever we see them in shops. It's a great help to have them on hand when needed and fun to select something suitable when going to a party. As with any gift, the giving is as much fun for the giver as for the recipient.

Gifting for the Weekend Hostess. The gift that is a token of your appreciation for a weekend visit, or longer, can be a little more impressive than for just a party, but any gift that is too lavish would embarrass a hostess. Also, any gift that strains your pocketbook would cause embarrassment, but here again you can resort to something you have created through your own efforts, even though it may be very inexpensive.

If it's a first visit to a home, you may prefer to send a small gift after your visit, when you know what might appeal to the family. The better you know home, hosts, and hobbies, the easier it is to select a gift. Take cards and scorepads to cardsharps, a good book to the avid reader, a small piece of old glass or a candlestick to the collector of antiques, a recording for the hi-fii addict, a flat of petunias to the compulsive gardener, a tote bag for the knitter, or a floating key ring for the boating enthusiast. Books are available on every interest imaginable, from archery to Zen Buddhism. Of course, any of the gifts for the party hostess would be appropriate for a weekend hostess, but perhaps in a larger way. Instead of taking pretty paper napkins, why not hem a dozen polished-cotton or linen napkins in assorted colors?

If you visit a home frequently, you learn to know the household needs and what would make acceptable gifts. One that particularly impressed us was a much-needed luggage rack for the guest room. Later a second guest "gilded the lily" by making exquisite needlepoint straps to replace the original ones on the rack. Some of the little luxuries we don't buy for ourselves please us considerably when received as gifts—scented drawer liners, especially pretty shelf papers, a fitted sewing basket, a hand-painted tray, place card holders, velvet- or satin-covered hangers. And being cat lovers, we adore gifts for our cat!

Bread-and-Butters

We're all a little like children in our desire for a pat on the back. Consequently, something more than the brief thank-you when you leave a party is a joy to any hostess; it brings such a nice warm feeling to receive a note several days later. Writing is not always obligatory, but the unexpected letter, like the unexpected gift, is often the most gratifying. If you have visited someone overnight, you do have an obligation to write a thank-you note as soon as you return home. And if you are an honored guest at a party, you certainly would wish to thank the hostess by note or telephone after the party. The note can be short; the important thing is the thought behind it.

Here again we have a little rule we try to follow: always write or telephone after a brunch, lunch, dinner or supper party, but not necessarily after more impersonal affairs, such as a cocktail party, open house, tea, or coffee. However, even with the latter group, if there is a special reason to write, we do. Another ground rule is: when in doubt about writing, *do* rather than *don't*, for you'll never go wrong in going the extra mile. Even when a written note isn't called for, next time you talk with the hostess, tell her what a nice party she gave.

~~~ *ABC'S of the Good Guest* ~~~

A rrive on time.

B e agreeable even though you've had a hard day. You might enjoy it if you give yourself a chance.

C irculate and contribute. Don't confine your conversation to the one person you know and see every day.

D on't leave a permanent reminder in the form of cigarette burns or rings from glasses on the furniture.

E at whatever the hostess serves. It's no time to be picky.

F lowers are flattering, but not if you arrive with them at a large party and expect the hostess to stop everything to arrange them.

G lamorize yourself for the party. It's a compliment to the hostess to look your best.

H ave grip, will travel—but only if you're invited.

I mitations never equal the genuine article, so be yourself.

J okes are fun only in small doses. Slightly risqué stories are acceptable sometimes, but never dirty jokes.

K eep your chin up. Even if the party is a dud, grin and bear it. (Every party director has a "turkey" occasionally, even you.)

L imit your conversation to topics of general interest. Private jokes and inside stories are discourteous.

M onopolizing the conversation or the hosts is rude.

N ame-dropping breeds contempt.

O ffer to help. If the hostess declines, she wants to be alone— so let her be.

411

P ut your best foot forward, but avoid stepping on someone else's toes.

Q uench your thirst, but don't become pixilated.

R. s.v.p. promptly on receipt of an invitation, not the day of the party.

S ing the praises of the hostess subtly. Avoid insincere raves, but don't ignore her efforts.

T read softly when politics or religion is discussed. You may be in the enemy camp.

U gly is as ugly does, so try to "do" pretty.

V icious gossip is taboo. Watch out—you may be the subject next time.

W ives and husbands belong to each other, so hands off someone else's, except as a dinner partner.

X marks the spot where braggarts fall. Don't bore others with how great you *think* you are.

Y oungsters are adorable, but not at adult parties, so leave yours at home.

Z ero out when it's time to depart—and before your welcome cools to zero.

 *I*ndex

413